THE MERCHANT OF VENICE

WILLIAM SHAKESPEARE

THE MERCHANT OF VENICE

With Contemporary Criticism

Edited by JOSEPH PEARCE

IGNATIUS PRESS   SAN FRANCISCO

Cover art:
Bonifacio de' Pitati (1487–1553), *Justice*
Location: Ca' d'Oro, Venice, Italy

Photo credit: Cameraphoto Arte, Venice / Art Resource, N.Y.

Cover design by John Herreid

© 2009 Ignatius Press, San Francisco
All rights reserved
ISBN 978-1-58617-320-3
Library of Congress Control Number 2008933487
Printed in India

Tradition is the extension of Democracy through time; it is the proxy of the dead and the enfranchisement of the unborn.

Tradition may be defined as the extension of the franchise. Tradition means giving votes to the most obscure of all classes, our ancestors. It is the democracy of the dead. Tradition refuses to submit to the small and arrogant oligarchy of those who merely happen to be walking about. All democrats object to men being disqualified by the accident of birth; tradition objects to their being disqualified by the accident of death. Democracy tells us not to neglect a good man's opinion, even if he is our groom; tradition asks us not to neglect a good man's opinion, even if he is our father. I, at any rate, cannot separate the two ideas of democracy and tradition.

—G. K. Chesterton

Ignatius Critical Editions—Tradition-Oriented Criticism for a new generation

CONTENTS

INTRODUCTION

Joseph Pearce
Ave Maria University

The Merchant of Venice was first registered[1] on July 22, 1598, but was probably written and first performed a few years earlier, perhaps as early as 1594 or 1595. It is likely that Shakespeare's initial inspiration for writing the play arose, in part, from the gruesome executions of two "traitors" on the orders of Queen Elizabeth. The first "traitor" was Roderigo López, the queen's personal physician, who was hanged, drawn, and quartered on June 7, 1594; the second was Robert Southwell, the Jesuit priest and poet who was hanged, drawn, and quartered on February 20, 1595. Whereas the former may have served as the inspiration for Shylock, the latter can be seen as a ghostly presence flitting through the play as an allusion to the deeper meanings to be gleaned from the drama.

Roderigo López, a converted Portuguese Jew, had been appointed personal physician to the queen in 1586. Two years later he became official interpreter to Antonio Perez, pretender to the throne of Portugal, after Perez had sought sanctuary in England from the clutches of his enemy, King Philip of Spain. In 1590 López seems to have become embroiled in a Spanish plot to assassinate both Antonio Perez and Queen Elizabeth. Although he protested his innocence, he was found guilty and was sentenced to death. At his execution a large crowd bayed for his blood and bellowed anti-Semitic abuse.

In the wake of López's trial and execution, the Admiral's Men, an acting company, revived Christopher Marlowe's *Jew*

---

[1] All plays had to be registered with the Stationers' Company, an organization of printers and publishers that held a monopoly of the printing trade in Tudor England.

of Malta as an entrepreneurial response to the tide of anti-Semitism that was sweeping through London. The play was a huge success, playing fifteen times to packed houses during 1594. It seems reasonable to assume, therefore, that Shakespeare wrote *The Merchant of Venice* in the same entrepreneurial spirit, seeking to cash in on the upsurge of anti-Semitism by writing his own play about a villainous Jew. Such a supposition is supported by the fact that many critics have identified "the Venesyon Comodye", staged at the Rose Theatre in August 1594, with Shakespeare's play. From a purely business perspective, it makes sense that Shakespeare might write a play for his own company of players, the Lord Chamberlain's Men, to compete with the success of the revival of Marlowe's play by the Admiral's Men. Even if "the Venesyon Comodye" has nothing to do with Shakespeare's play but is merely a comedy set in Venice by an unknown playwright, it still seems likely that *The Merchant of Venice* was written as a response or reaction to López's conviction for treachery. Such a view is supported by a clue embedded within the text of the play that seems to connect López to Shylock. In Act 4 of *The Merchant of Venice*, Gratiano describes Shylock as "a wolf ... hang'd for human slaughter" (4.1.134),[2] which appears to be a pun on López's name, the Latin for "wolf" being *lupus*. López was indeed hanged for plotting human slaughter, and it is difficult to conclude anything but the obvious with regard to the connection between the real-life Jewish villain and Shakespeare's counterpart, especially considering that someone named Antonio is the intended victim in both cases.

Much more needs to be said about the alleged anti-Semitism of *The Merchant of Venice*, which has been greatly exaggerated.[3] First, however, let us look at the other real-life character who seems to have influenced the writing of the play.

---

[2] All quotations from *The Merchant of Venice* are from the edition published by Ignatius Press: *The Merchant of Venice*, ed. Joseph Pearce (San Francisco: Ignatius, 2009).

[3] The whole issue of anti-Semitism in *The Merchant of Venice* is dealt with at considerable length in Joseph Pearce's forthcoming book, *Seeing through*

There is an abundance of evidence to show that Shakespeare knew the Jesuit poet Robert Southwell prior to the latter's arrest in 1592, and it is possible that Shakespeare might have been among the large crowd that witnessed Southwell's brutal execution in 1595.[4] Furthermore, Shakespeare would have been writing *The Merchant of Venice* shortly after Southwell's execution or, if we accept the earliest possible dates for the play's composition, during the period in which the Jesuit was being tortured repeatedly by Richard Topcliffe, Elizabeth's sadistic chief interrogator. It should not surprise us, therefore, that we see Southwell's shadow, or shade, in Shakespeare's play. It is present most palpably in the haunting echoes of Southwell's own poetry, which Shakespeare evidently knew well and which he introduces into *The Merchant of Venice* on numerous occasions.[5] Take, for instance, Portia's words after the Prince of Arragon's failure in the test of the caskets: "Thus hath the candle sing'd the moth" (2.9.79). And compare it to lines from Southwell's "Lewd Love is Losse":

> So long the flie doth dallie with the flame,
> Untill his singed wings doe force his fall.[6]

Not only does the phraseology suggest Shakespeare's indebtedness to Southwell, but the very title of the poem from which the phrase is extracted suggests a connection to Shakespeare's

Shakespeare's Eyes (San Francisco: Ignatius Press, 2010), and the issue of usury is discussed in James E. Hartley's essay "Breeding Barren Metal: Usury and *The Merchant of Venice*", pp. 201–16 below.

[4] For full details of the solid historical evidence for Shakespeare's friendship with Robert Southwell, see chap. 9 of *The Quest for Shakespeare* by Joseph Pearce (San Francisco: Ignatius, 2008), pp. 107–17.

[5] I am indebted in this discussion of St. Robert Southwell's influence on *The Merchant of Venice* to the diligent research of John Klause. See John Klause, "Catholic and Protestant, Jesuit and Jew: Historical Religion in *The Merchant of Venice*", in *Shakespeare and the Culture of Christianity in Early Modern England*, edited by Dennis Taylor and David N. Beauregard (New York: Fordham University Press, 2003), pp. 180–221.

[6] James H. McDonald and Nancy Pollard Brown, eds., *The Poems of Robert Southwell, S.J.* (Oxford: Clarendon Press, 1967), quoted in Taylor and Beauregard, *Shakespeare and the Culture of Christianity*, p. 187.

theme that lewd love is loss. Arragon's love is lewdly self-interested, and his choice leads to the loss of his hopes to marry Portia. Shakespeare is not simply taking lines from Southwell; he is apparently taking his very theme from him.

In the final act, as Portia and Nerissa return to Belmont, they see a candle burning in the darkness. "When the moon shone, we did not see the candle", says Nerissa, to which the sagacious Portia responds: "So doth the greater glory dim the less" (5.1.92–93). Compare this to Southwell's "seeking the sunne it is . . . booteles to borrowe the light of a candle".[7]

It is also intriguing that an expression ascribed by the *Oxford English Dictionary* to Shakespeare's coinage was actually coined originally by Southwell, to whom Shakespeare was presumably indebted. The phrase is Shylock's "a wilderness of monkeys" (subsequent to "a wilderness of Tygers" in *Titus Andronicus*), which presumably owed its original source to Southwell's "a wilderness of serpents" in his *Epistle unto His Father*.[8]

If the foregoing should fail to convince the skeptical reader of Southwell's ghostly presence, the pivotal scene in which Bassanio triumphs in the wisdom of his choice to "hazard all he hath", i.e., lay down his life for his love, should prove sufficient to allay the most hardened skepticism. The Shakespeare scholar John Klause has shown how this scene resonates as an echo of Southwell's *Marie Magdalens Funeral Teares*, in which the saint is of a mind to "venture [her] life" for her love of her Lord. Klause shows many suggestive parallels between Shakespeare's scene and Southwell's earlier work, and yet nowhere is the allusion to Southwell more evident than in the exchange between Bassanio and Portia before Bassanio makes his choice:

[7] Robert Southwell, *Marie Magdalens Funeral Teares*, ed. Vincent B. Leitch (Delmar, N.Y.: Scholars' Facsimiles and Reprints, 1974), quoted in Taylor and Beauregard, *Shakespeare and the Culture of Christianity*, p. 187.

[8] Taylor and Beauregard, *Shakespeare and the Culture of Christianity*, p. 187. Southwell's *Epistle unto His Father* was written in 1588 or 1589, five years or so before Shakespeare used the similar phrase in *Titus Andronicus*.

Bassanio.   Let me choose,
　　For as I am, I live upon the rack.

Portia. Upon the rack, Bassanio! then confess
　　What treason there is mingled with your love.

Bassanio. None but that ugly treason of mistrust,
　　Which makes me fear th' enjoying of my love;
　　There may as well be amity and life
　　'Tween snow and fire, as treason and my love.

Portia. Ay, but I fear you speak upon the rack,
　　Where men enforced do speak any thing.

Bassanio. Promise me life, and I'll confess the truth.

Portia. Well then, confess and live.

Bassanio.   Confess and love
　　Had been the very sum of my confession.
　　O happy torment, when my torturer
　　Doth teach me answers for deliverance!
　　But let me to my fortune and the caskets.

Portia. Away then! I am lock'd in one of them;
　　If you do love me, you will find me out.

                              (3.2.24–41)

Since this exchange between the lover and the longed-for beloved comes in the midst of an array of references to Southwell's poem, it is difficult to avoid the conclusion that it represents a clear allusion to Southwell's own recent experience "upon the rack" at the hands of a torturer seeking to force him into a confession of the alleged crime of "treason" with which he had been charged. Such a conclusion is reinforced still further when juxtaposed with Southwell's own words in his *Humble Supplication to Her Maiestie:*

What unsufferable Agonies we have bene put to upon the Rack…. [One so tortured] is apt to utter anything to abridge the sharpnes and severity of paine. [Yet even an] unskillful Lay man ... [would] rather venture his life by saying too much, then hazard his Conscience in not answering sufficient.[9]

What else is Bassanio doing, as he ponders the choices presented to him by the caskets, if not venturing his very life in the choice of death (lead) over worldly temptations (gold and silver)? He is willing to "hazard all he hath", as the casket demands, if it is the only way to gain his love. The parallels with Robert Southwell's willingness to die for his faith, hazarding all he has in his willingness to lay down his life for his friends, is obvious. And it is made even more so by the way in which Shakespeare artfully intersperses phrases from yet another Southwell poem, *Saint Peters Complaint*, into the words that Portia sings as Bassanio prepares to make his choice.[10]

It has been necessary to commence our exploration of *The Merchant of Venice* with the role that the Jew and the Jesuit played in its inspiration because, as we shall see, many of the mistakes made about the play have been the result of seeing the Jew and not the Jesuit. So much of the nonsense written about this most controversial of Shakespeare's plays arises from the opening of the wrong casket by worldly minded critics. The truth of the play, and the key to understanding it, is not to be found in the golden gaudiness of a materialistic perception of its meaning but from the lead-laden truth of the play's underlying Christian message. If we wish to understand where Shakespeare is leading us, we have to take up our cross and follow him. In doing so, we will be led by him to a region where hazarding all we have is the path to perception.

Before we follow Shakespeare to where he seeks to take us, let us take a short detour in the company of the critics. We will begin by taking a look at the literary sources for *The Merchant of Venice* and will continue by examining the way in which

---

[9] Robert Southwell, *An Humble Supplication to Her Maiestie*, ed. R.C. Bald (Cambridge: Cambridge University Press, 1953), pp. 34–35.

[10] For details of the similarities between Portia's song and *Saint Peters Complaint*, see Taylor and Beauregard, *Shakespeare and the Culture of Christianity*, p. 196.

the play has been perceived throughout the four centuries of its dramatic and critical history.

There is no single source for *The Merchant of Venice*, the plot of which seems to be a melding of three distinct stories: the story of the suitor and the usurer, the story of the caskets, and the story of the pound of flesh. It seems, however, that Shakespeare's principal source was *Il pecorone* (The dunce or The simpleton), a fourteenth-century story by Ser Giovanni Fiorentino. This is set in "Belmonte" and involves a quest by a suitor to win his mystical, otherworldly bride. As in Shakespeare's play, the suitor (Giannetto) receives money, in this case from his godfather, which has been borrowed from a Jewish usurer. Giannetto wins his bride with the assistance of the treachery of the lady's maid; the usurer demands payment, a lawyer intercedes, the lady appears in disguise, and the play ends with the business of the ring. It is, however, interesting that Shakespeare injects a specifically Christian morality into his recasting of the tale. Neither the hero nor the heroine is particularly devout in *Il pecorone*, and they choose to affront Christian morality by casually fornicating prior to their marriage. In comparison, the chastity of Portia and the chivalry of Bassanio stand in stark contrast to the moral obliquity of their literary prototypes, indicating Shakespeare's conscious decision to "baptize" his hero and heroine with Christian virtue.

Although the bare bones of much of the plot of *The Merchant of Venice* is to be found in *Il pecorone*, there is no trial of the suitors by means of the caskets in the earlier tale. This aspect of the drama might have been derived from any of several well-known versions of the casket story, such as John Gower's *Confessio amantis*, Boccacio's *Decameron*, or the anonymous *Gesta Romanorum*. In any event, as we have seen above, Shakespeare retold the casket story in his own inimitable fashion, injecting a Jesuitical metadramatic subtext into the tale.

The pound-of-flesh story was also widely known. Shakespeare might have read it in the anonymously authored "Ballad of the Crueltie of Geruntus" or in an "oration", recently translated from the French, entitled "Of a Jew, who would for his debt have a pound of flesh of a Christian". It was also included in the *Gesta Romanorum*, suggesting that this might have been the single source for both the casket and the pound-of-flesh stories. An earlier version appears in the tale of the fourth wise master in the "Seven Wise Masters of Rome" in *The Thousand and One Nights*, but since the *Nights* were not translated from the Arabic until the early eighteenth century, this version was presumably unknown to Shakespeare.

There is also the beguiling possibility that Shakespeare might have derived his own plot from an earlier play called simply *The Jew*, which was described by the English satirist Stephen Gosson in 1579 as "representing the greediness of worldly choosers and the bloody minds of usurers".[11] This description would suggest that the earlier play had a version of both the casket and the pound-of-flesh stories, but since the play is no longer extant, any further speculation is fruitless.

Finally, of course, there is the presence of Christopher Marlowe's *Jew of Malta*, which Shakespeare must have known very well. Although it seems likely that the successful revival of Marlowe's *Jew* in the wake of the López trial served as the motivation for Shakespeare's decision to write his own "Jewish" play, it would be a mistake to conflate the two plays. They have much in common, but it is in their differences, as distinct from their similarities, that we begin to perceive the injustice that has been done to Shakespeare's play by its critical misinterpretation over the centuries.

John Klause highlights "the moral vision of *The Merchant of Venice*, which is in some ways as idealistic as the ethos of Marlowe's play is cynical".[12] Whereas Marlowe made the antagonism between Christian and Jew the central element of his play, "cynically portraying Christian, Jew, and Turk as villains all",[13] the conflict between the two religions is very much a

---

[11] Stephen Gosson, *The School of Abuse* (1579), quoted in *The Reader's Encyclopedia of Shakespeare*, ed. Oscar James Campbell (New York: MJF Books, 1966), p. 522.

[12] Taylor and Beauregard, *Shakespeare and the Culture of Christianity*, p. 185.

[13] Ibid., p. 183.

secondary theme in Shakespeare's play, subsumed within the main episodes of the story line and subservient to the dominant moral theme. Take, for instance, the three main points of dramatic focus: the test of the caskets, the test of the trial, and the test of the rings. The conflict between Christian and Jew is entirely absent from the first and last of these dramatic nodal points, and it is present as a foil and not as the focus of the trial scene.

The moral focus during the drama of the trial revolves around notions of justice and mercy, or questions concerning the nature of law and ethics, and not about the hostilities between gentile and Jew. These hostilities are present, of course, and even prominent, but they are present as *accidents*, philosophically speaking,[14] and are not *essential* to the moral thrust of the plot. Unfortunately, the expression of these hostilities has distracted most critics from the essential morality of the play in pursuit of the red herring of its accidental qualities. Uncomfortable with the invective leveled against Shylock, the critics have leapt to his defense, enthroning him as the play's downtrodden hero and as its principal focus. This is absurd. Shylock is entirely uninvolved in two of the three pivotal turns in the plot and is only marginally and implicitly involved in the play's climactic denouement. To make Shylock the hero or the principal focus is to miss the whole point of the play. The play, we should remember, is called *The Merchant of Venice*, the merchant in question being Antonio and not Shylock, and is not called *The Jew of Venice* as an echo of Marlowe's *Jew of Malta*. Marlowe's play focuses on the Jew; Shakespeare's does not. In focusing too closely on Shylock, we lose the wider focus necessary to see the play as a whole.

This Shylockian heresy, to give it a name, is nothing less than a critical blindness. By way of analogy, let us look at two parallel characters in the works of Dickens that might be said to exhibit Shylockian attributes. The character of Ebenezer

---

[14] An accident, following the logic of Aristotle, is something that is irrelevant to the defining principle of a thing.

Scrooge in *A Christmas Carol* is so much at the center of the story line that stage and screen adaptations have adopted the title *Scrooge*. Though something of the artistic integrity of the work is lost in such a use of literary or dramatic license, one's critical sensibilities are not overly affronted by such an imposition. Scrooge is the principal focus of the work and his becoming its eponymous hero seems understandable enough. If, on the other hand, screen adaptations of *Oliver Twist* had altered the focus of the story to such an extent that Fagin became the principal focus, we would immediately protest that an act of gross literary vandalism had been committed against the meaning and integrity of Dickens' novel. Since Fagin is not the principal character or focus but merely a powerful and integral part of the wider plot, we would be justifiably out-raged at the grotesque parody of the original work inherent in such a shift of focus. And yet Shylock's role in *The Merchant of Venice* is much more akin to that of Fagin in *Oliver Twist* than it is to that of Scrooge in *A Christmas Carol*. It is, there-fore, shocking that it has been the sad fate of *The Merchant of Venice* to suffer from the effects of the blindness of this Shy-lockian heresy on the part of those who have read the play and staged it down the years.

From William Hazlitt's critical inversion of the play's deeper meaning in his defense of Shylock[15] to Henry Irving's cel-ebrated stage portrayal of a Jew who is "conscious of his own superiority in all but circumstance to the oppressor",[16] it has been the play's fate to have its heroes demonized and its vil-lain lionized. Perhaps this is the price that Shakespeare had to pay for his pandering to the anti-Semitic prejudices of his audience in the wake of the López trial. If so, after two hun-dred years of "substance abuse", in which the substantial mean-ing has been abused by the elevation of the accidental, it is

---

[15] William Hazlitt, *Characters of Shakespear's Plays* (London: George Bell and Sons, 1881), pp. 189–95. The work was first published by the London publisher Taylor and Hessey in 1817.

[16] From a review of Irving's performance of Shylock at London's Lyceum The-atre published in the *Saturday Review*, November 8, 1879.

surely time to insist that Shakespeare's debt has been paid. His words, having been made a pound of flesh, must now regain the spirit that gave life to the flesh in the first place. It is assuredly time to see *The Merchant of Venice* as Shakespeare saw it, as a work overflowing with Christian morality. In order to do so, we must shift our attention from the play's villain to its heroes.

If Antonio is the eponymous hero of *The Merchant of Venice*, it is generally agreed that he is upstaged by the play's heroine, the fairer-than-fair Portia.

Among Portia's numerous admirers is Fanny Kemble, the celebrated Shakespearean actress and sometime critic, who waxed lyrical, elevating Portia's "wondrous virtues" until she seems a veritable icon of idealized femininity:

> I chose Portia [as] my ideal of a perfect woman ... the wise, witty woman, loving with all her soul, and submitting with all her heart to a man whom everybody but herself (who was the best judge) would have judged her inferior; the laughter-loving, light-hearted, true-hearted, deep-hearted woman, full of keen perception, of active efficiency, of wisdom prompted by love, of tenderest unselfishness, of generous magnanimity; noble, simple, humble, pure; true, dutiful, religious, and full of fun; delightful above all others, the woman of women.[17]

Such effusiveness is echoed by characters in the play itself, most particularly by Bassanio and Jessica, and is reinforced by the name assigned to Portia's home.[18] The atmosphere of

[17] *Atlantic Monthly*, June 1876.

[18] Although "Belmonte" is the setting for *Il pecorone*, the source play for *The Merchant of Venice*, it is significant that Shakespeare chooses to retain the name, signaling his desire that the allegorical allusions with which it is pregnant are given birth within his own play. For those seeking biographical connections with Shakespeare's Catholicism, it is noteworthy that Belmont was also the Hampshire home of Thomas Pounde (1539–1615), a cousin of Shakespeare's benefactor, the Earl of Southampton, who had been an actor as a young man but was imprisoned for his active Catholicism and became a Jesuit lay brother in prison. He was still a prisoner at the time that Shakespeare was writing *The Merchant of Venice*, and it is entirely feasible, given what we know of Shakespeare's own Catholicism, that this was a further reason for his retaining Belmont as the home of his heroine.

Belmont is so different from the worldly dross that preoccupies the residents of Venice that its literal meaning, "mountain of beauty", seems singularly appropriate. The perspective of life that we attain from the beautiful heights of Belmont, in the company of the "heavenly" Portia, is so different from the venality and vendettas of Venice. If Venice wallows in the gutters of life, Belmont seems to point to the stars, and to the heaven beyond the stars, and ultimately, suggests Shakespeare scholar Fernando de Mello Moser, to the Love that moves the heaven and the stars:

> It is surely significant that Shakespeare kept the place-name of Bel-mont, implying Beauty and the Heights! Poetically and symbolically, Belmont stands for a state of overpowering Joy, a joy that grows with Love and through Love, and—as elsewhere in Shakespeare—is revealed and communicated primarily through the heroine. Because Shakespeare, different as he is from Dante in so many ways, is like the great Florentine ... both seem to have experienced what may be described as the "Beatrician vision" ... and Shakespeare, again and again, wrote about Love in terms that imply something more than merely human love, rather, beyond it, something like "l'amor che move il sole e l'altre stele".[19]

Fernando de Mello Moser's appraisal of the moral dimension of the play is as fresh and refreshing as it is rare and unusual. The problem that afflicts so much other Shakespearean criticism is that the so-called post-Christian age has lost the ability to see as Shakespeare sees, from the beautiful heights of Belmont. Lacking perspective, these critics are left with nothing but the perplexity that leads to apoplexy. They do not see Venice, as Portia sees it, from the heights of Belmont; they see only Belmont from the gutters of Venice. And from the gutters of Venice you cannot really see Belmont at

[19] Fernando de Mello Moser, *Dilecta Britannia: Estudos de cultura inglesa* (Lisbon, Portugal: Fundação Calouste Gulbenkian, 2004), p. 294. "L'amor che move il sole e l'altre stele" ("The Love that moves the sun and the other stars") is the final line and climax of Dante's *Divine Comedy*.

all. You have to hike to the heights to get Portia's perspective, and the true perspective of Portia's character. The *bella vista* can be seen only from the summit, and the summit can be reached only through an understanding of Christianity and an appreciation and apprehension of the Christian imagination that Shakespeare shared with his audience.

From a worldly perspective, and particularly from a post-modern worldly perspective, the whole business of the caskets is nothing less than a denial of Portia's freedom to make her own choices. And from a feminist perspective, it is a patriarchal denial of a woman's right to choose. And yet this is not the way that Portia sees it. In an act of outrageous "political incorrectness", she *freely chooses* to do the will of her father. "I will die as chaste as Diana, unless I be obtain'd by the manner of my father's will" (1.2.106–8). In *freely choosing* this limitation on her freedom, Portia is not succumbing to a patriarchal imposition but is merely conforming her will to correct reason. Portia knows that to *choose* evil is not only wrong but irrational. And to be irrational is to be a slave to the "madness" of one's passions. Liberty and the libertine are at war with each other. This is one of the ironies and paradoxes at the heart of the whole drama and is the very gist of Portia's discourse on the importance of prudence and temperance in the face of unruly passion. By contrast, the world chooses as it has ever chosen, following its unruly passions and binding itself with chains of gold and silver. Enslaving itself to its selfishness, it remains bereft of the joy it has not chosen. In the eyes of the world, Bassanio's choice of the "lead" of voluntary poverty over the gaudy pomp of temporal riches is but foolish. Yet it is the worldly choosers, and not Bassanio, who leave empty-handed, bereft of the pearl of great price that is beyond the reach of gold or silver; and it is Bassanio, and not the worldly choosers, who achieves the joy of his heart's desire. Led by the light of his own humility, he sees beneath the superficial surface to the very heart of reality.

But is this serious moral meaning not negated by the seemingly frivolous form that Shakespeare adopts for the play as a whole and the last scene in particular? Can a play that culminates in a riot of double entendres and sexual innuendo be taken seriously as a conveyer of any meaningful moral? Does the farce not remove the force of the morality? Does it not render any apparent moral null and void? Does it not perhaps even invert the moral, turning it into nothing more than an ironic sneer at convention? Such are the questions raised by some postmodern critics. Yet there is, for Portia, and for Shakespeare, no friction between the light of faith and the lightheartedness of humor. For the Christian, *joie de vivre* and *joie de foi* go hand in hand. They are very comfortable bedfellows. It is only the nonplussed nonbeliever who thinks that Christians need to "lighten up", whereas, in fact, the nonbeliever is far more uptight about the presence of morality than is the Christian about the presence of bawdy humor. "Angels can fly because they take themselves lightly", wrote G. K. Chesterton, whereas "the Devil fell by force of gravity." Nobody takes himself more seriously than the Devil, and this diabolical tendency is evident in those postmodern Shakespeare critics who, knowingly or unknowingly, are of the Devil's party. Such people take the jokes too seriously and the moral not seriously enough. This is a serious flaw that leaves those so afflicted utterly unable to read the Bard objectively.

The tragedy of the postmodern critic is that he cannot rise above the nihilistic sneer that is the nearest that the wingless humor of irony ever gets to laughter. Here we shall leave them, grounded in the gutters of Venice, while the true Shakespearean flies with Portia beyond the bounds of Belmont to the realm from whence all healthy Comedy finds its source.

TEXTUAL NOTE

The authoritative text of *The Merchant of Venice* is the First Quarto, published in 1600. The Second Quarto is a pirated edition, published in 1619 but fraudulently dated 1600. The First Folio text, printed from the First Quarto, was published in 1623. Although there are some minor edits of the First Quarto in the First Folio, the two texts are substantially the same. This edition is based on the First Quarto, the earliest and most authoritative text.

The Text of

THE MERCHANT OF VENICE

DRAMATIS PERSONAE

The Duke of Venice
The Prince of Morocco } Suitors to Portia
The Prince of Arragon
Antonio, a merchant of Venice
Bassanio, his friend, suitor to Portia
Solanio
Gratiano } friends to Antonio and Bassanio
Salerio
Lorenzo, in love with Jessica
Shylock, a rich Jew
Tubal, a Jew, Shylock's friend
Launcelot Gobbo, a clown, servant to Shylock
Old Gobbo, father to Launcelot
Leonardo, servant to Bassanio
Balthazar
Stephano } servants to Portia
Portia, a rich heiress, of Belmont
Nerissa, her waiting-gentlewoman
Jessica, daughter to Shylock
Magnificoes of Venice, Officers of the Court of Justice, Jailer,
   Servants to Portia, and other Attendants

ACT 1

Scene 1.   *Venice. A street.*

Enter Antonio, Salerio, and Solanio.

Antonio. In sooth,[1] I know not why I am so sad;[2]
   It wearies me, you say it wearies you;
   But how I caught it, found it, or came by it,
   What stuff 'tis made of, whereof it is born,
   I am to learn;[3]   5
   And such a want-wit[4] sadness makes of me,
   That I have much ado to know myself.

Salerio. Your mind is tossing on the ocean,[5]
   There where your argosies[6] with portly[7] sail
   Like signiors[8] and rich burghers[9] on the flood,   10
   Or as it were the pageants[10] of the sea,
   Do overpeer[11] the petty traffickers[12]
   That cur'sy[13] to them, do them reverence,[14]
   As they fly by them with their woven wings.[15]

---

[1] *In sooth:* truly.

[2] *sad:* melancholy.

[3] *I am to learn:* I have yet to learn; i.e., I do not know.

[4] *want-wit:* man out of his senses.

[5] *ocean:* a trisyllable (pronounced as if rhyming with "began").

[6] *argosies:* large merchant ships.

[7] *portly:* billowing, stately.

[8] *signiors:* wealthy, influential gentlemen.

[9] *burghers:* citizens of a town or city.

[10] *pageants:* costly scenes or festive public entertainment, as in the masques performed by the Elizabethan court.

[11] *overpeer:* tower over.

[12] *traffickers:* traders.

[13] *cur'sy:* curtsy; bow or dip (i.e., as ships moving on the waves or as is the fashion of courtiers).

[14] *do them reverence:* make a gesture signifying respect or deference.

[15] *woven wings:* i.e., sails.

Solanio. Believe me, sir, had I such venture[16] forth, 15
    The better part of my affections[17] would
    Be with my hopes abroad. I should be still[18]
    Plucking the grass to know where sits the wind,
    Piring[19] in maps for ports and piers and roads;[20]
    And every object that might make me fear 20
    Misfortune to my ventures, out of doubt[21]
    Would make me sad.

Salerio.   My wind cooling my broth[22]
    Would blow me to an ague[23] when I thought
    What harm a wind too great might do at sea.
    I should not see the sandy hour-glass run 25
    But I should think of shallows and of flats,[24]
    And see my wealthy *Andrew*[25] [dock'd] in sand,
    Vailing her high top lower than her ribs[26]
    To kiss her burial.[27] Should I go to church
    And see the holy edifice of stone, 30
    And not bethink me straight[28] of dangerous rocks,
    Which touching but my gentle[29] vessel's side
    Would scatter all her spices[30] on the stream,

---

[16] *venture*: commercial speculation.

[17] *affections*: thoughts and feelings.

[18] *still*: constantly.

[19] *Piring*: peering.

[20] *ports and piers and roads*: places of anchorage.

[21] *out of doubt*: doubtless.

[22] My *wind cooling my broth*: refers to the popular saying "Keep your breath to cool your broth" (i.e., do not waste breath in unnecessary argument).

[23] *ague*: illness involving fever and shivering (for example, malaria).

[24] *flats*: shoals.

[25] Andrew: name of a ship, possibly given in memory of a Genoese admiral, Andrea Doria. It was also the name of a Spanish galleon captured by the English in 1596.

[26] *Vailing . . . lower than her ribs*: "bowing" her topmast and breaking up (as in a shipwreck).

[27] *kiss her burial*: pay respects to the place of burial.

[28] *bethink me straight*: immediately put me in mind.

[29] *gentle*: noble.

[30] *spices*: cargo (spices were common commerce between Asia and Venice at the time).

Enrobe the roaring waters with my silks,
And in a word, but even now[31] worth this,   35
And now worth nothing? Shall I have the thought
To think on this, and shall I lack the thought
That such a thing bechanc'd[32] would make me sad?
But tell not me; I know Antonio
Is sad to think upon his merchandise.   40

Antonio. Believe me, no. I thank my fortune for it,
My ventures are not in one bottom[33] trusted,
Nor to one place; nor is my whole estate
Upon the fortune of this present year:[34]
Therefore my merchandise makes me not sad.   45

Solanio. Why then you are in love.

Antonio.   Fie, fie!

Solanio. Not in love neither? Then let us say you
    are sad
Because you are not merry; and 'twere as easy
For you to laugh and leap, and say you are merry
Because you are not sad. Now by two-headed Janus,[35]
Nature hath fram'd[36] strange fellows in her time: 51
Some that will evermore peep through their eyes,[37]
And laugh like parrots[38] at a bagpiper;[39]
And other[40] of such vinegar aspect[41]

---

[31] *but even now*: i.e., just a moment ago.

[32] *bechanc'd*: having happened.

[33] *one bottom*: one source (here, one ship or group of ships).

[34] *nor is . . . year*: Antonio's wealth is not all risked at this one time.

[35] *two-headed Janus*: in classical mythology, Roman god with two faces (facing past and future), patron of doors and openings; also a reference to the classical masks of comedy and tragedy (one smiling, one sad).

[36] *fram'd*: framed.

[37] *peep through their eyes*: i.e., look through half-closed eyes (half-closed because of laughter).

[38] *like parrots*: raucously.

[39] *bagpiper*: Bagpipe music was considered melancholy.

[40] *other*: used in a plural sense.

[41] *vinegar aspect*: sour or bitter facial expressions.

That they'll not show their teeth in way of smile   55
Though Nestor[42] swear the jest be laughable.

Enter Bassanio, Lorenzo, and Gratiano.

Solanio. Here comes Bassanio, your most noble kinsman,
   Gratiano, and Lorenzo. Fare ye well,
   We leave you now with better company.

Salerio. I would have stay'd till I had made you
     merry,   60
   If worthier friends had not prevented[43] me.

Antonio. Your worth is very dear in my regard.
   I take it your own business calls on you,
   And you embrace th' occasion[44] to depart.

Salerio. Good morrow, my good lords.   65

Bassanio. Good signiors both, when shall we laugh?[45]
     say, when?
   You grow exceeding strange.[46] Must it be so?

Salerio. We'll make our leisures to attend on[47]
     yours.

                           [Exeunt Salerio and Solanio.]

Lorenzo. My Lord Bassanio, since you have found
     Antonio,
   We two will leave you, but at dinner-time   70
   I pray you have in mind where we must meet.

Bassanio. I will not fail you.

---

[42] *Nestor:* in classical mythology, wise, solemn orator of the Trojan War.
[43] *prevented:* forestalled.
[44] *embrace th' occasion:* take advantage of the opportunity.
[45] *when shall we laugh?* when shall we laugh and be merry together?
[46] *strange:* like strangers.
[47] *attend on:* wait on, match.

Gratiano. You look not well, Signior Antonio,
  You have too much respect upon[48] the world.
  They lose it that do buy it with much care.   75
  Believe me you are marvellously chang'd.

Antonio. I hold the world but as the world, Gratiano,
  A stage, where every man must play a part,
  And mine a sad one.

Gratiano.   Let me play the fool,
  With mirth and laughter let old wrinkles come,   80
  And let my liver[49] rather heat with wine
  Than my heart cool with mortifying[50] groans.
  Why should a man, whose blood is warm within,
  Sit like his grandsire cut in alabaster?[51]
  Sleep when he wakes? and creep into the jaundies[52]   85
  By being peevish? I tell thee what, Antonio—
  I love thee, and 'tis my love that speaks—
  There are a sort of men whose visages
  Do cream and mantle[53] like a standing pond,
  And do a willful stillness entertain,[54]   90
  With purpose to be dress'd in an opinion[55]
  Of wisdom, gravity, profound conceit,[56]
  As who should say, "I am Sir Oracle,[57]
  And when I ope[58] my lips let no dog bark!"
  O my Antonio, I do know of these   95

[48] *respect upon*: concern for, mindfulness of.
[49] *liver*: considered by Elizabethans to be the seat of the emotions.
[50] *mortifying*: death-causing (according to the belief that the expenditure of breath shortened life).
[51] *alabaster*: stone used for graveyard monuments.
[52] *jaundies*: yellowing of the skin caused by an excess of bile pigments, associated by the Elizabethans with a troubled state of mind (bitterness, grief, resentment, etc.).
[53] *cream and mantle*: grow stagnant, build up scum.
[54] *entertain*: keep up.
[55] *opinion*: reputation.
[56] *conceit*: conception, notion.
[57] *Sir Oracle*: a mock title.
[58] *ope*: open.

That therefore only are reputed wise
For saying nothing; when I am very sure
If they should speak, would almost damn those ears
Which hearing them would call their brothers fools.[59]
I'll tell thee more of this another time;   100
But fish not with this melancholy bait[60]
For this fool gudgeon,[61] this opinion.[62]
Come, good Lorenzo. Fare ye well a while,
I'll end my exhortation[63] after dinner.

Lorenzo. Well, we will leave you then till dinner-time.
I must be one of these same dumb wise men,   106
For Gratiano never lets me speak.

Gratiano. Well, keep me company but two years moe,[64]
Thou shalt not know the sound of thine own tongue.

Antonio. Fare you well! I'll grow a talker for this gear.[65]

Gratiano. Thanks, i' faith,[66] for silence is only
commendable.   111
In a neat's tongue[67] dried and a maid not vendible.[68]

[*Exeunt Gratiano and Lorenzo.*]

Antonio. It is that—any thing now!

Bassanio. Gratiano speaks an infinite deal of nothing,
more than any man in all Venice. His reasons are as
two grains of wheat hid in two bushels of chaff;   116

---

[59] *If they . . . fools:* Cf. Matthew 5:22: "[W]hoever says, 'You fool!' shall be liable to the hell of fire."

[60] *Fish not . . . bait:* The fishing motif is taken further in the following lines.

[61] *fool gudgeon:* credulous person. A gudgeon is a small, easily caught fish.

[62] *opinion:* reputation.

[63] *exhortation:* strong encouragement or urging argument.

[64] *moe:* more.

[65] *for this gear:* because of what you just said.

[66] *i' faith:* a colloquial expression, literally, "in faith".

[67] *neat's tongue:* ox's tongue.

[68] *vendible:* sellable, i.e., marriageable.

you shall seek all day ere[69] you find them, and when
you have them, they are not worth the search.

Antonio. Well, tell me now what lady is the same
    To whom you swore a secret pilgrimage,   120
    That you to-day promis'd to tell me of?

Bassanio. 'Tis not unknown to you, Antonio,
    How much I have disabled[70] mine estate,
    By something showing a more swelling[71] port[72]
    Than my faint means would grant continuance.[73]   125
    Nor do I now make moan[74] to be abridg'd[75]
    From such a noble rate,[76] but my chief care
    Is to come fairly off from the great debts
    Wherein my time something too prodigal
    Hath left me gag'd.[77] To you, Antonio,   130
    I owe the most in money and in love,
    And from your love I have a warranty[78]
    To unburthen[79] all my plots and purposes
    How to get clear of all the debts I owe.

Antonio. I pray you, good Bassanio, let me know it,[80]
    And if it stand, as you yourself still do,   136
    Within the eye of honor,[81] be assur'd
    My purse, my person,[82] my extremest means,
    Lie all unlock'd to your occasions.[83]

---

[69] ere: before.
[70] disabled: constricted, reduced.
[71] swelling: extravagant.
[72] port: bearing, conduct of life.
[73] grant continuance: allow to continue.
[74] make moan: complain.
[75] abridg'd: reduced (the lavishness of his lifestyle).
[76] noble rate: lavish scale (of living).
[77] gag'd: gaged; engaged, pledged (financially).
[78] from . . . warranty: your love, in which I have full confidence, warrants me.
[79] unburthen: unburden.
[80] it: your plan or purposed enterprise.
[81] if . . . honor: if your plan is as honorable as you.
[82] person: reputation (as collateral).
[83] Lie . . . occasions: are completely available to you according to your necessities.

Bassanio. In my school-days, when I had lost one shaft,[84]
    I shot his fellow of the self-same flight   141
    The self-same way with more advised[85] watch
    To find the other forth, and by adventuring[86] both
    I oft found both. I urge this childhood proof,
    Because what follows is pure innocence.[87]   145
    I owe you much, and like a willful youth,
    That which I owe is lost, but if you please
    To shoot another arrow that self way
    Which you did shoot the first, I do not doubt,
    As I will watch the aim, or to find both   150
    Or bring your latter hazard back again,[88]
    And thankfully rest debtor for the first.

Antonio. You know me well, and herein spend but time
    To wind about my love with circumstance,[89]
    And out of doubt you do me now more wrong   155
    In making question of my uttermost[90]
    Than if you had made waste of all I have.
    Then do but say to me what I should do
    That in your knowledge may by me be done,
    And I am prest unto it;[91] therefore speak.   160

Bassanio. In Belmont is a lady richly left,[92]
    And she is fair and, fairer than that word,
    Of wondrous virtues. Sometimes[93] from her eyes

---

[84] *shaft*: arrow.

[85] *advised*: careful.

[86] *adventuring*: hazarding (in an adventure).

[87] *innocence*: childlike faith or earnestness.

[88] *Or . . . again*: either regaining both arrows (loans) or at least recovering the second (arrow).

[89] *spend . . . circumstance*: expend unnecessary breath (words) in circumlocution, seeking to persuade me.

[90] *making . . . uttermost*: questioning that I will do all I can.

[91] *prest unto it*: ready for it.

[92] *richly left*: wealthy by inheritance.

[93] *Sometimes*: formerly, at a particular time in the past.

I did receive fair speechless messages.
Her name is Portia, nothing undervalu'd[94]   165
To Cato's daughter, Brutus' Portia.[95]
Nor is the wide world ignorant of her worth,
For the four winds blow in from every coast
Renowned suitors, and her sunny[96] locks
Hang on her temples like a golden fleece,   170
Which makes her seat[97] of Belmont Colchis'[98]
    strond,[99]
And many Jasons[100] come in quest of her.[101]
O my Antonio, had I but the means
To hold a rival place with one of them,
I have a mind presages[102] me such thrift[103]   175
That I should questionless be fortunate!

Antonio. Thou know'st that all my fortunes are at sea,
Neither have I money nor commodity[104]
To raise a present sum; therefore go forth,
Try what my credit can in Venice do.   180
That shall be rack'd,[105] even to the uttermost,
To furnish thee to Belmont, to fair Portia.
Go presently[106] inquire, and so will I,

---

[94] *nothing undervalu'd*: not inferior.

[95] *Cato's daughter, Brutus' Portia*: daughter of Cato Uticensis, an honest tribune, and later wife of Brutus, conspirator against Julius Caesar.

[96] *sunny*: blonde. Elizabethans prized blonde (or red-golden) hair very highly.

[97] *seat*: residence, holding.

[98] *Colchis'*: Colchis was a city at the eastern end of the Black Sea, where Jason sailed to steal the golden fleece.

[99] *strond*: shore.

[100] *Jasons*: In classical mythology, Jason was the hero of the Argonautic quest for the golden fleece.

[101] *her*: Portia (like the golden fleece).

[102] *presages*: foretells, promises.

[103] *thrift*: profit, prosperity.

[104] *commodity*: goods.

[105] *rack'd*: stretched, as on the rack.

[106] *presently*: immediately.

Where money is, and I no question make
To have it of my trust,[107] or for my sake.[108] [*Exeunt.*] 185

Scene 2.   *Belmont. A room in Portia's house.*

Enter Portia with her waiting-woman, Nerissa.

Portia. By my troth,[109] Nerissa, my little body is
a-weary of this great world.

Nerissa. You would be, sweet madam, if your
miseries were in the same abundance as your good
fortunes are; and yet for aught I see, they are as   5
sick that surfeit with too much as they that starve
with nothing. It is no mean[110] happiness therefore
to be seated in the mean:[111] superfluity comes sooner
by white hairs,[112] but competency[113] lives longer.

Portia. Good sentences,[114] and well pronounc'd.   10

Nerissa. They would be better if well follow'd.

Portia. If to do were as easy as to know what were
good to do, chapels had been churches, and poor
men's cottages princes' palaces. It is a good divine[115]
that[116] follows his own instructions; I can easier   15
teach twenty what were good to be done, than to
be one of the twenty to follow mine own teaching.

---

[107] *my trust:* my credit (on a financial basis).

[108] *for my sake:* as a personal favor (based on reputation).

[109] *troth:* faith.

[110] *mean:* small.

[111] *in the mean:* in the middle (with neither too much nor too little).

[112] *comes sooner by white hairs:* comes sooner to older, wiser men; also, ages men more quickly.

[113] *competency:* modest or adequate means.

[114] *sentences:* wise sayings, maxims.

[115] *divine:* cleric, preacher.

[116] *that:* who.

The brain may devise laws for the blood, but a hot
temper[117] leaps o'er a cold decree[118]—such a hare
is madness the youth, to skip o'er the meshes[119] of   20
good counsel the cripple.[120] But this reasoning is not
in the fashion[121] to choose me a husband. O me,
the word choose! I may neither choose who I would,
nor refuse who I dislike; so is the will of a living
daughter curb'd by the will of a dead father.[122] Is it   25
not hard, Nerissa, that I cannot choose one, nor
refuse none?

Nerissa. Your father was ever virtuous, and holy
men at their death have good inspirations;
therefore the lott'ry[123] that he hath devis'd in these
three chests of gold, silver, and lead, whereof who   30
chooses his[124] meaning chooses you, will no doubt
never be chosen by any rightly but one who you shall
rightly[125] love. But what warmth is there in your
affection towards any of these princely suitors that
are already come?   35

Portia. I pray thee over-name them,[126] and as thou
namest them, I will describe them; and according to
my description level at my affection.[127]

---

[117] *temper:* temperament.

[118] *cold decree:* i.e., her father's bequest; also, cold reason (contrasting the hot-
ness of desire, "temper").

[119] *meshes:* snares for catching hares.

[120] *such a hare . . . good counsel the cripple:* the madness of youth skips lightly
(as a hare) over wisdom or counsel (equated to a cripple in contrast to the limber-
ness of youth).

[121] *not in the fashion:* not the way.

[122] *will of a dead father:* dead father's bequest; also, his determination (as to
her future).

[123] *lott'ry:* lottery, game of chance.

[124] *his:* i.e., her father's.

[125] *rightly . . . rightly:* correctly . . . truly.

[126] *over-name them:* list their names.

[127] *level at my affection:* aim at (as with an arrow), meaning to try to discern
my feelings toward them.

Nerissa. First, there is the Neapolitan prince.   39

Portia. Ay, that's a colt[128] indeed, for he doth nothing
     but talk of his horse, and he makes it a great
     appropriation[129] to his own good parts[130] that he
     can shoe him himself. I am much afeard my lady his
     mother play'd false with a smith.[131]

Nerissa. Then there is the County[132] Palentine.   45

Portia. He doth nothing but frown, as who should
     say, "And you will not have me, choose."[133] He hears
     merry tales and smiles not. I fear he will prove the
     weeping philosopher[134] when he grows old, being
     so full of unmannerly sadness in his youth. I had   50
     rather be married to a death's-head with a bone in
     his mouth than to either of these. God defend me
     from these two!

Nerissa. How say you by the French lord, Monsieur
     Le [Bon]?   55

Portia. God made him, and therefore let him pass
     for a man. In truth, I know it is a sin to be a mocker,
     but he! why, he hath a horse better than the
     Neapolitan's, a better bad habit of frowning than the
     Count Palentine; he is every man in no man. If a   60
     throstle[135] sing, he falls straight a cap'ring.[136] He
     will fence with his own shadow. If I should marry

128 *colt*: witless adolescent.
129 *appropriation*: addition.
130 *parts*: abilities, talents.
131 *my lady . . . a smith*: She suggests that he is the illegitimate son of a black-smith (thus his "genetic" preoccupation with horses).
132 *County*: Count.
133 *choose*: choose whom you will (i.e., "If I don't suit you, use your pleasure!").
134 *the weeping philosopher*: Heraclitus of Ephesus (c. 535–475 B.C.), Greek philosopher distinguished for his melancholy disposition.
135 *throstle*: song thrush.
136 *a cap'ring*: to capering; dancing.

him, I should marry twenty husbands. If he would
despise me, I would forgive him, for if he love me to
madness, I shall never requite him.   65

Nerissa. What say you then to Falconbridge, the
young baron of England?

Portia. You know I say nothing to him, for he
understands not me, nor I him. He hath neither
Latin, French, nor Italian, and you will come into   70
the court and swear that I have a poor
pennyworth[137] in the English. He is a proper[138]
man's picture, but alas, who can converse with a
dumb show?[139] How oddly he is suited![140] I think
he bought his doublet[141] in Italy, his round hose[142]
in France, his bonnet[143] in Germany, and his
behavior every where.[144]   76

Nerissa. What think you of the Scottish lord, his
neighbor?

Portia. That he hath a neighborly charity in him, for
he borrow'd a box of the ear of the Englishman,   80
and swore he would pay him again when he was able.
I think the Frenchman became his surety and seal'd
under[145] for another.

[137] poor pennyworth: poor value of money (as much as can be purchased for a penny).

[138] proper: handsome.

[139] dumb show: mime, made up of gestures to convey something without using speech.

[140] suited: dressed.

[141] doublet: coat.

[142] round hose: trunk hose, stuffed breeches.

[143] bonnet: hat.

[144] and his behavior every where: The assertion is that he is so weak of character that he assimilates the fashions and behaviors of anyone around him.

[145] seal'd under: put his seal under the Scot's (as a secondary guarantor of the loan). This playfully alludes to the traditional alliance between France and Scotland and their joint hostility to England.

Nerissa. How like you the young German, the Duke
of Saxony's nephew? 85

Portia. Very vildly[146] in the morning, when he is sober,
and most vildly in the afternoon, when he is drunk.
When he is best, he is a little worse than a man,
and when he is worst, he is little better than a beast.
And the worst fall that ever fell,[147] I hope I shall
make shift[148] to go without him. 91

Nerissa. If he should offer to choose, and choose the
right casket, you should refuse to perform your
father's will, if you should refuse to accept him. 94

Portia. Therefore for fear of the worst, I pray thee set
a deep glass of Rhenish wine[149] on the contrary[150]
casket, for if the devil be within, and that
temptation without, I know he will choose it. I
will do any thing, Nerissa, ere[151] I'll be married to a
spunge. 99

Nerissa. You need not fear, lady, the having any of
these lords. They have acquainted me with their
determinations, which is indeed to return to their
home, and to trouble you with no more suit, unless
you may be won by some other sort[152] than your
father's imposition depending on the caskets. 105

Portia. If I live to be as old as Sibylla,[153] I will die as
chaste as Diana,[154] unless I be obtain'd by the

[146] *vildly:* vilely.
[147] *And . . . ever fell:* if the worst befall.
[148] *make shift:* manage to do something.
[149] *Rhenish wine:* Rhine wine.
[150] *contrary:* other, or "wrong".
[151] *ere:* before.
[152] *by some other sort:* by some other way, in some other manner.
[153] *Sibylla:* In classical mythology, the Cumæan Sibyl was a wise prophetess, to whom Apollo promised years as numerous as the grains of sand in her grasp.
[154] *Diana:* in classical mythology, virginal goddess of the hunt.

manner of my father's will. I am glad this parcel[155]
of wooers are so reasonable, for there is not one
among them but I dote on his very absence, and I
pray God grant them a fair departure.   111

Nerissa. Do you not remember, lady, in your father's
time, a Venetian, a scholar and a soldier, that came
hither in company of the Marquis of Montferrat?

Portia. Yes, yes, it was Bassanio—as I think, so was
he call'd.   116

Nerissa. True, madam; he, of all the men that ever
my foolish eyes look'd upon, was the best deserving
a fair lady.

Portia. I remember him well, and I remember him
worthy of thy praise.   121

Enter a Servingman.

How now, what news?

Servingman. The four strangers seek for you, madam,
to take their leave; and there is a forerunner come
from a fift,[156] the Prince of Morocco, who brings
word the Prince his master will be here to-night.   126

Portia. If I could bid the fift welcome with so good
heart as I can bid the other four farewell, I should
be glad of his approach. If he have the condition[157]
of a saint, and the complexion of a devil, I had rather
he should shrive[158] me than wive[159] me.   131

---

[155] *parcel*: set, company.
[156] *fift*: fifth.
[157] *condition*: disposition, temper.
[158] *shrive*: absolve (perform the office of a confessor).
[159] *wive*: marry.

Come, Nerissa. Sirrah,[160] go before.
Whiles we shut the gate upon one wooer, another
knocks at the door.   [*Exeunt.*]

Scene 3.   *Venice. A public place.*

Enter Bassanio with Shylock the Jew.

Shylock. Three thousand ducats,[161] well.

Bassanio. Ay, sir, for three months.

Shylock. For three months, well.

Bassanio. For the which, as I told you, Antonio shall
be bound.[162]   5

Shylock. Antonio shall become bound, well.

Bassanio. May you stead[163] me? Will you pleasure me?
Shall I know your answer?

Shylock. Three thousand ducats for three months, and
Antonio bound.   10

Bassanio. Your answer to that.

Shylock. Antonio is a good[164] man.

Bassanio. Have you heard any imputation to the
contrary?   14

Shylock. Ho, no, no, no, no! my meaning in saying
he is a good man is to have you understand me that
he is sufficient.[165] Yet his means are in supposition:[166]
he hath an argosy[167] bound to Tripolis,

---

[160] *Sirrah:* form of address to servants.

[161] *ducats:* gold coins (literally, a ducat is a coin issued by a duke).

[162] *bound:* held as surety of the loan.

[163] *stead:* accommodate, assist.

[164] *good:* of sound credit.

[165] *sufficient:* legally satisfactory, safe as guarantor of the loan.

[166] *in supposition:* uncertain, hypothetical (not safe or concrete).

[167] *argosy:* merchant ship.

another to the Indies; I understand moreover upon
the Rialto,[168] he hath a third at Mexico, a fourth   20
for England, and other ventures he hath,
squand'red[169] abroad. But ships are but boards,
sailors but men; there be land-rats and water-rats,
water-thieves and land-thieves, I mean pirates, and
then there is the peril of waters, winds, and rocks.   25
The man is notwithstanding sufficient. Three
thousand ducats: I think I may take his bond.

Bassanio. Be assur'd you may.

Shylock. I will be assur'd I may; and that I may
be assur'd, I will bethink me. May I speak with
Antonio?   31

Bassanio. If it please you to dine with us.

Shylock. Yes, to smell pork, to eat of the habitation[170]
which your prophet the Nazarite conjur'd the devil
into.[171] I will buy with you, sell with you, talk   35
with you, walk with you, and so following; but I
will not eat with you, drink with you, nor pray with
you. What news on the Rialto? Who is he comes
here?

Enter Antonio.

Bassanio. This is Signior Antonio.   40

Shylock. [*Aside.*] How like a fawning publican[172] he
looks!

---

[168] *Rialto:* location of the Venetian stock exchange.

[169] *squand'red:* scattered.

[170] *habitation:* body.

[171] *your prophet . . . into:* reference to Jesus casting evil spirits into a herd of
swine (cf. Luke 8:26–33; Matthew 8:28–32).

[172] *publican:* farmer of taxes under Roman government, also an innkeeper. (It
has been hypothesized by some that this term results from a corruption of the
text.)

I hate him for[173] he is a Christian;
But more, for that in low simplicity
He lends out money gratis, and brings down
The rate of usance[174] here with us in Venice.   45
If I can catch him once upon the hip,[175]
I will feed fat the ancient grudge I bear him.
He hates our sacred nation, and he rails
Even there where merchants most do congregate
On me, my bargains, and my well-won thrift,   50
Which he calls interest. Cursed be my tribe
If I forgive him!

Bassanio.   Shylock, do you hear?

Shylock. I am debating of my present store,[176]
And by the near guess of my memory,
I cannot instantly raise up the gross   55
Of full three thousand ducats. What of that?
Tubal, a wealthy Hebrew of my tribe,
Will furnish me. But soft, how many months
Do you desire? [*To Antonio.*] Rest you fair, good
      signior,
Your worship was the last man in our mouths.   60

Antonio. Shylock, albeit I neither lend nor borrow
By taking nor by giving of excess,[177]
Yet to supply the ripe[178] wants of my friend,
I'll break a custom. [*To Bassanio.*] Is he yet possess'd
How much ye would?[179]

Shylock.   Ay, ay, three thousand ducats.

Antonio. And for three months.   66

---

[173] *for*: because.
[174] *usance*: interest, usury.
[175] *catch . . . hip*: get advantage of him (wrestling figure of speech).
[176] *store*: holdings, wealth.
[177] *excess*: interest.
[178] *ripe*: immediate.
[179] *possess'd . . . would*: informed of how much you want.

Shylock. I had forgot—three months—[*to Bassanio*]
    you told me so.
  Well then, your bond; and let me see—but hear you,[180]
  Methoughts[181] you said you neither lend nor borrow
  Upon advantage.

Antonio.   I do never use it.   70

Shylock. When Jacob graz'd his uncle Laban's sheep—[182]
  This Jacob from our holy Abram was
  (As his wise mother wrought in his behalf)
  The third possessor;[183] ay, he was the third—

Antonio. And what of him? did he take interest?   75

Shylock. No, not take interest, not as you would say
  Directly int'rest. Mark what Jacob did:
  When Laban and himself were compremis'd[184]
  That all the eanlings[185] which were streak'd and pied[186]
  Should fall as Jacob's hire, the ewes being rank[187]   80
  In end of autumn turned to the rams,
  And when the work of generation was
  Between these woolly breeders in the act,
  The skillful shepherd pill'd[188] me certain wands,
  And in the doing of the deed of kind,   85
  He stuck them up before the fulsome ewes,
  Who then conceiving did in eaning[189] time

---

[180] *but hear you*: figure of speech, essentially "wait a minute".

[181] *Methoughts*: I thought, I recall.

[182] *When Jacob graz'd . . . sheep*: Jacob was an Old Testament patriarch; Laban was his uncle and father-in-law. A paraphrase of the Old Testament story follows (cf. Genesis 30:25–43).

[183] *third possessor*: of Abraham's birthright (the third generation, as Abraham was his grandfather).

[184] *were compremis'd*: had made an agreement (cf. Genesis 30).

[185] *eanlings*: newborn lambs.

[186] *streak'd and pied*: streaked (striped) and spotted.

[187] *rank*: receptive to breeding.

[188] *pill'd*: peeled.

[189] *eaning*: lambing.

Fall[190] parti-color'd lambs, and those were Jacob's.
This was a way to thrive, and he was blest;
And thrift is blessing, if men steal it not.   90

Antonio. This was a venture, sir, that Jacob serv'd for,
A thing not in his power to bring to pass,
But sway'd and fashion'd by the hand of heaven.
Was this inserted to make interest good?[191]
Or is your gold and silver ewes and rams?   95

Shylock. I cannot tell, I make it breed as fast.[192]
But note me, signior.

Antonio.   Mark you this, Bassanio,
The devil can cite Scripture for his purpose.
An evil soul producing holy witness
Is like a villain with a smiling cheek,   100
A goodly[193] apple rotten at the heart.
O, what a goodly outside falsehood hath!

Shylock. Three thousand ducats—'tis a good round
        sum.
Three months from twelve; then let me see, the
        rate—

Antonio. Well, Shylock, shall we be beholding[194] to you?

Shylock. Signior Antonio, many a time and oft   106
In the Rialto you have rated[195] me
About my moneys and my usances.
Still have I borne it with a patient shrug

---

[190] *Fall*: give birth to.

[191] *inserted . . . good*: brought in to justify charging interest.

[192] *I make it breed as fast*: A main Elizabethan argument against usury was that it blasphemously caused inanimate metal to multiply as living creatures did at God's command (cf. Genesis 8:17; 9:1).

[193] *goodly*: attractive.

[194] *beholding*: beholden, indebted.

[195] *rated*: harshly reproved, railed at.

(For suff'rance is the badge[196] of all our tribe).[197]   110
You call me misbeliever, cut-throat dog,
And spet upon my Jewish gaberdine,[198]
And all for use of that which is mine own.
Well then, it now appears you need my help.
Go to[199] then, you come to me, and you say,   115
"Shylock, we would have moneys," you say so—
You, that did void[200] your rheum[201] upon my beard,
And foot[202] me as you spurn a stranger cur[203]
Over your threshold; moneys is your suit.
What should I say to you? Should I not say,   120
"Hath a dog money? Is it possible
A cur can lend three thousand ducats?" Or
Shall I bend low and in a bondman's key,
With bated breath and whisp'ring humbleness,
Say this: 125
"Fair sir, you spet[204] on me on Wednesday last,
You spurn'd me such a day, another time
You call'd me dog; and for these courtesies
I'll lend you thus much moneys"?

Antonio. I am as like to call thee so again,   130
To spet on thee again, to spurn thee too.
If thou wilt lend this money, lend it not
As to thy friends, for when did friendship take
A breed for barren metal of his friend?
But lend it rather to thine enemy,   135

[196] badge: distinctive mark, perhaps an actual metal or cloth emblem indicative of familial associations or, in this case, of Judaism.
[197] our tribe: the Jewish nation.
[198] gaberdine: cloak.
[199] Go to: colloquial expression, often an exclamation of impatience.
[200] void: vomit.
[201] rheum: spittle.
[202] foot: kick.
[203] stranger cur: mongrel dog.
[204] spet: spat.

Who if he break,[205] thou mayst with better face
Exact the penalty.

Shylock. Why, look you how you storm!
I would be friends with you, and have your love,
Forget the shames that you have stain'd me with,
Supply your present wants, and take no doit[206]　　　140
Of usance for my moneys, and you'll not hear me.
This is kind I offer.[207]

Bassanio. This were kindness.

Shylock. This kindness will I show.
Go with me to a notary, seal me there
Your single[208] bond; and in a merry sport　　　145
If you repay me not on such a day,
In such a place, such sum or sums as are
Express'd in the condition, let the forfeit
Be nominated[209] for an equal[210] pound
Of your fair flesh, to be cut off and taken　　　150
In what part of your body pleaseth me.

Antonio. Content, in faith, I'll seal to such a bond,
And say there is much kindness in the Jew.

Bassanio. You shall not seal to such a bond for me,
I'll rather dwell in my necessity.[211]　　　155

Antonio. Why, fear not, man, I will not forfeit it.
Within these two months, that's a month before
This bond expires, I do expect return
Of thrice three times the value of this bond.

---

[205] *break*: go bankrupt.
[206] *doit*: Dutch coin of very small value.
[207] *kind I offer*: i.e., a kindly offer.
[208] *single*: without conditions attached.
[209] *nominated*: named.
[210] *equal*: just, exact.
[211] *dwell in my necessity*: i.e., remain in my need.

Shylock. O father Abram, what these Christians are,
    Whose own hard dealings teaches them suspect   *161*
    The thoughts of others! Pray you tell me this:
    If he should break his day,[212] what should I gain
    By the exaction of the forfeiture?
    A pound of man's flesh taken from a man   *165*
    Is not so estimable, profitable neither,
    As flesh of muttons, beefs, or goats. I say,
    To buy his favor, I extend this friendship.
    If he will take it, so, if not, adieu;
    And for my love I pray you wrong me not.   *170*

Antonio. Yes, Shylock, I will seal unto this bond.

Shylock. Then meet me forthwith at the notary's;
    Give him direction for this merry bond,
    And I will go and purse[213] the ducats straight,
    See to my house, left in the fearful[214] guard   *175*
    Of an unthrifty knave, and presently
    I'll be with you.   *[Exit.]*

Antonio.   Hie thee, gentle[215] Jew.
    The Hebrew will turn Christian, he grows kind.

Bassanio. I like not fair terms and a villain's mind.

Antonio. Come on, in this there can be no dismay,   *180*
    My ships come home a month before the day.
    [Exeunt.]

---

[212] *break his day*: fail to pay by the due date.
[213] *purse*: procure, gather.
[214] *fearful*: causing (me) fear.
[215] *gentle*: potentially with pun on "gentile".

ACT 2

Scene 1.   *Belmont. A room in Portia's house.*

Flourish[1] *cornets.*[2] *Enter the Prince of Morocco,
a tawny Moor, all in white, and three or four Followers
accordingly, with Portia, Nerissa, and their Train.*

Morocco. Mislike[3] me not for my complexion,
　The shadowed livery[4] of the burnish'd sun,
　To whom I am a neighbor and near bred.
　Bring me the fairest creature northward born,
　Where Phoebus'[5] fire scarce thaws the icicles,　　　　　5
　And let us make incision[6] for your love,
　To prove whose blood is reddest, his or mine.
　I tell thee, lady, this aspect[7] of mine
　Hath fear'd[8] the valiant; by my love, I swear
　The best-regarded virgins of our clime　　　　　10
　Have lov'd it too. I would not change this hue,
　Except to steal your thoughts,[9] my gentle queen.

Portia. In terms of choice I am not soly led
　By nice[10] direction of a maiden's eyes;
　Besides, the lott'ry of my destiny　　　　　15
　Bars me the right of voluntary choosing.
　But if my father had not scanted[11] me,
　And hedg'd me by his wit to yield myself
　His wife who wins me by that means I told you,

---

[1] *Flourish:* fanfare.

[2] *cornets:* brass instruments like trumpets.

[3] *Mislike:* dislike.

[4] *livery:* distinctive clothes, often denoting association or allegiance.

[5] *Phoebus':* In classical mythology, Phoebus was god of the sun.

[6] *make incision:* cut to draw blood (a violent proof of love sometimes adopted by Elizabethan gallants).

[7] *aspect:* countenance.

[8] *fear'd:* feared; frightened, made afraid.

[9] *steal your thoughts:* i.e., win your favor.

[10] *nice:* fastidious.

[11] *scanted:* restricted.

Yourself, renowned Prince, then stood as fair   20
As any comer I have look'd on yet
For my affection.

Morocco.   Even for that I thank you;
Therefore I pray you lead me to the caskets
To try my fortune. By this scimitar
That slew the Sophy[12] and a Persian prince   25
That won three fields of Sultan Solyman,[13]
I would o'erstare the sternest eyes that look,
Outbrave the heart most daring on the earth,
Pluck the young sucking cubs from the she-bear,
Yea, mock the lion when 'a[14] roars for prey,   30
To win [thee], lady. But alas the while![15]
If Hercules and Lichas[16] play at dice
Which is the better man, the greater throw
May turn by fortune from the weaker hand:
So is Alcides[17] beaten by his [page],[18]   35
And so may I, blind fortune leading me,
Miss that which one unworthier may attain,
And die with grieving.

Portia.   You must take your chance,
And either not attempt to choose at all,
Or swear before you choose, if you choose wrong   40
Never to speak to lady afterward
In way of marriage; therefore be advis'd.

Morocco. Nor will not.[19] Come bring me unto my chance.

---

[12] Sophy: shah of Persia.

[13] Sultan Solyman: Suleiman the Magnificent (1494–1566), sultan of Turkey under whose governance the Ottoman Empire reached the peak of its power and influence.

[14] 'a: he.

[15] alas the while: alas, or alas for this time.

[16] Lichas: servant of Hercules who unwittingly gave his master a poisoned shirt that drove him to madness and death.

[17] Alcides: Hercules.

[18] his page: i.e., Lichas.

[19] Nor will not: He is promising to abide by the terms of the lottery.

Portia. First, forward to the temple;[20] after dinner
    Your hazard shall be made.

Morocco.   Good fortune then!   45
    To make me blest or cursed'st among men.

                          [*Cornets. Exeunt.*]

           Scene 2.   *Venice. A street.*

       Enter the Clown [Launcelot Gobbo] alone.

Launcelot. Certainly my conscience will serve me to
    run from this Jew my master. The fiend is at mine
    elbow and tempts me, saying to me, "[Gobbo],
    Launcelot [Gobbo], good Launcelot," or "good
    [Gobbo]," or "good Launcelot [Gobbo], use your   5
    legs, take the start, run away." My conscience
    says, "No; take heed, honest Launcelot, take heed,
    honest [Gobbo]," or as aforesaid, "honest Launcelot
    [Gobbo], do not run, scorn running with thy heels."[21]
    Well, the most courageous fiend bids me pack.[22]   10
    "Fia!"[23] says the fiend; "away!" says the fiend;
    "for the heavens,[24] rouse up a brave mind," says the
    fiend, "and run." Well, my conscience, hanging
    about the neck of my heart, says very wisely to me,
    "My honest friend Launcelot, being an honest   15
    man's son"—or rather an honest woman's son, for
    indeed my father did something smack, something
    grow to, he had a kind of taste—well, my
    conscience says, "Launcelot, bouge[25] not." "Bouge,"

---

[20] *the temple:* loosely used to mean the church. Morocco is to take a solemn
vow.

[21] *scorn running with thy heels:* spurn, reject running (with pun on "kick at").

[22] *pack:* begone, pack yourself off.

[23] *Fia!* command addressed to horses (probably from the Italian *via*—"away!").

[24] *for the heavens:* for Heaven's sake.

[25] *bouge:* budge.

says the fiend. "Bouge not," says my conscience.   20
"Conscience," say I, "you counsel well." "Fiend,"
say I, "you counsel well." To be rul'd by my
conscience, I should stay with the Jew my master,
who (God bless the mark)²⁶ is a kind of devil; and
to run away from the Jew, I should be rul'd²⁷ by   25
the fiend, who, saving your reverence,²⁸ is the devil
himself. Certainly the Jew is the very devil
incarnation,²⁹ and in my conscience,³⁰ my
conscience is but a kind of hard conscience, to offer
to counsel me to stay with the Jew. The fiend gives   30
the more friendly counsel: I will run, fiend; my heels
are at your commandement, I will run.

                          Enter Old Gobbo with a basket.

Gobbo. Master young man, you, I pray you, which
           is the way to Master Jew's?   34

Launcelot. [*Aside.*] O heavens, this is my true-
           begotten father, who being more than sand-blind,³¹
           high gravel-blind,³² knows me not. I will try
           confusions³³ with him.

Gobbo. Master young gentleman, I pray you, which
           is the way to Master Jew's?   40

Launcelot. Turn up on your right hand at the next
           turning, but at the next turning of all, on your left;

²⁶ *God bless the mark*: colloquial phrase used to avert evil (here possibly anticipating the mention of the Devil).
²⁷ *rul'd*: ruled.
²⁸ *saving your reverence*: with all due respect (excusing himself in advance for
what he is about to say).
²⁹ *incarnation*: incarnate.
³⁰ *in my conscience*: in my conception (wordplay).
³¹ *sand-blind*: half-blind.
³² *high gravel-blind*: blinder than sand-blind (a condition made up by Launcelot).
³³ *try confusions*: argue.

marry,[34] at the very next turning, turn of no hand,
but turn down indirectly to the Jew's house. 44

Gobbo. By God's sonties,[35] 'twill be a hard way to
hit. Can you tell me whether one Launcelot, that
dwells with him, dwell with him or no?

Launcelot. Talk you of young Master Launcelot?
[*Aside.*] Mark[36] me now, now will I raise the
waters.[37]—Talk you of young Master[38] Launcelot? 50

Gobbo. No master, sir, but a poor man's son. His
father, though I say 't, is an honest exceeding poor
man and, God be thank'd, well to live.[39]

Launcelot. Well, let his father be what 'a[40] will, we talk
of young Master Launcelot. 55

Gobbo. Your worship's friend and Launcelot, sir.

Launcelot. But I pray you, *ergo*,[41] old man, *ergo*, I
beseech you, talk you of young Master Launcelot.

Gobbo. Of Launcelot, an't please your mastership.

Launcelot. Ergo, Master Launcelot. Talk not of 60
Master Launcelot, father,[42] for the young
gentleman, according to Fates and Destinies, and such
odd sayings, the Sisters Three,[43] and such branches

---

[34] *marry*: indeed, to be sure.
[35] *sonties*: a word of doubtful meaning; perhaps health or sanctities or little
saints.
[36] *Mark*: attend.
[37] *raise the waters*: i.e., start something, perhaps raise tears.
[38] *Master*: a title applied to young gentlemen.
[39] *well to live*: likely to live long.
[40] *'a*: he.
[41] *ergo*: therefore (Latin), used flippantly here.
[42] *father*: familiar form of address to the old man, not an acknowledgment of
Gobbo as his father.
[43] *Sisters Three*: in classical mythology, the three Fates.

of learning, is indeed deceas'd, or as you would say
in plain terms, gone to heaven.   65

Gobbo. Marry, God forbid, the boy was the very
staff of my age, my very prop.

Launcelot. [*Aside.*] Do I look like a cudgel or a hovel-
post,[44] a staff, or a prop?—Do you know me, father?

Gobbo. Alack the day, I know you not, young
gentleman, but I pray you tell me, is my boy, God
rest his soul, alive or dead?   72

Launcelot. Do you not know me, father?

Gobbo. Alack, sir, I am sand-blind, I know you not.

Launcelot. Nay, indeed if you had your eyes   75
you might fail of the knowing me; it is a wise father
that knows his own child. Well, old man, I will
tell you news of your son. Give me your blessing;
truth will come to light; murder cannot be hid long;
a man's son may, but in the end truth will out.   80

Gobbo. Pray you, sir, stand up. I am sure you are
not Launcelot, my boy.

Launcelot. Pray you let's have no more fooling about
it, but give me your blessing. I am Launcelot, your
boy that was, your son that is, your child that shall
be.   86

Gobbo. I cannot think you are my son.

Launcelot. I know not what I shall think of that; but
I am Launcelot, the Jew's man, and I am sure
Margery your wife is my mother.   90

---

[44] *hovel-post:* timber supporting a shack.

Gobbo. Her name is Margery indeed. I'll be sworn,
    if thou be Launcelot, thou art mine own flesh and
    blood. Lord worshipp'd might he be,[45] what a beard[46]
    hast thou got! Thou hast got more hair on thy
    chin than Dobbin my fill-horse[47] has on his tail.   95

Launcelot. It should seem then that Dobbin's tail grows
    backward. I am sure he had more hair of his tail than
    I have of my face when I [last] saw him.

Gobbo. Lord, how art thou chang'd! How dost
    thou and thy master agree? I have brought him a
    present. How 'gree you now?   101

Launcelot. Well, well; but for mine own part, as I
    have set up my rest[48] to run away, so I will not rest
    till I have run some ground. My master's a very
    Jew. Give him a present! give him a halter.[49]   105
    I am famish'd in his service; you may tell[50] every
    finger I have with my ribs. Father, I am glad you
    are come; give me your present to one Master
    Bassanio, who indeed gives rare new liveries. If
    I serve not him, I will run as far as God has any   110
    ground. O rare fortune, here comes the man. To
    him, father, for I am a Jew if I serve the Jew any
    longer.

Enter Bassanio with a follower or two, [one of them Leonardo].

Bassanio. You may do so, but let it be so hasted that
    supper be ready at the farthest by five of the   115

---

[45] *Lord worship'd might he be*: exclamation of surprise and delight, where "might" means "may" ("The Lord be worshipped!").

[46] *beard*: According to stage tradition, Launcelot kneels with his back to his father so that Gobbo feels his son's hair and mistakes it for a beard.

[47] *fill-horse*: thill horse (horse that goes in the shafts or thills), cart horse.

[48] *set up my rest*: made up my mind, determined.

[49] *halter*: hangman's noose.

[50] *tell*: count.

clock. See these letters deliver'd, put the liveries to
making,[51] and desire Gratiano to come anon[52] to
my lodging.

[Exit one of his men.]

Launcelot. To him, father.

Gobbo. God bless your worship!   120

Bassanio. Gramercy,[53] wouldst thou aught with me?

Gobbo. Here's my son, sir, a poor boy—

Launcelot. Not a poor boy, sir, but the rich Jew's man,
    that would, sir, as my father shall specify—

Gobbo. He hath a great infection,[54] sir, as one would
    say, to serve—   126

Launcelot. Indeed the short and the long is, I serve
    the Jew, and have a desire, as my father shall
    specify—

Gobbo. His master and he (saving your worship's
    reverence) are scarce cater-cousins—[55]   131

Launcelot. To be brief, the very truth is that the Jew,
    having done me wrong, doth cause me, as my father,
    being I hope an old man, shall frutify[56] unto you—

Gobbo. I have here a dish of doves that I would
    bestow upon your worship, and my suit is—   136

---

[51] *put the liveries to making:* set the tailor to sewing the liveries.
[52] *anon:* presently, immediately.
[53] *Gramercy:* many thanks (from the French *grand merci*).
[54] *infection:* affection (desire).
[55] *cater-cousins:* close friends.
[56] *frutify:* fructify; become fruitful.

Launcelot. In very brief, the suit is impertinent[57] to
    myself, as your worship shall know by this honest
    old man, and though I say it, though old man, yet
    poor man, my father.   140

Bassanio. One speak for both. What would you?

Launcelot. Serve you, sir.

Gobbo. That is the very defect[58] of the matter, sir.

Bassanio. I know thee well, thou hast obtain'd thy suit.
    Shylock thy master spoke with me this day,   145
    And hath preferr'd[59] thee, if it be preferment
    To leave a rich Jew's service, to become
    The follower of so poor a gentleman.

Launcelot. The old proverb is very well parted between
    my master Shylock and you, sir: you have the grace
    of God, sir, and he hath enough.[60]   151

Bassanio. Thou speak'st it well. Go, father, with thy son.
    Take leave of thy old master, and inquire
    My lodging out.—Give him a livery
    More guarded[61] than his fellows'; see it done.   155

Launcelot. Father, in.[62] I cannot get a service, no, I
    have ne'er a tongue in my head, well! [*Looking
    on his palm.*] If any man in Italy hath a fairer table,[63]
    which doth offer to swear upon a book, I shall have
    good fortune. Go to,[64] here's a simple line of   160
    life! Here's a small trifle of wives! Alas, fifteen

---

[57] *impertinent*: i.e., pertinent.
[58] *defect*: i.e., effect.
[59] *preferr'd*: recommended for advancement, transferred.
[60] *proverb . . . enough*: play on the proverb "God's grace is gear enough."
[61] *guarded*: ornamented with a braid or lace.
[62] *in*: into the house with you, go in.
[63] *table*: palm of the hand.
[64] *Go to*: colloquial expression, essentially "get along", "go on".

wives is nothing! Aleven[65] widows and nine maids
is a simple coming-in[66] for one man. And then to
scape[67] drowning thrice, and to be in peril of my
life with the edge of a feather-bed,[68] here are   165
simple scapes.[69] Well, if Fortune be a woman, she's
a good wench for this gear.[70] Father, come, I'll take
my leave of the Jew in the twinkling.

                    [*Exit Clown with old Gobbo.*]

Bassanio. I pray thee, good Leonardo, think on this:
These things being bought and orderly bestowed,   170
Return in haste, for I do feast to-night
My best-esteem'd acquaintance. Hie thee, go.

Leonardo. My best endeavors shall be done herein.

                       Enter Gratiano.

Gratiano. Where's your master?

Leonardo.   Yonder, sir, he walks.   [*Exit Leonardo.*]

Gratiano. Signior Bassanio!   175

Bassanio. Gratiano!

Gratiano. I have a suit to you.

Bassanio.   You have obtain'd it.

Gratiano. You must not deny me; I must go with you to
    Belmont.

---

[65] *Aleven:* eleven.
[66] *coming-in:* inheritance.
[67] *scape:* escape.
[68] *in peril . . . feather-bed:* This may be an allusion to the danger of an angry cuckolded spouse (the feather bed representing someone else's marriage bed).
[69] *scapes:* escapes.
[70] *this gear:* this business, these matters.

Bassanio. Why then you must. But hear thee, Gratiano: 180
    Thou art too wild, too rude, and bold of voice—
    Parts that become thee happily enough,
    And in such eyes as ours appear not faults,
    But where thou art not known, why, there they show
    Something too liberal.[71] Pray thee take pain   185
    To allay with some cold drops of modesty
    Thy skipping spirit, lest through thy wild behavior
    I be misconst'red[72] in the place I go to,
    And lose my hopes.

Gratiano.   Signior Bassanio, hear me:
    If I do not put on a sober habit,[73]   190
    Talk with respect, and swear but now and then,
    Wear prayer-books in my pocket, look demurely,
    Nay more, while grace is saying[74] hood mine eyes
    Thus with my hat, and sigh and say amen,
    Use all the observance of civility,   195
    Like one well studied in a sad ostent[75]
    To please his grandam, never trust me more.

Bassanio. Well, we shall see your bearing.

Gratiano. Nay, but I bar to-night, you shall not gauge me
    By what we do to-night.

Bassanio.   No, that were pity.   200
    I would entreat you rather to put on
    Your boldest suit of mirth, for we have friends
    That purpose merriment. But fare you well,
    I have some business.

---

[71] *liberal*: free.

[72] *misconst'red*: misconstrued.

[73] *habit*: clothing or demeanor.

[74] *while grace is saying*: while grace is being said before a meal. Hats were worn during meals but removed during grace.

[75] *ostent*: appearance, display.

Gratiano. And I must to Lorenzo and the rest,   205
    But we will visit you at supper-time.   [*Exeunt.*]

Scene 3.   *The same. A room in Shylock's house.*

Enter Jessica and the Clown Launcelot.

Jessica. I am sorry thou wilt leave my father so.
    Our house is hell, and thou, a merry devil,
    Didst rob it of some taste of tediousness.
    But fare thee well, there is a ducat for thee,
    And, Launcelot, soon at supper shalt thou see   5
    Lorenzo, who is thy new master's guest.
    Give him this letter, do it secretly,
    And so farewell. I would not have my father
    See me in talk with thee.

Launcelot. Adieu, tears exhibit[76] my tongue. Most   10
       beautiful pagan, most sweet Jew! if a Christian do
       not play the knave and get thee, I am much deceiv'd.
       But adieu, these foolish drops do something drown
       my manly spirit. Adieu!   14

Jessica. Farewell, good Launcelot.   [*Exit Launcelot.*]
    Alack, what heinous sin[77] is it in me
    To be ashamed to be my father's child!
    But though I am a daughter to his blood,
    I am not to his manners. O Lorenzo,
    If thou keep promise, I shall end this strife,   20
    Become a Christian and thy loving wife.   [*Exit.*]

[76] *exhibit:* inhibit or prohibit (perhaps meaning "tears forbid me to speak").

[77] *heinous sin:* i.e., against the Fourth Commandment: "Honor thy father and thy mother."

Scene 4.   *The same. A street.*

Enter Gratiano, Lorenzo, Salerio, and Solanio.

Lorenzo. Nay, we will slink away in supper-time,
Disguise us at my lodging, and return
All in an hour.

Gratiano. We have not made good preparation.   4

Salerio. We have not spoke us yet of torch-bearers.

Solanio. 'Tis vile, unless it may be quaintly ordered,[78]
And better in my mind not undertook.

Lorenzo. 'Tis now but four of clock, we have two hours
To furnish us.

Enter Launcelot [with a letter].

Friend Launcelot, what's the news?

Launcelot. And it shall please you to break up[79] this, it
shall seem to signify.   11

Lorenzo. I know the hand; in faith, 'tis a fair hand,
And whiter than the paper it writ on
Is the fair hand that writ.

Gratiano.   Love-news, in faith.

Launcelot. By your leave, sir.   15

Lorenzo. Whither goest thou?

Launcelot. Marry, sir, to bid my old master the Jew
to sup to-night with my new master the Christian.

---

[78] *quaintly ordered:* artistically contrived.
[79] *break up:* break open.

Lorenzo. Hold here, take this. Tell gentle Jessica
   I will not fail her, speak it privately.   20
                       [*Exit Clown.*]

   Go, gentlemen,
   Will you prepare you for this masque to-night?
   I am provided of a torch-bearer.

Salerio. Ay, marry, I'll be gone about it straight.[80]

Solanio. And so will I.

Lorenzo.   Meet me and Gratiano   25
   At Gratiano's lodging some hour hence.

Salerio. 'Tis good we do so.   [*Exit with Solanio.*]

Gratiano. Was not that letter from fair Jessica?

Lorenzo. I must needs tell thee all. She hath directed
   How I shall take her from her father's house,   30
   What gold and jewels she is furnish'd with,
   What page's[81] suit she hath in readiness.
   If e'er the Jew her father come to heaven,
   It will be for his gentle daughter's sake,
   And never dare misfortune cross her foot,[82]   35
   Unless she[83] do it under this excuse,
   That she[84] is issue to a faithless[85] Jew.
   Come go with me, peruse this as thou goest.
   Fair Jessica shall be my torch-bearer.   [*Exeunt.*]

---

[80] *straight:* immediately.

[81] *page's:* A page was a young man training for knighthood (ranking below a squire).

[82] *cross her foot:* cross her path.

[83] *she:* i.e., misfortune.

[84] *she:* i.e., Jessica.

[85] *faithless:* i.e., not Christian.

Scene 5.   *The same. Before Shylock's house.*

Enter Shylock the Jew and his man that was, the Clown
Launcelot.

Shylock. Well, thou shalt see, thy eyes shall be thy judge,
The difference of old Shylock and Bassanio.—
What, Jessica!—Thou shalt not gurmandize,[86]
As thou hast done with me—What, Jessica!—
And sleep and snore, and rend apparel out—   5
Why, Jessica, I say!

Launcelot.   Why, Jessica!

Shylock. Who bids thee call? I do not bid thee call.

Launcelot. Your worship was wont to tell me I could
do nothing without bidding.

Enter Jessica.

Jessica. Call you? what is your will?   10

Shylock. I am bid forth to supper, Jessica.
There are my keys. But wherefore should I go?
I am not bid for love, they flatter me,
But yet I'll go in hate, to feed upon
The prodigal Christian. Jessica, my girl,   15
Look to my house. I am right loath to go;
There is some ill a-brewing towards my rest,
For I did dream of money-bags[87] to-night.[88]

Launcelot. I beseech you, sir, go. My young master
doth expect your reproach.[89]   20

Shylock. So do I his.

---

[86] *gurmandize:* gourmandize; eat good food (with a nuance of eating to excess).
[87] *money-bags:* According to Elizabethan traditions, dreams predicted contraries, so dreaming of money predicted its loss.
[88] *to-night:* last night.
[89] *reproach:* approach, but also anticipating Shylock's angry disapproval.

Launcelot. And they have conspir'd together. I will
  not say you shall see a masque, but if you do, then
  it was not for nothing that my nose fell a-bleeding
  on Black Monday[90] last at six o'clock i' th'   25
  morning, falling out that year on Ash We'n'sday was
  four year in th' afternoon.[91]

Shylock. What, are there masques? Hear you me, Jessica:
  Lock up my doors, and when you hear the drum
  And the vile squealing of the wry-neck'd fife,[92] 30
  Clamber not you up to the casements then,
  Nor thrust your head into the public street
  To gaze on Christian fools with varnish'd faces;[93]
  But stop my house's ears, I mean my casements;
  Let not the sound of shallow fopp'ry[94] enter 35
  My sober house. By Jacob's staff[95] I swear
  I have no mind of[96] feasting forth to-night;
  But I will go. Go you before me, sirrah,
  Say I will come.

Launcelot. I will go before, sir. Mistress, look out at
  window for all this—   41

    There will come a Christian by,
    Will be worth a Jewess' eye.[97]   [*Exit.*]

---

[90] *Black Monday:* Easter Monday.

[91] *falling . . . afternoon:* This is all nonsensical gibberish of omens and fortune-telling, involving liturgical high days (Black Monday and Ash Wednesday).

[92] *wry-neck'd fife:* a twisted instrument, or a fife played with a musician's head awry.

[93] *varnish'd faces:* painted masks (in the masques).

[94] *fopp'ry:* foppery.

[95] *By Jacob's staff:* Jacob set out from his homeland with only a staff and returned twenty years later a wealthy man.

[96] *I have no mind of:* I am not inclined toward.

[97] *Jewess' eye:* a proverbial phrase, also ("Jewès eye") object of great value. The disyllabic form of "Jew-es" is needed for the meter. Here the phrase signifies to Jessica that her lover is coming.

Shylock. What says that fool of Hagar's offspring,[98] ha?

Jessica. His words were "Farewell mistress!"—nothing else.   45

Shylock. The patch[99] is kind enough, but a huge feeder,
Snail-slow in profit, and he sleeps by day
More than the wild-cat. Drones hive not with me,
Therefore I part with him, and part with him
To one that I would have him help to waste   50
His borrowed purse. Well, Jessica, go in,
Perhaps I will return immediately.
Do as I bid you, shut doors after you;
Fast[100] bind, fast find—
A proverb never stale in thrifty mind.   [*Exit.*]   55

Jessica. Farewell, and if my fortune be not cross'd,
I have a father, you a daughter, lost.   [*Exit.*]

Scene 6.   *The same.*

Enter two of the masquers, Gratiano and Salerio.

Gratiano. This is the penthouse[101] under which Lorenzo
Desir'd us to make stand.[102]

Salerio.   His hour is almost past.

Gratiano. And it is marvel he out-dwells his hour,
For lovers ever run before the clock.

Salerio. O, ten times faster Venus' pigeons[103] fly   5
To seal love's bonds new made, than they are wont
To keep obliged[104] faith unforfeited!

[98] *Hagar's offspring*: a gentile and an outcast (cf. Genesis 16; 21:9).
[99] *patch*: fool.
[100] *Fast*: secure.
[101] *penthouse*: shed.
[102] *make stand*: wait.
[103] *Venus' pigeons*: doves that draw her chariot.
[104] *obliged*: bound, due.

Gratiano. That ever holds. Who riseth from a feast
   With that keen appetite that he sits down?
   Where is the horse that doth untread[105] again   10
   His tedious measures with the unbated[106] fire
   That he did pace them first? All things that are,
   Are with more spirit chased than enjoy'd.
   How like a younger or a prodigal
   The scarfed[107] bark puts from her native bay,   15
   Hugg'd and embraced by the strumpet wind!
   How like the prodigal doth she return,[108]
   With over-weather'd ribs and ragged sails,
   Lean, rent, and beggar'd by the strumpet wind!

                            Enter Lorenzo.

Salerio. Here comes Lorenzo, more of this hereafter.

Lorenzo. Sweet friends, your patience for my long abode;[109]   21
   Not I but my affairs have made you wait.
   When you shall please to play the thieves for wives,
   I'll watch as long for you then. Approach,
   Here dwells my father[110] Jew. Ho! who's within?   25

           Enter Jessica above in boy's clothes.

Jessica. Who are you? tell me for more certainty,
   Albeit I'll swear that I do know your tongue.

Lorenzo. Lorenzo, and thy love.

Jessica. Lorenzo, certain, and my love indeed,
   For who love I so much? And now who knows   30
   But you, Lorenzo, whether I am yours?

---

[105] *untread:* retrace.
[106] *unbated:* undiminished.
[107] *scarfed:* decked with flags or streamers.
[108] *How . . . return:* Cf. Luke 15:11–32, the parable of the Prodigal Son.
[109] *abode:* abiding, stay.
[110] *father:* i.e., future father-in-law.

Lorenzo. Heaven and thy thoughts are witness that thou
     art.

Jessica. Here, catch this casket, it is worth the pains.
     I am glad 'tis night, you do not look on me,
     For I am much asham'd of my exchange.[111]   35
     But love is blind, and lovers cannot see
     The pretty follies that themselves commit,
     For if they could, Cupid himself would blush
     To see me thus transformed to a boy.   39

Lorenzo. Descend, for you must be my torch-bearer.

Jessica. What, must I hold a candle to my shames?
     They in themselves, good sooth,[112] are too too[113]
          light.[114]
     Why, 'tis an office of discovery, love,
     And I should be obscur'd.

Lorenzo.   So are you, sweet,
     Even in the lovely garnish of a boy.   45
     But come at once,
     For the close[115] night doth play the runaway,
     And we are stay'd for[116] at Bassanio's feast.

Jessica. I will make fast the doors, and gild myself
     With some moe ducats, and be with you straight.

                                              [*Exit above.*]

Gratiano. Now by my hood,[117] a gentle,[118] and no Jew.   51

---

[111] *exchange:* change of clothes (perhaps too her theft and elopement).
[112] *sooth:* truth.
[113] *too too:* The repetition is for emphasis.
[114] *light:* illumined, frivolous, or immodest.
[115] *close:* secret (i.e., as in a secret closely kept).
[116] *stay'd for:* awaited.
[117] *by my hood:* meaningless oath, used to give emphasis.
[118] *gentle:* gentle woman, also a pun on "gentile".

Lorenzo. Beshrow me[119] but I love her heartily,
    For she is wise, if I can judge of her,
    And fair she is, if that mine eyes be true,
    And true she is, as she hath prov'd herself;   55
    And therefore, like herself, wise, fair, and true,
    Shall she be placed in my constant soul.

                           Enter Jessica.

What, art thou come? On, [gentlemen], away!
Our masquing mates by this time for us stay.

             [Exit with Jessica and Salerio.]

                        Enter Antonio.

Antonio. Who's there?   60

Gratiano. Signior Antonio!

Antonio. Fie, fie, Gratiano, where are all the rest?
    'Tis nine a' clock—our friends all stay for you.
    No masque to-night, the wind is come about,
    Bassanio presently[120] will go aboard.   65
    I have sent twenty out to seek for you.

Gratiano. I am glad on't.[121] I desire no more delight
    Than to be under sail, and gone to-night.

                          [Exeunt.]

---

[119] *Beshrow me:* Beshrew me; i.e., curse me, a generic oath.
[120] *presently:* immediately.
[121] *on't:* on it; about it.

Scene 7.   *Belmont. A room in Portia's house.*

Flourish cornets. Enter Portia with the Prince of
Morocco and both their Trains.

Portia. Go, draw aside the curtains and discover[122]
  The several[123] caskets to this noble prince.
  Now make your choice.

Morocco. The first, of gold, who this inscription bears,
  "Who chooseth me shall gain what many men desire";   5
  The second, silver, which this promise carries,
  "Who chooseth me shall get as much as he deserves";
  This third, dull lead, with warning all as blunt,[124]
  "Who chooseth me must give and hazard all he hath."
  How shall I know if I do choose the right?   10

Portia. The one of them contains my picture, Prince:
  If you choose that, then I am yours withal.[125]

Morocco. Some god direct my judgment! Let me see,
  I will survey th' inscriptions back again.
  What says this leaden casket?   15
  "Who chooseth me must give and hazard all he hath."
  Must give—for what? for lead, hazard for lead?
  This casket threatens. Men that hazard all
  Do it in hope of fair advantages;
  A golden mind stoops not to shows of dross.   20
  I'll then nor give nor[126] hazard aught for lead.
  What says the silver with her virgin hue?
  "Who chooseth me shall get as much as he deserves."
  As much as he deserves! pause there, Morocco,

---

[122] *discover*: reveal.

[123] *several*: various.

[124] *This third . . . blunt*: I.e., the lead casket is plain and dull (or blunt). The
message of the casket is clearly implied by its outside appearance.

[125] *withal*: therewith.

[126] *nor . . . nor*: neither . . . nor.

And weigh thy value with an even hand.[127]   25
If thou beest rated[128] by thy estimation,
Thou dost deserve enough, and yet enough
May not extend so far as to the lady;
And yet to be afeard of my deserving
Were but a weak disabling[129] of myself.   30
As much as I deserve! why, that's the lady.
I do in birth deserve her, and in fortunes,
In graces, and in qualities of breeding;
But more than these, in love I do deserve.
What if I stray'd no farther, but chose here?   35
Let's see once more this saying grav'd[130] in gold:
"Who chooseth me shall gain what many men desire."
Why, that's the lady, all the world desires her.
From the four corners of the earth they come
To kiss this shrine, this mortal breathing[131] saint.   40
The Hyrcanian deserts[132] and the vasty wilds
Of wide Arabia are as throughfares now
For princes to come view fair Portia.
The watery kingdom,[133] whose ambitious head[134]
Spets in the face of heaven, is no bar   45
To stop the foreign spirits,[135] but they come
As o'er a brook to see fair Portia.
One of these three contains her heavenly picture.
Is't like that lead contains her? 'Twere damnation
To think so base a thought; it[136] were too gross   50

---

[127] *with an even hand*: impartially.

[128] *rated*: estimated.

[129] *disabling*: disparaging, underrating.

[130] *grav'd*: engraved.

[131] *mortal breathing*: living.

[132] *Hyrcanian deserts*: area southeast of the Caspian Sea, supposedly haunted by fierce tigers.

[133] *watery kingdom*: i.e, the sea; in classical mythology, the sea was considered the kingdom of the water god (Neptune or Poseidon).

[134] *head*: insurgent force (i.e., the waves).

[135] *foreign spirits*: spirited foreigners (perhaps Portia's other suitors).

[136] *it*: i.e., lead.

To rib[137] her cerecloth[138] in the obscure grave.
Or shall I think in silver she's immur'd,
Being ten times undervalued to tried gold?
O sinful thought! never so rich a gem
Was set in worse than gold. They have in England
A coin that bears the figure of an angel[139]   56
Stamp'd in gold, but that's insculp'd upon;[140]
But here an angel in a golden bed
Lies all within. Deliver me the key.
Here do I choose, and thrive I as I may!   60

Portia. There take it, Prince, and if my form lie there,
    Then I am yours.   [*He unlocks the golden casket.*]

Morocco.   O hell! what have we here?
A carrion Death,[141] within whose empty eye
There is a written scroll! I'll read the writing.

[*Reads.*]   "All that glisters[142] is not gold,   65
        Often have you heard that told;
        Many a man his life hath sold
        But my outside to behold.
        Gilded [tombs] do worms infold.
        Had you been as wise as bold,   70
        Young in limbs, in judgment old,
        Your answer had not been inscroll'd.[143]
        Fare you well, your suit is cold."

Cold indeed, and labor lost:
Then farewell heat, and welcome frost!   75

---

[137] *rib*: cover, enclose.
[138] *cerecloth*: waxed cloth used in embalming.
[139] *coin . . . angel*: coin with Saint Michael's image, worth about ten shillings.
[140] *insculp'd upon*: engraved on the surface.
[141] *A carrion Death*: death's-head, skull.
[142] *glisters*: glitters.
[143] *inscroll'd*: thus inscribed.

Portia, adieu. I have too griev'd a heart
To take a tedious leave; thus losers part.[144]

[*Exit with his Train.*]

Portia. A gentle riddance. Draw the curtains, go.
Let all of his complexion[145] choose me so.

[*Exeunt.*]

Scene 8. *Venice. A street.*

Enter Salerio and Solanio.

Salerio. Why, man, I saw Bassanio under sail,
With him is Gratiano gone along;
And in their ship I am sure Lorenzo is not.

Solanio. The villain Jew with outcries rais'd the Duke,
Who went with him to search Bassanio's ship. 5

Salerio. He came too late, the ship was under sail,
But there the Duke was given to understand
That in a gondilo[146] were seen together
Lorenzo and his amorous Jessica.
Besides, Antonio certified[147] the Duke 10
They were not with Bassanio in his ship.

Solanio. I never heard a passion so confus'd,
So strange, outrageous, and so variable,
As the dog Jew did utter in the streets.
"My daughter! O my ducats! O my daughter! 15
Fled with a Christian! O my Christian ducats!
Justice! the law! my ducats, and my daughter!

[144] *part*: depart.
[145] *complexion*: often glossed as skin color but more probably temperament
(i.e., someone who would choose the gold casket).
[146] *gondilo*: gondola.
[147] *certified*: guaranteed, attested.

A sealed bag, two sealed bags of ducats,
Of double ducats, stol'n from me by my daughter!
And jewels, two stones, two rich and precious stones,
Stol'n by my daughter! Justice! find the girl,   21
She hath the stones upon her, and the ducats."

Salerio. Why, all the boys in Venice follow him,
Crying, his stones, his daughter, and his ducats.

Solanio. Let good Antonio look[148] he keep his day,   25
Or he shall pay for this.

Salerio.   Marry, well rememb'red.
I reason'd[149] with a Frenchman yesterday,
Who told me, in the Narrow Seas[150] that part
The French and English, there miscarried
A vessel of our country richly fraught.[151]   30
I thought upon Antonio when he told me,
And wish'd in silence that it were not his.

Solanio. You were best to tell Antonio what you hear,
Yet do not suddenly, for it may grieve him.

Salerio. A kinder gentleman treads not the earth.   35
I saw Bassanio and Antonio part:
Bassanio told him he would make some speed
Of his return; he answered, "Do not so,
[Slubber][152] not business for my sake, Bassanio,
But stay the very riping of the time;   40
And for the Jew's bond which he hath of me,
Let it not enter in your mind of love.[153]
Be merry, and employ your chiefest thoughts

[148] *look*: take care.
[149] *reason'd*: spoke.
[150] *Narrow Seas*: English Channel.
[151] *fraught*: loaded.
[152] *Slubber*: slur over, perform hastily and ill.
[153] *mind of love*: thoughts of wooing.

To courtship, and such fair ostents[154] of love
As shall conveniently become you there."   45
And even there, his eye being big with tears,
Turning his face, he put his hand behind him,
And with affection wondrous sensible[155]
He wrung Bassanio's hand, and so they parted.

Solanio. I think he only loves the world for him.   50
I pray thee let us go and find him out
And quicken his embraced heaviness[156]
With some delight or other.

Salerio.   *Do we so.*   *Exeunt.*

Scene 9.   *Belmont. A room in Portia's house.*

Enter Nerissa and a Servitor.[157]

Nerissa. Quick, quick, I pray thee, draw[158] the
    curtain[159] straight;[160]
The Prince of Arragon hath ta'en his oath,
And comes to his election[161] presently.[162]

                   Flourish cornets. Enter the Prince of
                   Arragon, his Train, and Portia.

Portia. Behold, there stand the caskets, noble Prince.
If you choose that wherein I am contain'd,   5

---

[154] *ostents:* appearances, displays.
[155] *wondrous sensible:* wonderfully strong in feeling, wonderfully apparent in
his behavior.
[156] *quicken . . . heaviness:* enliven (or dispel) his sadness.
[157] *Servitor:* attendant.
[158] *draw:* pull aside.
[159] *the curtain:* i.e., the one that covers the caskets.
[160] *straight:* immediately.
[161] *election:* selection (of a casket and subsequent fortune).
[162] *presently:* immediately.

Straight shall our nuptial rites[163] be solemniz'd;
But if you fail, without more speech, my lord,
You must be gone from hence immediately.

Arragon. I am enjoin'd by oath to observe three things:
First, never to unfold to any one   10
Which casket 'twas I chose; next, if I fail
Of the right casket, never in my life
To woo a maid in way of marriage;
Lastly,
If I do fail in fortune of my choice,   15
Immediately to leave you, and be gone.

Portia. To these injunctions every one doth swear
That comes to hazard for my worthless self.

Arragon. And so have I address'd[164] me. Fortune[165] now
To my heart's hope! Gold, silver, and base lead.   20
"Who chooseth me must give and hazard all he hath."
You shall look fairer ere[166] I give or hazard.[167]
What says the golden chest? Ha, let me see:
"Who chooseth me shall gain what many men desire."
What many men desire! That many may be meant   25
By[168] the fool multitude that choose by show,
Not learning more than the fond[169] eye doth teach,
Which pries not to th' interior, but like the martlet[170]
Builds in[171] the weather on the outward wall,
Even in the force and road of casualty.[172]   30
I will not choose what many men desire,

[163] *nuptial rites:* ceremony of marriage.
[164] *address'd:* prepared.
[165] *Fortune:* i.e., good fortune.
[166] *ere:* before.
[167] *You shall . . . hazard:* The Prince is speaking to the lead casket.
[168] *meant / By:* meant for.
[169] *fond:* foolish.
[170] *martlet:* a kind of swallow, associated with the virtue of prudence.
[171] *in:* exposed to.
[172] *force . . . casualty:* power and pain of mishap.

Because I will not jump with[173] common spirits,
And rank me with the barbarous multitudes.
Why then to thee, thou silver treasure house,
Tell me once more what title thou dost bear: 35
"Who chooseth me shall get as much as he deserves."
And well said too; for who shall go about
To cozen[174] fortune, and be honorable
Without the stamp of merit? Let none presume
To wear an undeserved dignity.   40
O that estates, degrees, and offices
Were not deriv'd corruptly, and that clear honor
Were purchas'd by the merit of the wearer!
How many then should cover that stand bare?
How many be commanded that command?   45
How much low peasantry would then be gleaned
From the true seed of honor? and how much honor
Pick'd from the chaff and ruin of the times
To be new varnish'd? Well, but to my choice:
"Who chooseth me shall get as much as he deserves."
I will assume desert. Give me a key for this,   51
And instantly unlock my fortunes here.
          [*He unlocks the silver casket.*]

Portia. Too long a pause for that which you find there.

Arragon. What's here? the portrait of a blinking idiot,
Presenting me a schedule![175] I will read it.   55
How much unlike art thou to Portia!
How much unlike my hopes and my deservings!
"Who chooseth me shall have as much as he deserves!"
Did I deserve no more than a fool's head?
Is that my prize? Are my deserts no better?   60

---

[173] *jump with:* agree with.
[174] *cozen:* cheat.
[175] *schedule:* scroll.

Portia. To offend and judge are distinct offices,
    And of opposed natures.[176]

Arragon.   What is here?

[*Reads.*]   "The fire seven times tried this:[177]
            Seven times tried that judgment is,
            That did never choose amiss.   65
            Some there be that shadows kiss,
            Such have but a shadow's bliss.
            There be fools alive, iwis,[178]
            Silver'd o'er, and so was this.
            Take what wife you will to bed,   70
            I will ever be your head.
            So be gone, you are sped."[179]

    Still more fool I shall appear
    By the time I linger here.
    With one fool's head I came to woo,   75
    But I go away with two.
    Sweet, adieu. I'll keep my oath,
    Patiently to bear my wroth.[180]

                       [*Exit with his Train.*]

Portia. Thus hath the candle sing'd the moth.
    O, these deliberate[181] fools, when they do choose,   80
    They have the wisdom by their wit to lose.

Nerissa. The ancient saying is no heresy,
    Hanging and wiving goes by destiny.

---

[176] *To offend . . . natures:* I.e., those subject to judgment may not be their own judges.
[177] *this:* i.e., the silver.
[178] *iwis:* I know, certainly.
[179] *sped:* done for.
[180] *wroth:* The quarto's word is ambiguous ("wroath") and could be wrath or grievance.
[181] *deliberate:* deliberating.

Portia. Come draw the curtain, Nerissa.

Enter Messenger.

Messenger. Where is my lady?

Portia.   Here; what would my lord?   85

Messenger. Madam, there is alighted at your gate
  A young Venetian, one that comes before
  To signify th' approaching of his lord,
  From whom he bringeth sensible regreets:[182]
  To wit (besides commends and courteous breath),   90
  Gifts of rich value. Yet I have not seen
  So likely an embassador of love.
  A day in April never came so sweet,
  To show how costly[183] summer was at hand,
  As this fore-spurrer[184] comes before his lord.   95

Portia. No more, I pray thee. I am half afeard
  Thou wilt say anon he is some kin to thee,
  Thou spend'st such high-day[185] wit in praising him.
  Come, come, Nerissa, for I long to see
  Quick Cupid's post[186] that comes so mannerly.   100

Nerissa. Bassanio, Lord Love,[187] if thy will it be!

                                    [*Exeunt.*]

---

[182] *sensible regreets*: tangible greetings (i.e., gifts).
[183] *costly*: rich, bountiful.
[184] *fore-spurrer*: forerunner.
[185] *high-day*: holy day, day of high feast, holiday.
[186] *post*: swift messenger.
[187] *Lord Love*: god of love (i.e., Cupid).

ACT 3

Scene 1. *Venice. A street.*

Enter Solanio and Salerio.

Solanio. Now what news on the Rialto?

Salerio. Why, yet it lives[1] there uncheck'd[2] that
    Antonio hath a ship of rich lading wrack'd on the
    Narrow Seas; the Goodwins[3] I think they call the
    place, a very dangerous flat, and fatal, where the   5
    carcasses of many a tall ship lie buried, as they say,
    if my gossip Report be an honest woman of her word.

Solanio. I would she were as lying a gossip in that
    as ever knapp'd[4] ginger or made her neighbors
    believe she wept for the death of a third husband.   10
    But it is true, without any slips of prolixity,[5] or
    crossing the plain highway of talk,[6] that the good
    Antonio, the honest Antonio—O that I had a title
    good enough to keep his name company!—

Salerio. Come, the full stop.[7]   15

Solanio. Ha, what sayest thou? Why, the end is,
    he hath lost a ship.

Salerio. I would it might prove the end of his losses.

---

    [1] *lives*: i.e., circulates.
    [2] *uncheck'd*: uncontradicted.
    [3] *Goodwins*: Goodwin Sands, treacherous sand bank off the southeastern English
coast.
    [4] *knapp'd*: nibbled, gnawed.
    [5] *slips of prolixity*: lapses into wordiness.
    [6] *crossing . . . talk*: i.e., deviation from plain speech.
    [7] *full stop*: period, end of statement.

Solanio. Let me say amen betimes,[8] lest the devil
     cross my prayer, for here he comes in the likeness of
     a Jew.   21

                                    Enter Shylock.

   How now, Shylock, what news among the
     merchants?

Shylock. You knew, none so well, none so well as you,
     of my daughter's flight.   25

Salerio. That's certain. I for my part knew the
     tailor that made the wings she flew withal.[9]

Solanio. And Shylock for his own part knew the
     bird was flidge, and then it is the complexion[10] of
     them all to leave the dam.[11]   30

Shylock. She is damn'd for it.

Salerio. That's certain, if the devil may be her
     judge.

Shylock. My own flesh and blood to rebel!

Solanio. Out upon it, old carrion, rebels it at these
     years?   36

Shylock. I say, my daughter is my flesh and my
     blood.

Salerio. There is more difference between thy flesh
     and hers than between jet and ivory, more between
     your bloods than there is between red wine and   41
     Rhenish. But tell us, do you hear whether Antonio
     have had any loss at sea or no?

---

    [8] *betimes*: in time, quickly.
    [9] *withal*: emphatic form of "with", placed after its object.
    [10] *complexion*: disposition.
    [11] *dam*: mother.

Shylock. There I have another bad match.[12] A
    bankrout, a prodigal, who dare scarce[13] show his   45
    head on the Rialto; a beggar, that was us'd[14] to come
    so smug upon the mart:[15] let him look to his bond.
    He was wont to call me usurer, let him look to his
    bond. He was wont to lend money for a Christian
    cur'sy,[16] let him look to his bond.   50

Salerio. Why, I am sure if he forfeit thou wilt not
    take his flesh. What's that good for?

Shylock. To bait fish withal—if it will feed nothing
    else, it will feed my revenge. He hath disgrac'd me,
    and hind'red me half a million, laugh'd at my   55
    losses, mock'd at my gains, scorn'd my nation,
    thwarted my bargains, cool'd my friends, heated
    mine enemies; and what's his reason? I am a Jew.
    Hath not a Jew eyes? Hath not a Jew hands, organs,
    dimensions,[17] senses, affections, passions; fed with   60
    the same food, hurt with the same weapons, subject
    to the same diseases, heal'd by the same means,
    warm'd and cool'd by the same winter and summer,
    as a Christian is? If you prick us, do we not bleed?
    If you tickle us, do we not laugh? If you poison   65
    us, do we not die? And if you wrong us, shall we not
    revenge? If we are like you in the rest, we will
    resemble you in that. If a Jew wrong a Christian,
    what is his humility? Revenge. If a Christian wrong
    a Jew, what should his[18] sufferance be by Christian   70
    example? Why, revenge. The villainy you teach

---

[12] *bad match:* bad bargain.
[13] *dare scarce:* scarce would dare.
[14] *was us'd:* used.
[15] *mart:* exchange.
[16] *cur'sy:* curtsy.
[17] *dimensions:* parts of the body.
[18] *his:* i.e., the Jew's.

me, I will execute, and it shall go hard but I will
better the instruction.

Enter a Servingman from Antonio.

[*Servingman.*] Gentlemen, my master Antonio is at his
house, and desires to speak with you both.   75

Salerio. We have been up and down to seek him.

Enter Tubal.

Solanio. Here comes another of the tribe; a third
cannot be match'd, unless the devil himself turn Jew.

Exeunt Gentlemen [*Solanio and Salerio, with Servingman.*]

Shylock. How now, Tubal, what news from Genoa?
Hast thou found my daughter?   80

Tubal. I often came where I did hear of her, but
cannot find her.

Shylock. Why, there, there, there, there! A diamond
gone, cost me two thousand ducats in Frankford!
The curse[19] never fell upon our nation till   85
now, I never felt it till now. Two thousand ducats
in that, and other precious, precious jewels. I
would my daughter were dead at my foot, and
the jewels in her ear! Would she were hears'd[20] at
my foot, and the ducats in her coffin! No news   90
of them? Why, so—and I know not what's spent
in the search. Why, thou loss upon loss! the thief
gone with so much, and so much to find the thief,
and no satisfaction, no revenge, nor no ill luck
stirring but what lights a' my shoulders, no sighs but
a' my breathing, no tears but a' my shedding.   96

---

[19] *curse*: perhaps the prophecy of Jerusalem's destruction (cf. Matthew 23:38).
[20] *hears'd*: in a hearse (i.e., dead).

Tubal. Yes, other men have ill luck too. Antonio,
     as I heard in Genoa—

Shylock. What, what, what? ill luck, ill luck?

Tubal. Hath an argosy cast away, coming from
     Tripolis.   101

Shylock. I thank God, I thank God. Is it true, is it
     true?

Tubal. I spoke with some of the sailors that escap'd
     the wrack.   105

Shylock. I thank thee, good Tubal, good news, good
     news! Ha, ha! [Heard] in Genoa?

Tubal. Your daughter spent in Genoa, as I heard,
     one night fourscore ducats.   109

Shylock. Thou stick'st a dagger in me. I shall never
     see my gold again. Fourscore ducats at a sitting,
     fourscore ducats!

Tubal. There came divers[21] of Antonio's creditors in
     my company to Venice that swear he cannot choose
     but break.[22]   115

Shylock. I am very glad of it. I'll plague him, I'll
     torture him. I am glad of it.

Tubal. One of them show'd me a ring that he had
     of your daughter for a monkey.   119

Shylock. Out upon her! Thou torturest me, Tubal.
     It was my turkis, I had it of Leah[23] when I was a
     bachelor. I would not have given it for a
     wilderness of monkeys.

[21] *divers:* diverse, several.
[22] *break:* go bankrupt.
[23] *Leah:* Shylock's wife.

Tubal. But Antonio is certainly undone.   124

Shylock. Nay, that's true, that's very true. Go, Tubal, fee[24]
   me an officer; bespeak[25] him a fortnight before.
   I will have the heart of him if he forfeit, for were
   he out of Venice I can make what merchandise I
   will. Go, Tubal, and meet me at our synagogue;
   go, good Tubal, at our synagogue, Tubal.   130

                                          [*Exeunt.*]

          Scene 2.   *Belmont. A room in Portia's house.*

          Enter Bassanio, Portia, Gratiano, Nerissa,
          and all their Trains.

Portia. I pray you tarry, pause a day or two
   Before you hazard, for in choosing wrong
   I lose your company; therefore forbear a while.
   There's something tells me (but it is not love)
   I would not lose you, and you know yourself,   5
   Hate counsels not in such a quality.[26]
   But lest you should not understand me well—
   And yet a maiden hath no tongue but thought—
   I would detain you here some month or two
   Before you venture for me. I could teach you   10
   How to choose right, but I am then forsworn.
   So will I never be, so may you miss me,
   But if you do, you'll make me wish a sin,
   That I had been forsworn. Beshrow your eyes,
   They have o'erlook'd me and divided me: 15
   One half of me is yours, the other half yours—
   Mine own, I would say; but if mine, then yours,

---

[24] *fee:* hire.
[25] *bespeak:* engage.
[26] *in such a quality:* thus, in such a way, to such a purpose.

And so all yours. O, these naughty[27] times
Put bars between the owners and their rights!
And so though yours, not yours. Prove it so,[28]   20
Let fortune go to hell for it, not I.
I speak too long, but 'tis to peize[29] the time,
To eche[30] it, and to draw it out in length,
To stay you from election.

Bassanio.   Let me choose,
For as I am, I live upon the rack.   25

Portia. Upon the rack, Bassanio! then confess
What treason[31] there is mingled with your love.

Bassanio. None but that ugly treason of mistrust,
Which makes me fear th' enjoying of my love;
There may as well be amity and life   30
'Tween snow and fire, as treason and my love.

Portia. Ay, but I fear you speak upon the rack,
Where men enforced do speak any thing.

Bassanio. Promise me life, and I'll confess the truth.

Portia. Well then, confess and live.

Bassanio.   Confess and love
Had been the very sum of my confession.   36
O happy torment, when my torturer
Doth teach me answers for deliverance!
But let me to my fortune and the caskets.

Portia. Away then! I am lock'd in one of them;
If you do love me, you will find me out.   41

---

[27] *naughty*: wicked.
[28] *Prove it so*: should it prove so.
[29] *peize*: weigh down, retard.
[30] *eche*: eke, augment.
[31] *Upon the rack . . . treason*: alludes to confessions of treason obtained by torture on the rack.

Nerissa and the rest, stand all aloof.
Let music sound while he doth make his choice;
Then if he lose he makes a swan-like end,[32]
Fading in music. That the comparison   45
May stand more proper, my eye shall be the stream
And wat'ry death-bed for him. He may win,
And what is music then? Then music is
Even as the flourish when true subjects bow
To a new-crowned monarch; such it is   50
As are those dulcet sounds in break of day
That creep into the dreaming bridegroom's ear,
And summon him to marriage. Now he goes,
With no less presence,[33] but with much more love,
Than young Alcides, when he did redeem   55
The virgin tribute paid by howling Troy
To the sea-monster.[34] I stand for sacrifice;[35]
The rest aloof are the Dardanian[36] wives,
With bleared[37] visages, come forth to view
The issue of th' exploit. Go, Hercules,   60
Live thou,[38] I live; with much, much more dismay
I view the fight than thou that mak'st the fray.
                                        [Here music.]

                [A song, the whilst Bassanio comments
                    on the caskets to himself.]

---

[32] swan-like end: Swans, usually mute, were thought to sing beautifully before
death.

[33] presence: dignity of bearing.

[34] Alcides . . . sea-monster: Alcides (Hercules) rescued Hesione, the virgin daughter of Leomedon, the Trojan king, who was going to be sacrificed to a sea monster. He does so, not out of love, but to win the horses that her father had promised
him as a reward.

[35] stand for sacrifice: represent the sacrificial victim.

[36] Dardanian: Trojan.

[37] bleared: weeping.

[38] Live thou: if you live.

Tell me where is fancy[39] bred,
Or in the heart or in the head?
How begot, how nourished?   65
            [*All*.] Reply, reply.
It is engend'red in the [eyes],
With gazing fed, and fancy dies
In the cradle where it lies.
Let us all ring fancy's knell.   70
I'll begin it. Ding, dong, bell.
            All. Ding, dong, bell.

Bassanio. So may the outward shows be least themselves—
The world is still deceiv'd with ornament.
In law, what plea so tainted and corrupt   75
But, being season'd with a gracious voice,
Obscures the show of evil? In religion,
What damned error but some sober brow
Will bless it, and approve[40] it with a text,
Hiding the grossness with fair ornament?   80
There is no [vice] so simple but assumes
Some mark of virtue on his outward parts.
How many cowards, whose hearts are all as false
As stairs of sand, wear yet upon their chins
The beards of Hercules and frowning Mars,   85
Who inward search'd, have livers white as milk,
And these assume but valor's excrement[41]
To render them redoubted![42] Look on beauty,
And you shall see 'tis purchased by the weight,[43]
Which therein works a miracle in nature,   90
Making them lightest[44] that wear most of it.
So are those crisped[45] snaky golden locks,

[39] *fancy*: fond love, liking.
[40] *approve*: confirm.
[41] *excrement*: outgrowth, beard.
[42] *redoubted*: feared.
[43] *weight*: e.g., of cosmetics.
[44] *lightest*: least heavy (with pun alluding to moral lightness).
[45] *crisped*: curled.

Which [make] such wanton gambols with the wind
Upon supposed fairness, often known
To be the dowry of a second head,   95
The skull that bred them in the sepulchre.[46]
Thus ornament is but the guiled[47] shore
To a most dangerous sea; the beauteous scarf
Veiling an Indian[48] beauty; in a word,
The seeming truth which cunning times put on   100
To entrap the wisest. Therefore then, thou gaudy gold,
Hard food for Midas,[49] I will none of thee;
Nor none of thee, thou pale and common drudge[50]
'Tween man and man; but thou, thou meagre lead,
Which rather threaten'st than dost promise aught,
Thy paleness moves me more than eloquence,   106
And here choose I. Joy be the consequence!

Portia. [*Aside.*] How all the other passions fleet to air,
As doubtful thoughts, and rash-embrac'd despair,
And shudd'ring fear, and green-eyed jealousy!   110
O love, be moderate, allay thy ecstasy,
In measure rain thy joy, scant this excess!
I feel too much thy blessing; make it less,
For fear I surfeit.

Bassanio.   What find I here?

                [*Opening the leaden casket.*]

Fair Portia's counterfeit![51] What demigod   115
Hath come so near creation? Move these eyes?
Or whether, riding on the balls of mine,
Seem they in motion? Here are sever'd lips,

---

[46] *dowry . . . sepulchre:* i.e., hair taken from a person now dead and buried.
[47] *guiled:* full of guile, treacherous.
[48] *Indian:* i.e., dark-skinned, not fair.
[49] *Midas:* In classical mythology, all that Midas touched (including food) turned to gold.
[50] *common drudge:* public slave.
[51] *counterfeit:* image, likeness.

Parted with sugar breath; so sweet a bar
Should sunder such sweet friends.[52] Here in her hairs
The painter plays the spider, and hath woven   *121*
A golden mesh t'entrap the hearts of men
Faster[53] than gnats in cobwebs. But her eyes—
How could he see to do them? Having made one,
Methinks it should have power to steal both his   *125*
And leave itself unfurnish'd.[54] Yet look how far
The substance of my praise doth wrong this shadow
In underprizing it, so far this shadow
Doth limp behind the substance. Here's the scroll,
The continent[55] and summary of my fortune.   *130*

[*Reads.*]   "You that choose not by the view,
                     Chance as fair,[56] and choose as true:
                     Since this fortune falls to you,
                     Be content, and seek no new.
                     If you be well pleas'd with this,   *135*
                     And hold your fortune for your bliss,
                     Turn you where your lady is,
                     And claim her with a loving kiss."

A gentle scroll. Fair lady, by your leave,
I come by note,[57] to give and to receive.   *140*
Like one of two contending in a prize,
That thinks he hath done well in people's eyes,
Hearing applause and universal shout,
Giddy in spirit, still gazing in a doubt
Whether those peals of praise be his[58] or no,   *145*
So, thrice-fair lady, stand I, even so,

---

[52] *sweet friends*: i.e., the two lips.
[53] *Faster*: more securely.
[54] *unfurnish'd*: without a companion, unfellowed.
[55] *continent*: container.
[56] *Chance as fair*: hazard as fortunately.
[57] *by note*: according to the scroll, with authorization.
[58] *his*: for him.

As doubtful whether what I see be true,
Until confirm'd, sign'd, ratified by you.

Portia. You see me, Lord Bassanio, where I stand,
    Such as I am. Though for myself alone   150
    I would not be ambitious in my wish
    To wish myself much better, yet for you,
    I would be trebled twenty times myself,
    A thousand times more fair, ten thousand times more
       rich,
    That only to stand high in your account,   155
    I might in virtues, beauties, livings,[59] friends,
    Exceed account. But the full sum of me
    Is sum of something;[60] which, to term in gross,[61]
    Is an unlesson'd girl, unschool'd, unpractic'd,
    Happy in this, she is not yet so old   160
    But she may learn; happier than this,
    She is not bred so dull but she can learn;
    Happiest of all, is that her gentle spirit
    Commits itself to yours to be directed,
    As from her lord, her governor, her king.   165
    Myself, and what is mine, to you and yours
    Is now converted. But now[62] I was the lord
    Of this fair mansion, master of my servants,
    Queen o'er myself; and even now, but now,
    This house, these servants, and this same myself   170
    Are yours—my lord's!—I give them with this ring,
    Which when you part from, lose, or give away,
    Let it presage the ruin of your love,
    And be my vantage to exclaim on you.[63]   174

---

[59] *livings:* possessions.

[60] *sum of something:* This is taken from the folios; the quartos give it as "sum of nothing".

[61] *term in gross:* state in full.

[62] *But now:* a moment ago.

[63] *vantage . . . you:* ground of advantage, opportunity to denounce you.

Bassanio. Madam, you have bereft me of all words,
  Only my blood speaks to you in my veins,
  And there is such confusion in my powers,[64]
  As after some oration fairly spoke
  By a beloved prince, there doth appear
  Among the buzzing pleased multitude,   180
  Where every something, being blent together,
  Turns to a wild of nothing, save of joy
  Express'd and not express'd. But when this ring
  Parts from this finger, then parts life from hence;
  O then be bold to say Bassanio's dead!   185

Nerissa. My lord and lady, it is now our time,
  That[65] have stood by and seen our wishes prosper,
  To cry good joy. Good joy, my lord and lady!

Gratiano. My Lord Bassanio and my gentle lady,
  I wish you all the joy that you can wish;   190
  For I am sure you can wish none from me;
  And when your honors mean to solemnize
  The bargain of your faith, I do beseech you
  Even at that time I may be married too.   194

Bassanio. With all my heart, so thou canst get a wife.

Gratiano. I thank your lordship, you have got me one.
  My eyes, my lord, can look as swift as yours:
  You saw the mistress, I beheld the maid;
  You lov'd, I lov'd; for intermission
  No more pertains to me, my lord, than you;   200
  Your fortune stood upon the caskets there,
  And so did mine too as the matter falls;
  For wooing here until I sweat again,
  And swearing till my very [roof][66] was dry
  With oaths of love, at last, if promise last,   205

[64] *powers:* faculties.
[65] *That:* who.
[66] *roof:* i.e., roof of the mouth.

I got a promise of this fair one here
To have her love—provided that your fortune
Achiev'd her mistress.

Portia.   Is this true, Nerissa?

Nerissa. Madam, it is, so you stand pleas'd withal.[67]

Bassanio. And do you, Gratiano, mean good faith?

Gratiano. Yes, faith, my lord.   211

Bassanio. Our feast shall be much honored in your
      marriage.

Gratiano. We'll play with them the first boy for a
      thousand ducats.

Nerissa. What, and stake down?   215

Gratiano. No, we shall ne'er win at that sport, and stake
      down.
   But who comes here? Lorenzo and his infidel?[68]
   What, and my old Venetian friend Salerio?

> *Enter Lorenzo, Jessica, and Salerio,*
> *a messenger from Venice.*

Bassanio. Lorenzo and Salerio, welcome hither,   220
   If that the youth of my new int'rest[69] here
   Have power to bid you welcome. By your leave,
   I bid my very[70] friends and countrymen,
   Sweet Portia, welcome.

Portia.   So do I, my lord,
   They are entirely welcome.   225

---

[67] *so . . . withal:* if it pleases you.
[68] *infidel:* i.e., Jessica.
[69] *int'rest:* position in the household.
[70] *very:* true.

Lorenzo. I thank your honor. For my part, my lord,
My purpose was not to have seen you here,
But meeting with Salerio by the way,
He did entreat me, past all saying nay,
To come with him along.

Salerio.   I did, my lord,   230
And I have reason for it. Signior Antonio
Commends him[71] to you.   [*Gives Bassanio a letter.*]

Bassanio.   Ere I ope his letter,
I pray you tell me how my good friend doth.

Salerio. Not sick, my lord, unless it be in mind,
Nor well, unless in mind. His letter there   235
Will show you his estate.[72]

                    [*Bassanio open the letter.*]

Gratiano. Nerissa, cheer yond stranger, bid her welcome.
Your hand, Salerio. What's the news from Venice?
How doth that royal merchant, good Antonio?
I know he will be glad of our success;   240
We are the Jasons, we have won the fleece.

Salerio. I would you had won the fleece that he hath lost.

Portia. There are some shrowd[73] contents in yond same
    paper
That steals the color from Bassanio's cheek—
Some dear friend dead, else nothing in the world   245
Could turn so much the constitution
Of any constant man. What, worse and worse!
With leave, Bassanio, I am half yourself,
And I must freely have the half of any thing
That this same paper brings you.

---

[71] *Commends him*: sends his greeting.
[72] *estate*: condition.
[73] *shrowd*: biting, sharp, bitter.

Bassanio.   O sweet Portia, 250
Here are a few of the unpleasant'st words
Than ever blotted paper! Gentle lady,
When I did first impart my love to you,
I freely told you all the wealth I had
Ran in my veins: I was a gentleman;   255
And then I told you true. And yet, dear lady,
Rating myself at nothing, you shall see
How much I was a braggart: when I told you
My state was nothing, I should then have told you
That I was worse than nothing; for indeed   260
I have engag'd myself[74] to a dear friend,
Engag'd my friend to his mere[75] enemy,
To feed my means. Here is a letter, lady,
The paper as the body of my friend,
And every word in it a gaping wound   265
Issuing life-blood. But is it true, Salerio?
Hath all his ventures fail'd? What, not one hit?
From Tripolis, from Mexico, and England,
From Lisbon, Barbary, and India,
And not one vessel scape the dreadful touch   270
Of merchant-marring rocks?

Salerio.   Not one, my lord.
Besides, it should appear, that if he had
The present money to discharge the Jew,
He[76] would not take it. Never did I know
A creature that did bear the shape of man   275
So keen and greedy to confound a man.
He plies the Duke at morning and at night,
And doth impeach[77] the freedom of the state,
If they deny him justice. Twenty merchants,

---

[74] *engag'd myself*: become indebted.
[75] *mere*: absolute, unqualified.
[76] *He*: i.e., Shylock.
[77] *impeach*: deny.

The Duke himself, and the magnificoes[78]   280
Of greatest port,[79] have all persuaded with him,
But none can drive him from the envious[80] plea
Of forfeiture, of justice, and his bond.

Jessica. When I was with him I have heard him swear
To Tubal and to Chus, his countrymen,   285
That he would rather have Antonio's flesh
Than twenty times the value of the sum
That he did owe him; and I know, my lord,
If law, authority, and power deny not,
It will go hard with poor Antonio.   290

Portia. Is it your dear friend that is thus in trouble?

Bassanio. The dearest friend to me, the kindest man,
The best-condition'd[81] and unwearied spirit
In doing courtesies, and one in whom
The ancient Roman honor more appears   295
Than any that draws breath in Italy.

Portia. What sum owes he the Jew?

Bassanio. For me, three thousand ducats.

Portia.   What, no more?
Pay him six thousand, and deface the bond;
Double six thousand, and then treble that,   300
Before a friend of this description
Shall lose a hair through Bassanio's fault.
First go with me to church and call me wife,
And then away to Venice to your friend;
For never shall you lie by Portia's side   305
With an unquiet soul. You shall have gold
To pay the petty debt twenty times over.

---

[78] *magnificoes:* chief men of Venice.
[79] *port:* importance, state, eminence.
[80] *envious:* malicious.
[81] *best-condition'd:* best-natured.

When it is paid, bring your true friend along.
My maid Nerissa and myself mean time
Will live as maids and widows. Come away!   310
For you shall hence[82] upon your wedding-day.
Bid your friends welcome, show a merry cheer—[83]
Since you are dear bought, I will love you dear.
But let me hear the letter of your friend.   314

[*Bassanio.* (*Reads.*)] "Sweet Bassanio, my ships have
     all miscarried, my creditors grow cruel, my estate
     is very low, my bond to the Jew is forfeit; and since
     in paying it, it is impossible I should live, all debts
     are clear'd between you and I, if I might but   319
     see you at my death. Notwithstanding, use your
     pleasure; if your love do not persuade you to come,
     let not my letter."

Portia. O love! dispatch all business and be gone.

Bassanio. Since I have your good leave to go away,
     I will make haste; but till I come again,   325
     No bed shall e'er be guilty of my stay,
     No rest be interposer 'twixt us twain.   [*Exeunt.*]

Scene 3.   *Venice. A street.*

*Enter Shylock the Jew and Solanio and Antonio
and the Jailer.*

Shylock. Jailer, look to him, tell not me of mercy.
     This is the fool that lent out money gratis.
     Jailer, look to him.

Antonio.   Hear me yet, good Shylock.

---

[82] *hence:* go hence.
[83] *merry cheer:* happy countenance.

Shylock. I'll have my bond, speak not against my bond,
 I have sworn an oath that I will have my bond.   5
 Thou call'dst me dog before thou hadst a cause,
 But since I am a dog, beware my fangs.
 The Duke shall grant me justice. I do wonder,
 Thou naughty[84] jailer, that thou art so fond[85]
 To come abroad with him at his request.   10

Antonio. I pray thee hear me speak.

Shylock. I'll have my bond; I will not hear thee speak.
 I'll have my bond, and therefore speak no more.
 I'll not be made a soft and dull-ey'd[86] fool
 To shake the head, relent, and sigh, and yield   15
 To Christian intercessors. Follow not,
 I'll have no speaking, I will have my bond
              [*Exit Jew.*]

Solanio. It is the most impenetrable cur
 That ever kept with[87] men.

Antonio.   Let him alone,
 I'll follow him no more with bootless[88] prayers.   20
 He seeks my life; his reason well I know:
 I oft deliver'd from his forfeitures
 Many that have at times made moan to me;
 Therefore he hates me.

[Solanio.]   I am sure the Duke
 Will never grant this forfeiture to hold.   25

Antonio. The Duke cannot deny the course of law;
 For the commodity that strangers[89] have
 With us in Venice, if it be denied,

---

[84] *naughty:* wicked or corrupt.
[85] *fond:* foolish, indulgent.
[86] *dull-ey'd:* easily deceived.
[87] *kept with:* dwelt among, associated with.
[88] *bootless:* fruitless.
[89] *strangers:* non-Venetians, including Jews.

Will much impeach the justice of the state,
Since that the trade and profit of the city   30
Consisteth of all nations. Therefore go.
These griefs and losses have so bated[90] me
That I shall hardly spare a pound of flesh
To-morrow to my bloody creditor.
Well, jailer, on. Pray God Bassanio come   35
To see me pay his debt, and then I care not!

[Exeunt.]

Scene 4.   *Belmont. A room in Portia's house.*

Enter Portia, Nerissa, Lorenzo, Jessica, and
Balthazar, a man of Portia's.

Lorenzo. Madam, although I speak it in your presence,
You have a noble and a true conceit[91]
Of godlike amity,[92] which appears most strongly
In bearing thus the absence of your lord.
But if you knew to whom you show this honor,   5
How true a gentleman you send relief,
How dear a lover of my lord your husband,
I know you would be prouder of the work
Than customary bounty can enforce you.[93]

Portia. I never did repent for doing good,   10
Nor shall not now: for in companions
That do converse and waste[94] the time together,
Whose souls do bear an egall yoke of love,
There must be needs a like proportion

---

[90] *bated:* reduced.
[91] *conceit:* understanding, conception.
[92] *amity:* friendship (i.e., that of Antonio and Bassanio).
[93] *Than . . . you:* than ordinary kindness or your usual charities will make you.
[94] *waste:* spend.

Of lineaments,[95] of manners, and of spirit;   15
Which makes me think that this Antonio,
Being the bosom lover of my lord,
Must needs be like my lord. If it be so,
How little is the cost I have bestowed
In purchasing the semblance of my soul,[96]   20
From out the state of hellish cruelty.
This comes too near the praising of myself,
Therefore no more of it. [Hear] other things:
Lorenzo, I commit into your hands
The husbandry[97] and manage of my house   25
Until my lord's return. For mine own part,
I have toward heaven breath'd a secret vow
To live in prayer and contemplation,
Only attended by Nerissa here,
Until her husband and my lord's return.   30
There is a monast'ry two miles off,
And there will we abide. I do desire you
Not to deny this imposition,[98]
The which my love and some necessity
Now lays upon you.

Lorenzo.   Madam, with all my heart,   35
I shall obey you in all fair commands.

Portia. My people do already know my mind,
And will acknowledge[99] you and Jessica
In place of Lord Bassanio and myself.
So fare you well till we shall meet again.   40

Lorenzo. Fair thoughts and happy hours attend on you!

Jessica. I wish your ladyship all heart's content.

---

[95] *lineaments:* characteristics.

[96] *purchasing . . . soul:* redeeming Antonio (as Bassanio's friend, he is the likeness of Bassanio, who, as her husband, is "my soul").

[97] *husbandry:* stewardship.

[98] *imposition:* duty, charge.

[99] *acknowledge:* obey.

Portia. I thank you for your wish, and am well pleas'd
  To wish it back on you. Fare you well, Jessica.

> [*Exeunt Jessica and Lorenzo.*]

Now, Balthazar,   45
As I have ever found thee honest-true,
So let me find thee still. Take this same letter,
And use thou all th' endeavor of a man
In speed to [Padua]. See thou render this
Into my [cousin's] hands, Doctor Bellario,   50
And look what notes and garments he doth give thee,
Bring them, I pray thee, with imagin'd speed[100]
Unto the [traject],[101] to the common ferry
Which trades to Venice. Waste no time in words,
But get thee gone. I shall be there before thee.   55

Balthazar. Madam, I go with all convenient speed.

> [*Exit.*]

Portia. Come on, Nerissa, I have work in hand
  That you yet know not of. We'll see our husbands
  Before they think of us.

Nerissa.   Shall they see us?

Portia. They shall, Nerissa; but in such a habit[102]   60
  That they shall think we are accomplished[103]
  With that we lack.[104] I'll hold thee any wager,
  When we are both accoutered[105] like young men,
  I'll prove the prettier fellow of the two,
  And wear my dagger with the braver grace,   65
  And speak between the change of man and boy

---

[100] *imagin'd speed*: all the speed imaginable.
[101] *traject*: ferryboat (perhaps derived from the Italian, *traghetto*).
[102] *habit*: costume, outfit.
[103] *accomplished*: fully equipped.
[104] *With that we lack*: i.e., manliness.
[105] *accoutered*: dressed.

With a reed voice, and turn two mincing steps
Into a manly stride; and speak of frays
Like a fine bragging youth, and tell quaint lies,
How honorable ladies sought my love,   70
Which I denying, they fell sick and died.
I could not do withal.[106] Then I'll repent,
And wish, for all that, that I had not kill'd them;
And twenty of these puny lies I'll tell,
That men shall swear I have discontinued school   75
Above a twelvemonth. I have within my mind
A thousand raw tricks of these bragging Jacks,[107]
Which I will practice.

Nerissa.   Why, shall we turn to men?

Portia. Fie, what a question's that,
If thou wert near a lewd interpreter!   80
But come, I'll tell thee all my whole device
When I am in my coach, which stays for us
At the park-gate; and therefore haste away,
For we must measure twenty miles to-day.

                                              [*Exeunt.*]

Scene 5.   *The same. A garden.*

Enter Clown [Launcelot] and Jessica.

Launcelot. Yes, truly, for look you, the sins of the
     father are to be laid upon the children; therefore, I
     promise you, I fear you.[108] I was always plain with
     you, and so now I speak my agitation[109] of the
     matter; therefore be a' good cheer, for truly I think   5
     you are damn'd. There is but one hope in it that

---

[106] *I could not do withal*: I couldn't help it.
[107] *Jacks*: knaves, fellows.
[108] *fear you*: fear for you.
[109] *agitation*: i.e., cogitation.

can do you any good, and that is but a kind of
bastard hope neither.

Jessica. And what hope is that, I pray thee?   9

Launcelot. Marry, you may partly hope that your
father got you not, that you are not the Jew's
daughter.

Jessica. That were a kind of bastard hope indeed;
So the sins of my mother should be visited upon me.

Launcelot. Truly then I fear you are damn'd both   15
by father and mother; thus when I shun Scylla, your
father, I fall into Charybdis,[110] your mother. Well,
you are gone both ways.

Jessica. I shall be sav'd by my husband, he hath
made me a Christian!   20

Launcelot. Truly, the more to blame he; we were
Christians enow[111] before, e'en as many as could well
live one by another. This making of Christians will
raise the price of hogs. If we grow all to be pork-
eaters, we shall not shortly have a rasher[112] on the
coals for money.   26

                                                    Enter Lorenzo.

Jessica. I'll tell my husband, Launcelot, what you say.
Here he [comes].

Lorenzo. I shall grow jealous of you shortly, Launcelot,
if you thus get my wife into corners!   30

---

[110] *Scylla . . . Charybdis*: In classical mythology, Scylla (who dwelled in a rock
and ate sailors) and Charybdis (who created whirlpools) were monstrous obsta-
cles in the Strait of Messina.

[111] *enow*: enough.

[112] *rasher*: thin slice of bacon.

Jessica. Nay, you need not fear us, Lorenzo, Launcelot
  and I are out.[113] He tells me flatly there's no mercy
  for me in heaven because I am a Jew's daughter; and
  he says you are no good member of the common
  wealth, for in converting Jews to Christians, you raise
  the price of pork.   36

Lorenzo. I shall answer that better to the commonwealth
  than you can the getting up of the Negro's
  belly; the Moor is with child by you, Launcelot.

Launcelot. It is much that the Moor should be   40
  more than reason; but if she be less than an honest
  woman, she is indeed more than I took her for.

Lorenzo. How every fool can play upon the word!
  I think the best grace of wit will shortly turn into
  silence, and discourse grow commendable in   45
  none only but parrots. Go in, sirrah, bid them
  prepare for dinner.

Launcelot. That is done, sir, they have all stomachs!

Lorenzo. Goodly Lord, what a wit-snapper are you!
  then bid them prepare dinner.   50

Launcelot. That is done too, sir, only "cover"[114] is the
  word.

Lorenzo. Will you cover them, sir?

Launcelot. Not so, sir, neither, I know my duty.   54

Lorenzo. Yet more quarrelling with occasion![115] wilt
  thou show the whole wealth of thy wit in an
  instant? I pray thee understand a plain man in his

---

[113] *are out:* have quarreled.
[114] *cover:* i.e., lay the table.
[115] *quarreling with occasion:* quibbling, picking quarrels with words at every
opportunity.

plain meaning: go to thy fellows; bid them cover
the table, serve in the meat, and we will come in to
dinner.   60

Launcelot. For the table, sir, it shall be serv'd in; for
the meat, sir, it shall be cover'd; for your coming in
to dinner, sir, why, let it be as humors and conceits
shall govern.   [*Exit Clown*.]   64

Lorenzo. O dear discretion, how his words are suited![116]
The fool hath planted in his memory
An army of good words, and I do know
A many[117] fools, that stand in better place,
Garnish'd like him, that for a tricksy word
Defy the matter. How cheer'st thou,[118] Jessica?   70
And now, good sweet, say thy opinion,
How dost thou like the Lord Bassanio's wife?

Jessica. Past all expressing. It is very meet
The Lord Bassanio live an upright life,
For having such a blessing in his lady,   75
He finds the joys of heaven here on earth,
And if on earth he do not [merit] it,
In reason he should never come to heaven!
Why, if two gods should play some heavenly match,
And on the wager lay two earthly women,   80
And Portia one, there must be something else
Pawn'd with the other, for the poor rude world
Hath not her fellow.

Lorenzo.   Even such a husband
Hast thou of me as she is for [a] wife.

Jessica. Nay, but ask my opinion too of that.   85

---

[116] *suited*: used to suit the occasion.
[117] *A many*: many.
[118] *How cheer'st thou*: Are you in good spirits?

Lorenzo. I will anon, first let us go to dinner.

Jessica. Nay, let me praise you while I have a stomach.[119]

Lorenzo. No, pray thee, let it serve for table-talk;
Then, howsome'er thou speak'st, 'mong other things
I shall digest it.

Jessica.   Well, I'll set you forth.[120]   90

                              [*Exuent.*]

---

[119] *a stomach:* an inclination, an appetite.
[120] *set you forth:* serve you up, as at a feast.

ACT 4

Scene 1. *Venice. A court of justice.*[1]

Enter the Duke, the Magnificoes, Antonio, Bassanio,
[Salerio,] and Gratiano [with others].

Duke. What, is Antonio here?

Antonio. Ready, so please your Grace.

Duke. I am sorry for thee. Thou art come to answer
  A stony adversary, an inhuman wretch,
  Uncapable of pity, void and empty   5
  From[2] any dram of mercy.

Antonio.   I have heard
  Your Grace hath ta'en great pains to qualify[3]
  His rigorous course; but since he stands obdurate,
  And that no lawful means can carry me
  Out of his envy's[4] reach, I do oppose   10
  My patience to his fury, and am arm'd
  To suffer, with a quietness of spirit,
  The very tyranny and rage of his.

Duke. Go one, and call the Jew into the court.

Salerio. He is ready at the door; he comes, my lord.

Enter Shylock.

Duke. Make room, and let him stand before our[5] face.   16
  Shylock, the world thinks, and I think so too,
  That thou but leadest this fashion[6] of thy malice
  To the last hour of act, and then 'tis thought

---

[1] This is often staged in a room in the doge's palace.
[2] *From*: of.
[3] *qualify*: moderate.
[4] *envy's*: malice's, hatred's.
[5] *our*: my (the "royal we").
[6] *fashion*: assumed appearance, pretense.

Thou'lt show thy mercy and remorse[7] more strange
Than is thy strange apparent cruelty;   21
And where thou now exacts the penalty,
Which is a pound of this poor merchant's flesh,
Thou wilt not only loose the forfeiture,
But touch'd with humane gentleness and love,   25
Forgive a moi'ty[8] of the principal,
Glancing an eye of pity on his losses,
That have of late so huddled on his back,
Enow[9] to press a royal merchant down,
And pluck commiseration of [his state]   30
From brassy bosoms and rough hearts of flints,
From stubborn Turks, and Tartars never train'd
To offices of tender courtesy.
We all expect a gentle answer, Jew!

Shylock. I have possess'd[10] your Grace of what I
    purpose,   35
And by our holy Sabaoth have I sworn
To have the due and forfeit of my bond.
If you deny it, let the danger light
Upon your charter and your city's freedom!
You'll ask me why I rather choose to have   40
A weight of carrion flesh than to receive
Three thousand ducats. I'll not answer that;
But say it is my humor,[11] is it answer'd?
What if my house be troubled with a rat,
And I be pleas'd to give ten thousand ducats   45
To have it ban'd?[12] What, are you answer'd yet?
Some men there are love not a gaping pig;[13]
Some that are mad if they behold a cat;

[7] *remorse*: pity.
[8] *moi'ty*: literally a half, but generally any portion.
[9] *Enow*: enough.
[10] *possess'd*: informed.
[11] *humor*: whim.
[12] *ban'd*: poisoned.
[13] *gaping pig*: roasted pig, with mouth open.

And others, when the bagpipe sings i' th' nose,
Cannot contain their urine: for affection,   50
[Mistress] of passion, sways it to the mood
Of what it likes or loathes. Now for your answer:
As there is no firm reason to be rend'red
Why he cannot abide a gaping pig;
Why he, a harmless necessary cat;   55
Why he, a woolen bagpipe, but of force
Must yield to such inevitable shame
As to offend, himself being offended;
So can I give no reason, nor I will not,
More than a lodg'd hate and a certain[14] loathing   60
I bear Antonio, that I follow thus
A losing suit against him. Are you answered?

Bassanio. This is no answer, thou unfeeling man,
To excuse the current of thy cruelty.

Shylock. I am not bound to please thee with my answers.   65

Bassanio. Do all men kill the things they do not love?

Shylock. Hates any man the thing he would not kill?

Bassanio. Every offence is not a hate at first.

Shylock. What, wouldst thou have a serpent sting thee
twice?

Antonio. I pray you think you question[15] with the Jew:
You may as well go stand upon the beach   71
And bid the main flood[16] bate[17] his usual height;
You may as well use question with the wolf
Why he hath made the ewe bleak for the lamb;
You may as well forbid the mountain pines   75

---

[14] *certain:* confirmed, rooted.
[15] *question:* argue.
[16] *main flood:* high tide.
[17] *bate:* diminish.

To wag their high tops, and to make no noise
When they are fretten[18] with the gusts of heaven;
You may as well do any thing most hard
As seek to soften that—than which what's harder?—
His Jewish heart! Therefore I do beseech you　　　80
Make no moe offers, use no farther means,
But with all brief and plain conveniency[19]
Let me have judgment and the Jew his will.

Bassanio. For thy three thousand ducats here is six.

Shylock. If every ducat in six thousand ducats　　　85
Were in six parts, and every part a ducat,
I would not draw[20] them, I would have my bond.

Duke. How shalt thou hope for mercy, rend'ring none?

Shylock. What judgment shall I dread, doing no wrong?
You have among you many a purchas'd slave,　　　90
Which like your asses, and your dogs and mules,
You use in abject and in slavish parts,[21]
Because you bought them. Shall I say to you,
"Let them be free! Marry them to your heirs!
Why sweat they under burthens? Let their beds　　　95
Be made as soft as yours, and let their palates
Be season'd with such viands"?[22] You will answer,
"The slaves are ours." So do I answer you:
The pound of flesh which I demand of him
Is dearly bought as mine, and I will have it.　　　100
If you deny me, fie upon your law!
There is no force in the decrees of Venice.
I stand for judgment. Answer—shall I have it?

---

[18] *fretten*: fretted.
[19] *conveniency*: propriety.
[20] *draw*: take.
[21] *parts*: offices, functions.
[22] *viands*: items of food.

Duke. Upon my power I may dismiss this court,
    Unless Bellario, a learned doctor,   105
    Whom I have sent for to determine this,
    Come here to-day.

Salerio.   My lord, here stays without
    A messenger with letters from the doctor,
    New come from Padua.

Duke. Bring us the letters; call the messenger.   110

Bassanio. Good cheer, Antonio! what, man, courage yet!
    The Jew shall have my flesh, blood, bones, and all,
    Ere thou shalt lose for me one drop of blood.

Antonio. I am a tainted wether[23] of the flock,
    Meetest for death;[24] the weakest kind of fruit   115
    Drops earliest to the ground, and so let me.
    You cannot better be employ'd, Bassanio,
    Than to live still and write mine epitaph.

        Enter Nerissa [dressed like a lawyer's clerk].

Duke. Came you from Padua, from Bellario?

Nerissa. From both, my lord. Bellario greets your Grace.
                   [Presenting a letter.]

Bassanio. Why dost thou whet thy knife so earnestly?   121

Shylock. To cut the forfeiture from that bankrout there.

Gratiano. Not on thy sole,[25] but on thy soul, harsh Jew,
    Thou mak'st thy knife keen; but no metal can,   124
    No, not the hangman's axe, bear half the keenness
    Of thy sharp envy. Can no prayers pierce thee?

Shylock. No, none that thou hast wit enough to make.

---

[23] *wether*: castrated ram.
[24] *Meetest for death*: most fit for slaughter.
[25] *sole*: Many productions have Shylock sharpen his knife on his shoe here.

Gratiano. O, be thou damn'd, inexecrable[26] dog!
    And for thy life[27] let justice be accus'd.
    Thou almost mak'st me waver in my faith   130
    To hold opinion with Pythagoras,[28]
    That souls of animals infuse themselves
    Into the trunks of men. Thy currish spirit
    Govern'd a wolf, who hang'd for human slaughter,
    Even from the gallows did his fell[29] soul fleet,[30]   135
    And whilst thou layest in thy unhallowed dam,[31]
    Infus'd itself in thee; for thy desires
    Are wolvish, bloody, starv'd, and ravenous.

Shylock. Till thou canst rail the seal from off my bond,
    Thou but offend'st thy lungs to speak so loud.   140
    Repair thy wit, good youth, or it will fall
    To cureless ruin. I stand here for law.

Duke. This letter from Bellario doth commend
    A young and learned doctor to our court.
    Where is he?

Nerissa.   He attendeth here hard by   145
    To know your answer, whether you'll admit him.

Duke. With all my heart. Some three or four of you
    Go give him courteous conduct to this place.
    Meantime the court shall hear Bellario's letter.   149

[*Reads.*][32] "Your Grace shall understand that at
    the receipt of your letter I am very sick, but in
    the instant that your messenger came, in loving

---

[26] *inexecrable*: unable to be execrated (cursed) enough.

[27] *for thy life*: i.e., for letting thee live.

[28] *Pythagoras*: Greek philosopher (c. 580–490 B.C.) who thought the soul migrated at death into another living creature.

[29] *fell*: cruel.

[30] *fleet*: pass.

[31] *dam*: mother.

[32] No reader is designated in early texts. The letter may be read by the Duke or by Nerissa, the "clerk".

visitation was with me a young doctor of Rome.
His name is Balthazar. I acquainted him with the
cause in controversy between the Jew and   155
Antonio the merchant. We turn'd o'er many books
together. He is furnish'd with my opinion, which
better'd with his own learning, the greatness
whereof I cannot enough commend, comes with
him,[33] at my importunity, to fill up your Grace's   160
request in my stead. I beseech you let his lack of
years be no impediment to let him lack a reverend
estimation, for I never knew so young a body with
so old a head. I leave him to your gracious
acceptance, whose trial shall better publish his
commendation."   166

Enter Portia for Balthazar.

You hear the learn'd Bellario, what he writes,
And here I take it is the doctor come.
Give me your hand. Come you from old Bellario?

Portia. I did, my lord.

Duke.   You are welcome, take your place.
Are you acquainted with the difference   171
That holds this present question in the court?

Portia. I am informed throughly[34] of the cause.[35]
Which is the merchant here? and which the Jew?   174

Duke. Antonio and old Shylock, both stand forth.

Portia. Is your name Shylock?

Shylock.   Shylock is my name.

---

[33] *comes with him:* i.e., brings my opinion.

[34] *throughly:* thoroughly. The quarto's obsolete "throughly" is important rhythmically.

[35] *cause:* case.

Portia. Of a strange nature is the suit you follow,
 Yet in such rule[36] that the Venetian law
 Cannot impugn you[37] as you do proceed.—
 You stand within his danger,[38] do you not?   *180*

Antonio. Ay, so he says.

Portia.   Do you confess the bond?

Antonio. I do.

Portia.   Then must[39] the Jew be merciful.

Shylock. On what compulsion must I? tell me that.

Portia. The quality of mercy is not strain'd,[40]
 It droppeth as the gentle rain from heaven   *185*
 Upon the place beneath. It is twice blest:
 It blesseth him that gives and him that takes.
 'Tis mightiest in the mightiest, it becomes
 The throned monarch better than his crown.
 His sceptre shows the force of temporal power,   *190*
 The attribute to[41] awe and majesty,
 Wherein doth sit the dread and fear of kings;
 But mercy is above this sceptred sway,
 It is enthroned in the hearts of kings,
 It is an attribute to God himself;   *195*
 And earthly power doth then show likest God's
 When mercy seasons[42] justice. Therefore, Jew,
 Though justice be thy plea, consider this,
 That in the course of justice, none of us

---

[36] *in such rule*: so within the rules.

[37] *impugn you*: oppose you, dispute your honesty.

[38] *within his danger*: in his debt, under his power.

[39] *must*: not a question of legal compulsion but of moral compulsion; indicative that only Shylock's mercy can save Antonio and that, therefore, he *should feel compelled* to do so.

[40] *strain'd*: constrained, forced.

[41] *The attribute to*: the property of.

[42] *seasons*: qualifies, moderates.

Should see salvation. We do pray for mercy,   200
And that same prayer doth teach us all to render
The deeds of mercy. I have spoke thus much
To mitigate[43] the justice of thy plea,[44]
Which if thou follow, this strict court of Venice   204
Must needs give sentence 'gainst the merchant there.

Shylock. My deeds upon my head! I crave the law,
The penalty and forfeit of my bond.

Portia. Is he not able to discharge the money?

Bassanio. Yes, here I tender it for him in the court,
Yea, twice the sum. If that will not suffice,   210
I will be bound to pay it ten times o'er,
On forfeit of my hands, my head, my heart.
If this will not suffice, it must appear
That malice bears down truth. [*To the Duke.*] And I
  beseech you
Wrest once the law to your authority: 215
To do a great right, do a little wrong,
And curb this cruel devil of his will.

Portia. It must not be, there is no power in Venice
Can alter a decree established.
'Twill be recorded for a precedent,   220
And many an error by the same example
Will rush into the state. It cannot be.

Shylock. A Daniel come to judgment![45] yea, a Daniel!
O wise young judge, how I do honor thee!

Portia. I pray you let me look upon the bond.   225

Shylock. Here 'tis, most reverend doctor, here it is.

---

[43] *mitigate:* moderate.
[44] *justice of thy plea:* your appeal to strict justice.
[45] *A Daniel come to judgement:* Daniel was the shrewd young man and judge who exposed the elders in their false charges against Susannah (cf. Daniel 6:3).

Portia. Shylock, there's thrice thy money off'red thee.

Shylock. An oath, an oath, I have an oath in heaven!
   Shall I lay perjury upon my soul?
   [No], not for Venice.

Portia.   Why, this bond is forfeit,   230
   And lawfully by this the Jew may claim
   A pound of flesh, to be by him cut off
   Nearest the merchant's heart. Be merciful,
   Take thrice thy money, bid me tear the bond.

Shylock. When it is paid according to the tenure.[46]   235
   It doth appear you are a worthy judge;
   You know the law, your exposition
   Hath been most sound. I charge you by the law,
   Whereof you are a well-deserving pillar,
   Proceed to judgment. By my soul I swear   240
   There is no power in the tongue of man
   To alter me: I stay here on my bond.

Antonio. Most heartily I do beseech the court
   To give the judgment.

Portia.   Why then thus it is:
   You must prepare your bosom for his knife—   245

Shylock. O noble judge, O excellent young man!

Portia. For the intent and purpose of the law
   Hath full relation to[47] the penalty,
   Which here appeareth due upon the bond.

Shylock. 'Tis very true. O wise and upright judge!
   How much more elder art thou than thy looks!   251

Portia. Therefore lay bare your bosom.

---

[46] *tenure:* substance of the terms.
[47] *Hath full relation to:* is in complete accord with.

Shylock.   Ay, his breast,
So says the bond, doth it not, noble judge?
"Nearest his heart," those are the very words.

Portia. It is so. Are there balance[48] here to weigh
The flesh?

Shylock.   I have them ready.   256

Portia. Have by some surgeon, Shylock, on your charge,[49]
To stop his wounds, lest he do bleed to death.

Shylock. Is it so nominated in the bond?

Portia. It is not so express'd, but what of that?   260
'Twere good you do so much for charity.

Shylock. I cannot find it, 'tis not in the bond.

Portia. You, merchant, have you any thing to say?

Antonio. But little; I am arm'd and well prepar'd.
Give me your hand, Bassanio, fare you well.   265
Grieve not that I am fall'n to this for you;
For herein Fortune shows herself more kind
Than is her custom. It is still her use
To let the wretched man outlive his wealth,
To view with hollow eye and wrinkled brow   270
An age of poverty; from which ling'ring penance
Of such a misery doth she cut me off.
Commend me to your honorable wife,
Tell her the process[50] of Antonio's end,
Say how I lov'd you, speak me fair[51] in death;   275
And when the tale is told, bid her be judge
Whether Bassanio had not once a love.

---

[48] *balance*: scales.
[49] *charge*: expense.
[50] *process*: course, also a pun on the word's meaning as a legal proceeding.
[51] *speak me fair*: speak well of me.

Repent but you[52] that you shall lose your friend,
And he repents not that he pays your debt;
For if the Jew do cut but deep enough,   280
I'll pay it instantly with all my heart.

Bassanio. Antonio, I am married to a wife
Which is as dear to me as life itself,
But life itself, my wife, and all the world,
Are not with me esteem'd above thy life.   285
I would lose all, ay, sacrifice them all
Here to this devil, to deliver you.

Portia. Your wife would give you little thanks for that
If she were by to hear you make the offer.

Gratiano. I have a wife who I protest I love;   290
I would she were in heaven, so she could
Entreat some power to change this currish Jew.

Nerissa. 'Tis well you offer it behind her back,
The wish would make else an unquiet house.

Shylock. [*Aside.*] These be the Christian husbands. I have
   a daughter—   295
Would any of the stock of Barrabas[53]
Had been her husband rather than a Christian!
—We trifle time. I pray thee pursue sentence.

Portia. A pound of that same merchant's flesh is thine,
The court awards it, and the law doth give it.   300

Shylock. Most rightful judge!

Portia. And you must cut this flesh from off his breast,
The law allows it, and the court awards it.

---

[52] *Repent but you:* i.e., if only you regret.
[53] *Barrabas:* a robber and murderer set free by Pontius Pilate when Jesus was condemned (cf. John 18:40); also the central character's name ("Barabas") in Christopher Marlowe's play *The Jew of Malta.*

Shylock. Most learned judge, a sentence! Come prepare!

Portia. Tarry a little, there is something else.   305
  This bond doth give thee here no jot of blood;
  The words expressly are "a pound of flesh."
  Take then thy bond, take thou thy pound of flesh,
  But in the cutting it, if thou dost shed
  One drop of Christian blood, thy lands and goods   310
  Are by the laws of Venice confiscate
  Unto the state of Venice.

Gratiano. O upright judge! Mark, Jew. O learned judge!

Shylock. Is that the law?

Portia.   Thyself shalt see the act;
  For as thou urgest justice, be assur'd   315
  Thou shalt have justice more than thou desir'st.

Gratiano. O learned judge! Mark, Jew, a learned judge!

Shylock. I take this offer then; pay the bond thrice
  And let the Christian go.

Bassanio.   Here is the money.

Portia. Soft,[54]   320
  The Jew shall have all justice. Soft, no haste.
  He shall have nothing but the penalty.

Gratiano. O Jew! an upright judge, a learned judge!

Portia. Therefore prepare thee to cut off the flesh.
  Shed thou no blood, nor cut thou less nor more   325
  But just a pound of flesh. If thou tak'st more
  Or less than a just[55] pound, be it but so much
  As makes it light or heavy in the substance
  Or the division of the twentieth part

---

[54] *Soft:* wait (injunction).
[55] *just:* exact.

Of one poor scruple,[56] nay, if the scale do turn   330
But in the estimation of a hair,[57]
Thou diest, and all thy goods are confiscate.

Gratiano. A second Daniel! a Daniel, Jew!
  Now, infidel, I have thee on the hip.[58]   334

Portia. Why doth the Jew pause? Take thy forfeiture.

Shylock. Give me my principal, and let me go.

Bassanio. I have it ready for thee, here it is.

Portia. He hath refus'd it in the open court;
  He shall have merely justice and his bond.

Gratiano. A Daniel, still say I, a second Daniel!   340
  I thank thee, Jew, for teaching me that word.

Shylock. Shall I not have barely[59] my principal?

Portia. Thou shalt have nothing but the forfeiture,
  To be so taken at thy peril, Jew.

Shylock. Why then the devil give him good of it!
  I'll stay no longer question.[60]

Portia.   Tarry, Jew,   346
  The law hath yet another hold on you.
  It is enacted in the laws of Venice,
  If it be proved against an alien,
  That by direct or indirect attempts   350
  He seek the life of any citizen,
  The party 'gainst the which he doth contrive
  Shall seize one half his goods; the other half

---

[56] *scruple*: according to apothecaries' weight, one gram (a very small amount).
[57] *the estimation of a hair*: a hair's breadth.
[58] *have thee on the hip*: have advantage of you (wrestling figure of speech).
[59] *barely*: even.
[60] *question*: argument, discussion.

Comes to the privy coffer of the state,[61]
And the offender's life lies in[62] the mercy   355
Of the Duke only, 'gainst all other voice:
In which predicament I say thou stand'st;
For it appears, by manifest proceeding,
That indirectly, and directly too,
Thou hast contrived against the very life   360
Of the defendant; and thou hast incurr'd
The danger formerly by me rehears'd.[63]
Down therefore, and beg mercy of the Duke.

Gratiano. Beg that thou mayst have leave to hang thyself,
And yet thy wealth being forfeit to the state,   365
Thou hast not left the value of a cord;
Therefore thou must be hang'd at the state's charge.[64]

Duke. That thou shalt see the difference of our spirit,
I pardon thee thy life before thou ask it.
For[65] half thy wealth, it is Antonio's;   370
The other half comes to the general state,
Which humbleness may drive unto a fine.[66]

Portia. Ay, for the state, not for Antonio.

Shylock. Nay, take my life and all, pardon not that:
You take my house when you do take the prop   375
That doth sustain my house; you take my life
When you do take the means whereby I live.

Portia. What mercy can you render him, Antonio?

Gratiano. A halter[67] gratis—nothing else, for God sake.

---

[61] *privy coffer of the state*: personal funds of the sovereign.
[62] *in*: at.
[63] *rehears'd*: cited.
[64] *charge*: expense.
[65] *For*: as for.
[66] *Which . . . fine*: which humility on your part may reduce to a fine.
[67] *halter*: hangman's noose.

Antonio. So please[68] my lord the Duke and all the court
  To quit[69] the fine for one half of his goods,   381
  I am content; so he will let me have
  The other half in use,[70] to render it
  Upon his death unto the gentleman
  That lately stole his daughter.   385
  Two things provided more, that for this favor
  He presently[71] become a Christian;
  The other, that he do record a gift,
  Here in the court, of all he dies possess'd
  Unto his son Lorenzo and his daughter.   390

Duke. He shall do this, or else I do recant[72]
  The pardon that I late pronounced here.

Portia. Art thou contented,[73] Jew? what dost thou say?

Shylock. I am content.

Portia.   Clerk, draw a deed of gift.

Shylock. I pray you give me leave to go from hence,
  I am not well. Send the deed after me,   396
  And I will sign it.

Duke.   Get thee gone, but do it.

[Gratiano.] In christ'ning shalt thou have two godfathers:
  Had I been judge, thou shouldst have had ten more,[74]
  To bring thee to the gallows, not to the font.   400

                          [Exit Shylock.]

Duke. Sir, I entreat you home with me to dinner.

[68] *So please:* if it please.
[69] *quit:* remit.
[70] *in use:* in trust (perhaps with legal associations, as in "at interest").
[71] *presently:* immediately.
[72] *recant:* withdraw.
[73] *contented:* satisfied (i.e., willing to accept these terms).
[74] *ten more:* i.e., twelve jurymen.

Portia. I humbly do desire your Grace of pardon,[75]
  I must away this night toward Padua,
  And it is meet I presently set forth.

Duke. I am sorry that your leisure serves you not.
  Antonio, gratify[76] this gentleman,   406
  For in my mind you are much bound to him.

               [*Exeunt Duke and his Train.*]

Bassanio. Most worthy gentleman, I and my friend
  Have by your wisdom been this day acquitted
  Of grievous penalties, in lieu whereof[77]   410
  Three thousand ducats, due unto the Jew,
  We freely cope[78] your courteous pains withal.

Antonio. And stand indebted, over and above,
  In love and service to you evermore.

Portia. He is well paid that is well satisfied,   415
  And I, delivering you, am satisfied,
  And therein do account myself well paid.
  My mind was never yet more mercenary.
  I pray you know me when we meet again;
  I wish you well, and so I take my leave.   420

Bassanio. Dear sir, of force I must attempt you[79] further.
  Take some remembrance of us as a tribute,
  Not as fee. Grant me two things, I pray you,
  Not to deny me, and to pardon me.   424

Portia. You press me far, and therefore I will yield.
  [*To Antonio.*] Give me your gloves, I'll wear them for
    your sake,

[75] *I . . . desire your Grace of pardon*: idiomatic Elizabethan construction meaning, "I desire pardon of Your Grace."

[76] *gratify*: reward.

[77] *in lieu whereof*: in return for which.

[78] *cope*: meet, requite.

[79] *attempt you*: try to persuade you.

[*To Bassanio.*] And for your love I'll take this ring from
   you.
Do not draw back your hand, I'll take no more,
And you in love shall not deny me this!

Bassanio. This ring, good sir, alas, it is a trifle! 430
I will not shame myself to give you this.

Portia. I will have nothing else but only this,
And now methinks I have a mind to it.

Bassanio. There's more depends on this than on the value.
The dearest ring in Venice will I give you, 435
And find it out by proclamation;
Only for this,[80] I pray you pardon me.

Portia. I see, sir, you are liberal in offers.
You taught me first to beg, and now methinks
You teach me how a beggar should be answer'd. 440

Bassanio. Good sir, this ring was given me by my wife,
And when she put it on, she made me vow
That I should neither sell, nor give, nor lose it.

Portia. That 'scuse[81] serves many men to save their gifts,
And if your wife be not a mad woman, 445
And know how well I have deserv'd this ring,
She would not hold out enemy for ever
For giving it to me. Well, peace be with you!

                     [*Exeunt Portia and Nerissa.*]

Antonio. My Lord Bassanio, let him have the ring.
Let his deservings and my love withal 450
Be valued 'gainst your wive's commandement.

---

[80] *for this:* as for this (i.e., the ring).
[81] *'scuse:* excuse.

Bassanio. Go, Gratiano, run and overtake him;
   Give him the ring, and bring him, if thou canst,
   Unto Antonio's house. Away, make haste.

                                  [*Exit Gratiano.*]

   Come, you and I will thither presently,   455
   And in the morning early will we both
   Fly toward Belmont. Come, Antonio.   [*Exeunt.*]

Scene 2.   *The same. A street.*

Enter Portia and Nerissa disguised as before.

Portia. Inquire the Jew's house out, give him this deed,[82]
   And let him sign it. We'll away to-night,
   And be a day before our husbands home.
   This deed will be well welcome to Lorenzo.

                              Enter Gratiano.

Gratiano. Fair sir, you are well o'erta'en.[83]   5
   My Lord Bassanio upon more advice
   Hath sent you here this ring, and doth entreat
   Your company at dinner.

Portia.   That cannot be.
   His ring I do accept most thankfully,
   And so I pray you tell him; furthermore,   10
   I pray you show my youth old Shylock's house.

Gratiano. That will I do.

Nerissa.   Sir, I would speak with you.
   [*Aside to Portia.*] I'll see if I can get my husband's ring,
   Which I did make him swear to keep for ever.

---

[82] *deed*: deed of gift.
[83] *o'erta'en*: overtaken.

Portia. [*Aside to Nerissa.*] Thou mayst, I warrant. We shall   15
    have old[84] swearing
That they did give the rings away to men;
But we'll outface them, and outswear them too.—
Away, make haste. Thou know'st where I will tarry.

Nerissa. Come, good sir, will you show me to this
    house?   [*Exeunt.*]

[84] *old:* plenty of (an augmentative, signifying "great").

ACT 5

Scene 1. *Belmont. Avenue to Portia's house.*

Enter Lorenzo and Jessica.

Lorenzo. The moon shines bright. In such a night as
    this,[1]
  When the sweet wind did gently kiss the trees,
  And they did make no noise, in such a night
  Troilus[2] methinks mounted the Troyan walls,
  And sigh'd his soul toward the Grecian tents,   *5*
  Where Cressid lay that night.

Jessica.   In such a night
  Did Thisby[3] fearfully o'ertrip the dew,
  And saw the lion's shadow ere[4] himself,
  And ran dismayed away.

Lorenzo.   In such a night
  Stood Dido[5] with a willow[6] in her hand   *10*
  Upon the wild sea-banks, and waft[7] her love
  To come again to Carthage.

Jessica.   In such a night
  Medea[8] gathered the enchanted herbs
  That did renew old Aeson.[9]

---

[1] The following allusions to classical stories of doomed lovers are all drawn from Ovid and Chaucer.

[2] *Troilus*: in classical mythology, Trojan whose beloved, Cressida, was sent unwillingly to the Greek camp. She later fell in love with a Greek chieftan, proving false to Troilus.

[3] *Thisby*: in classical mythology, beloved of Pyramus. She fled from the lovers' rendezvous when a lion approached.

[4] *ere*: before.

[5] *Dido*: in classical mythology, queen of Carthage whose love for Aeneas ends tragically.

[6] *willow*: A willow branch was symbolic of forsaken love.

[7] *waft*: beckon.

[8] *Medea*: in classical mythology, enchantress who fell in love with Jason and helped him gain the golden fleece.

[9] *Aeson*: in classical mythology, Jason's father.

Lorenzo.   In such a night
    Did Jessica steal[10] from the wealthy Jew,   15
    And with an unthrift love did run from Venice,
    As far as Belmont.

Jessica.   In such a night
    Did young Lorenzo swear he lov'd her well,
    Stealing her soul with many vows of faith,
    And ne'er a true one.

Lorenzo.   In such a night   20
    Did pretty Jessica (like a little shrow)
    Slander her love, and he forgave it her.

Jessica. I would out-night you, did nobody come;
    But hark, I hear the footing of a man.

                      Enter a Messenger.

Lorenzo. Who comes so fast in silence of the night?   25

Messenger. A friend.

Lorenzo. A friend! what friend? your name, I pray you,
    friend?

Messenger. Stephano is my name, and I bring word
    My mistress will before the break of day
    Be here at Belmont. She doth stray about   30
    By holy crosses,[11] where she kneels and prays
    For happy wedlock hours.

Lorenzo.   Who comes with her?

Messenger. None but a holy hermit and her maid.
    I pray you, is my master yet return'd?

Lorenzo. He is not, nor we have not heard from him.
    But go we in, I pray thee, Jessica,   36

---

[10] *steal:* slip away.
[11] *holy crosses:* wayside shrines marked with crosses.

And ceremoniously let us prepare
Some welcome for the mistress of the house.

Enter Clown [Launcelot].

Launcelot. Sola,[12] sola! wo ha, ho! sola, sola!

Lorenzo. Who calls?   40

Launcelot. Sola! did you see Master Lorenzo? Master
     Lorenzo, sola, sola!

Lorenzo. Leave hollowing, man—here.

Launcelot. Sola! where, where?

Lorenzo. Here!   45

Launcelot. Tell him there's a post come from my
     master, with his horn full of good news. My master
     will be here ere[13] morning.   [*Exit.*]

Lorenzo. Sweet soul, let's in, and there expect their
     coming.
     And yet no matter; why should we go in?   50
     My friend [Stephano], signify,[14] I pray you,
     Within the house, your mistress is at hand,
     And bring your music forth into the air.
                                        [*Exit Messenger.*]
     How sweet the moonlight sleeps upon this bank!
     Here will we sit, and let the sounds of music   55
     Creep in our ears. Soft stillness and the night
     Become[15] the touches[16] of sweet harmony.
     Sit, Jessica. Look how the floor of heaven

[12] *Sola:* sound imitating a post horn.
[13] *ere:* before.
[14] *signify:* announce.
[15] *Become:* befit, are appropriate to.
[16] *touches:* notes, strains.

Is thick inlaid with patens[17] of bright gold.
There's not the smallest orb which thou behold'st   60
But in his motion like an angel sings,[18]
Still quiring[19] to the young-ey'd cherubins;
Such harmony is in immortal souls,
But whilst this muddy vesture[20] of decay
Doth grossly close it in, we cannot hear it.   65

Enter Musicians.

Come ho, and wake Diana[21] with a hymn,
With sweetest touches pierce your mistress' ear
And draw her home with music.   [*Play Music.*]

Jessica. I am never merry when I hear sweet music.

Lorenzo. The reason is, your spirits are attentive;   70
For do but note a wild and wanton herd
Or race of youthful and unhandled colts,[22]
Fetching mad bounds, bellowing and neighing loud,
Which is the hot condition of their blood,
If they but hear perchance a trumpet sound,   75
Or any air of music touch their ears,
You shall perceive them make a mutual stand,[23]
Their savage eyes turn'd to a modest gaze,
By the sweet power of music; therefore the poet[24]
Did feign[25] that Orpheus[26] drew[27] trees, stones, and
          floods;

[17] *patens*: metal plates or tiling. The First Folio and two of the quartos read "pattens", while later folios have "patterns", and "patines" was later suggested.
[18] *motion . . . sings*: allusion to the music of the spheres.
[19] *quiring*: choiring, singing.
[20] *muddy vesture*: clay (i.e., flesh).
[21] *Diana*: in classical mythology, virginal goddess of the hunt.
[22] *unhandled colts*: unbroken young stallions.
[23] *make a mutual stand*: all stand still together.
[24] *poet*: Ovid, drawing from the *Metamorphoses*.
[25] *feign*: imagine.
[26] *Orpheus*: in classical mythology, legendary poet and musician whose music was so lovely that inanimate objects were drawn to it.
[27] *drew*: attracted, bent to his musical spell.

Since nought so stockish,[28] hard, and full of rage,   81
But music for the time doth change his nature.
The man that hath no music in himself,
Nor is not moved with concord of sweet sounds,
Is fit for treasons, stratagems, and spoils;[29]   85
The motions of his spirit are dull as night,
And his affections dark as [Erebus]:[30]
Let no such man be trusted. Mark the music.

Enter Portia and Nerissa.

Portia. That light we see is burning in my hall.
How far that little candle throws his beams!   90
So shines a good deed in a naughty[31] world.

Nerissa. When the moon shone, we did not see the candle.

Portia. So doth the greater glory dim the less:
A substitute[32] shines brightly as a king
Until a king be by, and then his state   95
Empties itself, as doth an inland brook
Into the main of waters. Music, hark!

Nerissa. It is your music,[33] madam, of the house.

Portia. Nothing is good, I see, without respect;[34]
Methinks it sounds much sweeter than by day.   100

Nerissa. Silence bestows that virtue on it, madam.

Portia. The crow doth sing as sweetly as the lark
When neither is attended;[35] and I think

---

[28] *stockish*: dull, blockish.

[29] *spoils*: plundering.

[30] *Erebus*: in classical mythology, offspring of Chaos and personification of utter darkness and shadow.

[31] *naughty*: wicked.

[32] *substitute*: deputy (of the king).

[33] *music*: group of musicians.

[34] *without respect*: without regard to the conditions.

[35] *attended*: listened to, attended by favorable circumstances.

The nightingale, if she should sing by day
When every goose is cackling, would be thought   *105*
No better a musician than the wren.
How many things by season season'd are
To their right praise and true perfection!
Peace ho! the Moon sleeps with Endymion,[36]
And would not be awak'd.   [*Music ceases.*]

Lorenzo.   That is the voice,   *110*
Or I am much deceiv'd, of Portia.

Portia. He knows me as the blind man knows the cuckoo,
By the bad voice!

Lorenzo.   Dear lady, welcome home!

Portia. We have been praying for our husbands' welfare,
Which speed we hope the better for our words.   *115*
Are they return'd?

Lorenzo.   Madam, they are not yet;
But there is come a messenger before,
To signify their coming.

Portia.   Go in, Nerissa.
Give order to my servants that they take
No note at all of our being absent hence—   *120*
Nor you, Lorenzo—Jessica, nor you.
                        [*A tucket*[37] *sounds.*]

Lorenzo. Your husband is at hand, I hear his trumpet.
We are no tell-tales, madam, fear you not.

Portia. This night methinks is but the daylight sick,
It looks a little paler. 'Tis a day,   *125*
Such as the day is when the sun is hid.

---

[36] *Endymion*: in classical mythology, beautiful shepherd loved by the moon
goddess. Here the reference implies that the moon has passed behind a cloud.
[37] *tucket*: flourish on a trumpet.

Enter Bassanio, Antonio, Gratiano,
and their Followers.

Bassanio. We should hold day with the Antipodes,[38]
　　If you would walk in absence of the sun.

Portia. Let me give light, but let me not be light,[39]
　　For a light wife doth make a heavy[40] husband,　　　*130*
　　And never be Bassanio so for me—
　　But God sort all! You are welcome home, my lord.

Bassanio. I thank you, madam. Give welcome to my friend;
　　This is the man, this is Antonio,
　　To whom I am so infinitely bound.　　　　　　　　*135*

Portia. You should in all[41] sense be much bound to him,
　　For as I hear he was much bound for you.

Antonio. No more than I am well acquitted of.[42]

Portia. Sir, you are very welcome to our house.
　　It must appear in other ways than words,　　　　*140*
　　Therefore I scant this breathing courtesy.[43]

Gratiano. [*To Nerissa.*] By yonder moon I swear you do
　　　　me wrong;
　　In faith, I gave it to the judge's clerk.
　　Would he were gelt that had it, for my part,
　　Since you do take it, love, so much at heart.　　*145*

Portia. A quarrel ho already! what's the matter?

---

[38] *hold . . . Antipodes:* i.e., share daylight with the other side of the earth.
[39] *light:* i.e., flighty, unfaithful.
[40] *heavy:* sorrowful.
[41] *all:* every.
[42] *acquitted of:* released from.
[43] *scant . . . courtesy:* cut short these courteous words (i.e., expenditure of breath).

Gratiano. About a hoop of gold, a paltry ring
  That she did give me, whose posy[44] was
  For all the world like cutler's poetry[45]
  Upon a knife, "Love me, and leave me not."   150

Nerissa. What[46] talk you of the posy or the value?
  You swore to me, when I did give [it] you,
  That you would wear it till your hour of death,
  And that it should lie with you in your grave.
  Though not for me, yet for your vehement oaths,   155
  You should have been respective[47] and have kept it.
  Gave it a judge's clerk! no, God's my judge,
  The clerk will ne'er wear hair on 's face that had it.

Gratiano. He will, and if[48] he live to be a man.

Nerissa. Ay, if a woman live to be a man.   160

Gratiano. Now, by this hand, I gave it to a youth,
  A kind of boy, a little scrubbed[49] boy,
  No higher than thyself, the judge's clerk,
  A prating boy, that begg'd it as a fee.
  I could not for my heart deny it him.   165

Portia. You were to blame, I must be plain with you,
  To part so slightly with your wive's first gift,
   A thing stuck on with oaths upon your finger,
  And so riveted with faith unto your flesh.
  I gave my love a ring, and made him swear   170
  Never to part with it, and here he stands.
  I dare be sworn for him he would not leave[50] it,
  Nor pluck it from his finger, for the wealth

---

[44] *posy:* inscription on the inside of a ring.
[45] *cutler's poetry:* banal verse of stale mottoes carved in a knife handle.
[46] *What:* why.
[47] *respective:* careful, mindful.
[48] *and if:* if.
[49] *scrubbed:* stunted, wretched, short.
[50] *leave:* give, part with.

That the world masters.[51] Now, in faith, Gratiano,
You give your wife too unkind a cause of grief;   175
And 'twere to me I should be mad[52] at it.

Bassanio. [*Aside.*] Why, I were best to cut my left hand off,
And swear I lost the ring defending it.

Gratiano. My Lord Bassanio gave his ring away
Unto the judge that begg'd it, and indeed   180
Deserv'd it too; and then the boy, his clerk,
That took some pains in writing, he begg'd mine,
And neither man nor master would take aught
But the two rings.

Portia.   What ring gave you, my lord?
Not that, I hope, which you receiv'd of me.   185

Bassanio. If I could add a lie unto a fault,
I would deny it; but you see my finger
Hath not the ring upon it, it is gone.

Portia. Even so void is your false heart of truth.
By heaven, I will ne'er come in your bed   190
Until I see the ring!

Nerissa.   Nor I in yours
Till I again see mine!

Bassanio.   Sweet Portia,
If you did know to whom I gave the ring,
If you did know for whom I gave the ring,
And would conceive for what I gave the ring,   195
And how unwillingly I left the ring,
When nought would be accepted but the ring,
You would abate the strength of your displeasure.

[51] *masters:* possesses.
[52] *mad:* furious, distracted.

Portia. If you had known the virtue[53] of the ring,
  Or half her worthiness that gave the ring,   200
  Or your own honor to contain[54] the ring,
  You would not then have parted with the ring.
  What man is there so much unreasonable,
  If you had pleas'd to have defended it
  With any terms of zeal, wanted the modesty   205
  To urge[55] the thing held as a ceremony?[56]
  Nerissa teaches me what to believe—
  I'll die for't but some woman had the ring!

Bassanio. No, by my honor, madam, by my soul,
  No woman had it, but a civil doctor,[57]   210
  Which did refuse three thousand ducats of me,
  And begg'd the ring, the which I did deny him,
  And suffer'd[58] him to go displeas'd away—
  Even he that had held up the very life
  Of my dear friend. What should I say, sweet lady?
  I was enforc'd to send it after him,   216
  I was beset with shame and courtesy,
  My honor would not let ingratitude
  So much besmear it. Pardon me, good lady,
  For by these blessed candles of the night,   220
  Had you been there, I think you would have begg'd
  The ring of me to give the worthy doctor.

Portia. Let not that doctor e'er come near my house.
  Since he hath got the jewel that I loved,
  And that which you did swear to keep for me,   225
  I will become as liberal as you,
  I'll not deny him any thing I have,

[53] *virtue*: power.
[54] *contain*: keep, retain.
[55] *wanted the modesty / To urge*: would have been so wanting in modesty as to demand as a gift.
[56] *ceremony*: token, sacred thing.
[57] *civil doctor*: doctor of civil law.
[58] *suffer'd*: allowed.

No, not my body nor my husband's bed.
Know him I shall, I am well sure of it.
Lie not a night from home. Watch me like Argus;
If you do not, if I be left alone,   231
Now by mine honor, which is yet mine own,
I'll have that doctor for [my] bedfellow.

Nerissa. And I his clerk; therefore be well advis'd
    How you do leave me to mine own protection.   235

Gratiano. Well, do you so; let not me take him then,
    For if I do, I'll mar the young clerk's pen.[59]

Antonio. I am th' unhappy subject of these quarrels.

Portia. Sir, grieve not you, you are welcome
    notwithstanding.

Bassanio. Portia, forgive me this enforced[60] wrong,   240
    And in the hearing of these many friends
    I swear to thee, even by thine own fair eyes,
    Wherein I see myself—

Portia.   Mark you but that!
    In both my eyes he doubly sees himself,
    In each eye, one. Swear by your double[61] self,   245
    And there's an oath of credit.[62]

Bassanio.   Nay, but hear me.
    Pardon this fault, and by my soul I swear
    I never more will break an oath with thee.

Antonio. I once did lend my body for his wealth,
    Which but for him that had your husband's ring   250
    Had quite miscarried. I dare be bound again,

---

[59] pen: with a bawdy secondary meaning.
[60] enforced: unavoidable.
[61] double: false, deceitful.
[62] of credit: creditable, believable.

My soul upon the forfeit, that your lord
Will never more break faith advisedly.[63]

Portia. Then you shall be his surety. Give him this,
And bid him keep it better than the other.   255

Antonio. Here, Lord Bassanio, swear to keep this ring.

Bassanio. By heaven, it is the same I gave the doctor!

Portia. I had it of him. Pardon me, Bassanio,
For by this ring, the doctor lay with me.

Nerissa. And pardon me, my gentle Gratiano,   260
For that same scrubbed boy, the doctor's clerk,
In lieu of this last night did lie with me.

Gratiano. Why, this is like the mending of highways
In summer, where the ways are fair enough.
What, are we cuckolds[64] ere[65] we have deserv'd it?   265

Portia. Speak not so grossly, you are all amaz'd.[66]
Here is a letter, read it at your leisure.
It comes from Padua, from Bellario.
There you shall find that Portia was the doctor,
Nerissa there her clerk. Lorenzo here   270
Shall witness I set forth as soon as you,
And even but now return'd; I have not yet
Enter'd my house. Antonio, you are welcome,
And I have better news in store for you
Than you expect. Unseal this letter soon;   275
There you shall find three of your argosies
Are richly come to harbour suddenly.
You shall not know by what strange accident
I chanced on this letter.

---

[63] *advisedly*: intentionally.
[64] *cuckolds*: rendered foolish by the unfaithfulness of our wives.
[65] *ere*: before.
[66] *amaz'd*: bewildered.

Antonio.   I am dumb.   279

Bassanio. Were you the doctor, and I knew you not?

Gratiano. Were you the clerk that is to make me cuckold?

Nerissa. Ay, but the clerk that never means to do it,
    Unless he live until he be a man.

Bassanio. Sweet doctor, you shall be my bedfellow—
    When I am absent, then lie with my wife.   285

Antonio. Sweet lady, you have given me life and living,[67]
    For here I read for certain that my ships
    Are safely come to road.[68]

Portia.   How now, Lorenzo?
    My clerk hath some good comforts too for you.

Nerissa. Ay, and I'll give them him without a fee.   290
    There do I give to you and Jessica,
    From the rich Jew, a special deed of gift,
    After his death, of all he dies possess'd of.

Lorenzo. Fair ladies, you drop manna[69] in the way
    Of starved people.

Portia.   It is almost morning,   295
    And yet I am sure you are not satisfied
    Of these events at full.[70] Let us go in,
    And charge us there upon inter'gatories,[71]
    And we will answer all things faithfully.

Gratiano. Let it be so. The first inter'gatory   300
    That my Nerissa shall be sworn on is,

[67] living: possessions.
[68] road: anchorage.
[69] manna: i.e., food from heaven (cf. Exodus 16:15).
[70] satisfied . . . full: fully satisfied with the explanation of these events.
[71] inter'gatories: interrogatories (legally framed questions answerable under oath).

Whether till the next night she had rather stay,
Or go to bed now, being two hours to day.
But were the day come, I should wish it dark
Till I were couching with the doctor's clerk.   305
Well, while I live I'll fear[72] no other thing
So sore, as keeping safe Nerissa's ring.   [*Exeunt.*]

[72] *fear*: be concerned about.

Contemporary Criticism

The Merchant of Venice on Film

James Bemis
California Political Review

Shakespeare's plays are often misunderstood, especially in today's semiliterate society. But none of the Bard's plays is as misread, misconstrued, misinterpreted, and subjected to so much mischief as *The Merchant of Venice*.

The Merchant of Venice is a profoundly Catholic play. The subjects dealt with by Shakespeare and the structure and outcomes of the play could have been the product only of a Catholic mind operating in a world still informed by the Church's teachings. Because the modern world has traveled so far from this perspective, this fact is easily overlooked by today's students.

For example, one of the great subjects dealt with in this play is the corruptive—and ultimately destructive—effects of usury, which is at the core of the conflict between Antonio and Shylock. This may shock many students, who have been programmed to believe that the fundamental disagreement between the two is religious, but such is not the case. As Shylock says in Act 1, scene 3,

> I hate him for he is a Christian;
> But more, for that in low simplicity
> He lends out money gratis, and brings down
> The rate of usance here with us in Venice.
> (42–45)*

* All quotations from *The Merchant of Venice* are from the edition published by Ignatius Press: *The Merchant of Venice*, ed. Joseph Pearce (San Francisco: Ignatius, 2009).

To understand the tension between these characters, one must be aware of the Catholic Church's teaching on usury. Many believe that usury involves the charging of excessive interest on a loan, but this is incorrect. As the 1515 Fifth Lateran Council defined it, "For that is the real meaning of usury: when, from its use, a thing which produces nothing is applied to the acquiring of gain and profit without any work, any expense or any risk."

Hence, the Church's prohibition on usury actually has to do with making money on an unproductive loan and is intended to protect the poor from the greed of the wealthy. Antonio's contempt for Shylock, then, originates in the natural disdain we have for the rich who exploit the needy. This puts the characters' mutual enmity—and our view of Antonio—in an entirely different light.

Two Plays in One

The Merchant of Venice is really two plays in one. The first takes place in the daytime working hours in Venice, a world of money, merchants, and commerce that reeks of business, borrowings, and bonds. It is a high-stakes society, full of huge risks and rewards, a place where if you do gamble, you had better win. The competition is cutthroat or—as Antonio finds—liable to cut out the heart of those who lose.

The play's other world is Belmont, meaning "beautiful mountain". It is a nighttime place of sweet music and romance, a place of casket games where true love triumphs, a place where ships unexpectedly come in, and a place of happy marriages and happy endings. Belmont has a fairy-tale atmosphere, and one easily can believe that its inhabitants will never grow old or unhappy.

This distinction between Venice and Belmont—so critical to the play's comedic essence—often is lost in modern productions, usually preoccupied by the titanic commercial struggle between Antonio and Shylock. But so important is Belmont in Shakespeare's view of the proper social order that the only major character who does not end up there is Shylock, the play's main threat and villain.

Several themes run prominently through the play:

a. *Charity overcomes greed.* Antonio is reviled by modern commentators as a crude anti-Semite. But this superficial view overlooks the kind and charitable nature of the title character, which Shakespeare so clearly conveys. In fact, in his willingness to sacrifice his treasure and even his life on behalf of his friends, Antonio can be seen as Christlike. Shylock's greed, on the other hand, proves his undoing as he loses first his daughter, Jessica, and then his livelihood because of his rapacity.

b. *True justice must be tempered with mercy.* This theme is best stated when, after Shylock insists, "I stand here for law", Portia tells him, "Thou shalt have justice more than thou desir'st" (4.1.142, 316). Truer words were never spoken: any man who asks for true justice for himself is a fool, as, in Portia's words, "in the course of justice, none of us / Should see salvation" (4.1.199–200).

Shakespeare's underlying theme is clear here. In Portia's magnificent speech in Act 4, scene 1, she says of mercy,

> 'Tis mightiest in the mightiest, it becomes
> The throned monarch better than his crown.
> . . . .
> It is enthroned in the hearts of kings,
> It is an attribute to God himself.
> (4.1.188–89, 194–95)

Conversely, when Shylock refuses to show mercy, the whole world, it seems, collapses down upon him.

c. *Love and forgiveness conquer all.* In keeping with *The Merchant's* comedic nature, the play concludes in reconciliation and romance. In the three subplots of the bond, the caskets, and the rings, those who love and forgive find happiness, while the one character that harbors hatred and pitilessness is destroyed.

Understanding the Main Characters in
The Merchant of Venice

Perhaps the best way to analyze the play is to understand its
three main characters, Antonio, Portia, and Shylock, by focusing on the scenes that best reflect their character.

Antonio

It is important to be mindful that Antonio—not Shylock—is
the "merchant" referred to in the play's title. Granted, he is a
rather indistinct character compared to Shylock and Portia and
certainly is not one of Shakespeare's great creations. Nevertheless, as the title character, it is vital to a proper compre-
hension of the play that Antonio's character be understood
and his role put in perspective.

The first of Antonio's virtues we learn of is his generosity. In the first act, when his friend Bassanio needs
money in order to court "a lady richly left,/And she is
fair .../Of wondrous virtues" (1.1.161–63), Antonio quickly
agrees to lend it, despite the inference that Bassanio still
owes him from previous borrowings. Nevertheless, Antonio
says,

> Go presently inquire, and so will I,
> Where money is, and I no question make
> To have it of my trust, or for my sake.
>   (1.1.183–85)

A second instance of Antonio's generosity comes in the
climactic Act 4, scene 1. When Shylock is undone, the Duke
awards half of the Jew's wealth to the state, the other half to
Antonio. Despite being nearly murdered by the villain,
Antonio refuses to take his portion of Shylock's wealth for
himself. Instead, he recommends that Shylock keep half his
goods and

> let me have
> The other half in use, to render it
> Upon his death unto the gentleman
> That lately stole his daughter.
>   (4.1.382–85)

In the play's last act, Antonio again displays his charitable nature. Despite nearly having lost his life once due to his generosity toward Bassanio, Antonio offers himself as surety to Portia after his friend gave away her engagement ring:

> I once did lend my body for his wealth,
> Which but for him that had your husband's ring
> Had quite miscarried. I dare be bound again,
> My soul upon the forfeit, that your lord
> Will never more break faith advisedly.
>   (5.1.249–53)

The second attribute of Antonio revealed in the play is his obvious courage, although this virtue is often overlooked by modern commentators and producers. When in Act 4, scene 1, his bond is forfeit, he does not argue or complain, as he tells the Duke,

> [S]ince he [Shylock] stands obdurate,
> And that no lawful means can carry me
> Out of his envy's reach, I do oppose
> My patience to his fury, and am arm'd
> To suffer, with a quietness of spirit,
> The very tyranny and rage of his.
>   (4.1.8–13)

Later, during a scene of unbearable tension, we see Shylock whetting his knife, preparing to cut out the heart of his adversary. As the moment of his own murder is at hand, the calmest voice in the courtroom is Antonio's, as, baring his breast, he says,

                            I am arm'd and well prepar'd.
Give me your hand, Bassanio, fare you well.
Grieve not that I am fall'n to this for you;

.   .   .   .

Repent but you that you shall lose your friend,
And he repents not that he pays your debt;
For if the Jew do cut but deep enough,
I'll pay it instantly with all my heart.
                            (4.1.264–66, 278–81)

Portia

Of Shakespeare's many marvelous female creations, *The Merchant*'s Portia stands very near the top. She is always warm, witty, and wise yet wholly feminine (except, of course, when displaying the dispassionate, cool logic of a judge when she enter the man's world of the law court).

In many ways, the play revolves around her more than any other character. She is the only one who figures centrally in all three of the interwoven plots: Antonio's bond, the casket scenes, and the ring plot. Further, her wisdom and patience ensure all three plots work out happily, central to a comedy like *The Merchant*. Certainly, she is the play's most sympathetic and admirable character.

Two scenes reveal particularly important insights into Portia's character. In Act 3, scene 2, Bassanio arrives to try his luck at selecting the right casket to win Portia's hand. She cannot help but show her partiality for Bassanio and asks him to "tarry, pause a day or two" (line 1) before making his choice, lest he fail and she lose his company. Interestingly, although she clearly favors Bassanio, she continues to respect her dead father's wishes by honoring the protocol of the casket contest, although the stakes in this for her are enormous.

This reveals another admirable trait in Portia—her devotion to her late father. While many observers dismiss the casket plot as trivial and not credible, it remains an important and telling component of the play's drama. This also provides an interesting contrast to Jessica's contempt for and desertion of Shylock, her tyrannical father.

Two suitors, the princes of Morocco and Arragon—each wholly unsuited for Portia—make wrong choices, as each is misled by appearances. On the other hand, Bassanio, the right match, is not "deceiv'd with ornament" but makes his selection of "meagre lead", which "rather threathen'st than dost promise aught, / Thy paleness moves me more than eloquence" (3.2.74, 104–6). Thus, as Portia's father realized when setting up the casket scheme, the true lover will not be fooled by appearances and will select the plainest casket.

Sometimes Father does indeed know best.

Another important scene in establishing Portia's character is the climactic trial in Act 4, scene 1. Here, Portia is disguised as the young and learned lawyer Balthazar, purportedly called to fill in for the sick attorney Bellario, who was scheduled to adjudicate the dispute. In a lesser playwright's hands, such a contrivance would be the stuff of either low comedy or would be wholly incredible. Instead, Shakespeare creates one of literature's most memorable scenes, full of dread, impending horror, suspense, comedy, and magnificent passages, including one of the greatest speeches in the English language.

Here we see Portia as wise and capable, her patient, methodical strategy ensuring that Shylock's insistence on the letter of the law backfires, resulting in his own undoing. Along the way, Portia is by turns cool, rational, eloquent, charming, witty, and humble.

Her signature speech—and one of Shakespeare's most quoted—comes as Shylock repeatedly disdains mercy in favor of the imposition of the letter of the law:

> The quality of mercy is not strain'd,
> It droppeth as the gentle rain from heaven
> Upon the place beneath. It is twice blest:
> It blesseth him that gives and him that takes.
> 'Tis mightiest in the mightiest, it becomes

The throned monarch better than his crown.
His sceptre shows the force of temporal power,
The attribute to awe and majesty,
Wherein doth sit the dread and fear of kings;
But mercy is above this sceptred sway,
It is enthroned in the hearts of kings,
It is an attribute to God himself;
And earthly power doth then show likest God's
When mercy seasons justice.

(4.1.184–97)

Yet Act 4 not only resolves the bond dilemma but also sets in motion another important element of the play, the ring plot. Here we see another aspect of Portia in her playful and somewhat cunning nature as she entraps Bassanio into giving up the betrothal ring she gave him, inspiring Nerissa to do the same with Gratiano. While accepting the ring as Balthazar and then charging Bassanio with disloyalty may seem arbitrary to some, it is important to remember that Portia eventually forgives her husband, in stark contrast with the villainous Shylock, reinforcing one of the play's themes that love and forgiveness conquer all.

Shylock

The Merchant of Venice, it cannot be too often stated, is a comedy, containing the comedic characteristics of social tension, exploration of human foibles, and a happy ending. Modern commentators have tried to turn the play into *The Tragedy of Shylock*, but the wise student always bears in mind the author's artistic intent and judges the work by how well the work attains the objectives of its creator.

The best comedy also often entails social conflict or tension, and this requires the dramatic artifice of either a buffoon or a villain. To accentuate a social conflict, Shakespeare frequently uses the device of an "outsider", someone whose presence poses a threat to the happiness or cohesion of the social order. In *Twelfth Night*, the puritanical Malvolio fulfills this role; in *As You Like It*, it is the cynical Jaques; and in *Much Ado about Nothing*, it is the bastard Don John.

Shylock fits neatly within this "outsider" tradition: a Jew in a Christian society, a man prepared to cut the heart out of an adversary in open court, a miser surrounded by generous souls such as Antonio and Portia, a father who makes his home, in his daughter's words, a "hell" (2.3.2). Yet Shakespeare rarely creates a motiveless villain, and Shylock is no exception. Spat upon, reviled, cursed, and hated, the "ancient grudge" Shylock carries is in some ways understandable. In fact, many try justifying Shylock's murderous villainy based on Elizabethan society's "anti-Semitism".

But this is an exceptionally superficial and narrow perspective from which to view the play. Clearly, Shakespeare's intent is for Shylock's villainy to shock the audience, building on this to an incredibly tense courtroom scene. Further, Shakespeare develops one of the play's themes by contrasting Shylock's merciless, rigid adherence to the letter of the law (resembling the Old Testament's dictum of "an eye for an eye") with Portia's more flexible and merciful (New Testament) administering of "the spirit of the law" that renders true justice.

Yet Shylock is so brilliantly created that it is hard not to feel some measure of sympathy for him. He has suffered grave humiliation at the hands of Christians, so his resentment is understandable, if not justification for murder. On a personal level, he is pained greatly at his daughter's loss, although he is the cause of her departure. Finally, he is obviously a highly intelligent and witty man and is given some of the play's most brilliant and unforgettable lines. In fact, he is so memorable and so much more distinctly drawn than Antonio that many mistake the "merchant" in the title for Shylock.

Two scenes are particularly revealing of Shylock's character. The first, occurring in Act 3, scene 1, is his great—but menacing—"Hath not a Jew?" speech. After reciting a litany of abuses aimed against him, Shylock makes a moving plea for recognizing his humanity:

Hath not a Jew eyes? Hath not a Jew hands, organs, dimensions, senses, affections, passions; fed with the same food, hurt with the same weapons, subject to the same diseases, heal'd by the same means, warm'd and cool'd by the same winter and summer, as a Christian is? If you prick us, do we not bleed? If you tickle us, do we not laugh? If you poison us, do we not die? And if you wrong us, shall we not revenge?

(3.1.59–67)

The second key scene for Shylock is, of course, the epic court battle. At the outset, Shylock is cool, calm, rational, and insistent that "I would have my bond." Further, the Jew is impervious to the insults and pleadings of the courtroom crowd. To the Duke's request for a reason for Shylock's "strange apparent cruelty", the villain responds,

> So can I give no reason, nor I will not,
> More than a lodg'd hate and a certain loathing
> I bear Antonio, that I follow thus
> A losing suit against him. Are you answered?
>
> (4.1.59–62)

When Gratiano angrily calls Shylock a "damn'd, inexecrable dog", Shylock calmly answers,

> Till thou canst rail the seal from off my bond,
> Thou but offend'st thy lungs to speak so loud.
> Repair thy wit, good youth, or it will fall
> To cureless ruin. I stand here for law.
>
> (4.1.139–42)

Shylock's long, taunting speeches and sharp replies reveal his deadly intent. Most chilling is his calm and earnest whetting of his knife as he patiently waits "[t]o cut the forfeiture from that bankrout there" (4.1.122).

Shylock's savage, fixed purpose is maintained until the last possible moment. He is confident and composed even as he prepares to commit a brutal murder, and his reversal that begins with Portia's "Tarry a little" (4.1.305) is as thrilling as anything in literature.

From that point to the end, Shylock has little to say, but his presence is still the focal point and subject of the action, whether of Portia's strict application of the law, the crowd's taunts, the Duke's rulings, or Antonio's mandates. Although Shylock's words are few, his physical presence must convey much, as Portia delivers blow after blow and his defeat goes from bad to absolute. First losing his victim, then his livelihood and possessions, and finally—to his horror—forced to convert to Christianity, his breakdown is swift and complete, both physical and spiritual. By the time he utters poignantly, "I am content", he is a thoroughly beaten and almost pathetic character.

This scene—given the complexities of Shylock's character and the extreme highs and lows he experiences—provides a rich setting for actors. Both in the transition from brash defiance to utter resignation and—especially—from confident, knife-sharpening executioner to physically broken wretch, the role rewards the actor with extraordinary range and ability to convey deep emotional changes physically. While many have attempted to portray Shylock's range of wit, intelligence, and comedic sense with the dark undertones of a true villain and to excite in the audience both an empathy for the outsider with the horror of his savage cruelty, only a handful can strike the delicate balance perfectly.

Many of today's commentators, so obsessed by politics, often attempt to frame *The Merchant of Venice* as anti-Semitic and emphasize the wrongs suffered by Shylock from Christians, especially Antonio. These efforts usually culminate in attempts to excuse Shylock's villainous attempt to murder Antonio and bemoan the scoundrel's "sad" fate of losing his wealth and—egad!—being forced to convert to Christianity.

Shakespeare's audiences would have seen Shylock's fate in an entirely different light. In fact, they would have cheered this outcome as a villain receiving his just desserts and rejoiced in Antonio's charitable attempt to save Shylock's soul. Needless to say, these two perspectives are not only centuries but worlds apart.

The Merchant of Venice on Film: Five Performances

Fortunately, many filmed performances of *The Merchant of Venice* are readily available. Let us look at how the main characters are developed in five films. The differences between the films are discussed below and summarized in table 1.

BBC (1972)

In 1972, the BBC filmed a production of *The Merchant of Venice*, directed by Cedric Messina. This version stars Maggie Smith as Portia and Frank Finlay as Shylock.

In Act 1, scene 1, we are introduced to Antonio (played by Charles Gray) and his friends. This Antonio immediately strikes us as a rather unlikable, somewhat sinister character, whose unexplained sadness seems to conceal ulterior motives. This exposes a major flaw in the production, as Antonio's kindness and charity toward his friends should be shining forth abundantly. Instead, we are left with an uneasiness regarding what this man is all about.

Shylock first appears talking to Bassanio about the loan of three thousand ducats. The veteran actor Frank Finlay plays Shylock brilliantly in this production. One senses he is a dangerous adversary, but in Finlay's capable hands, he also conjures up a measure of sympathy from the audience as one who has suffered much and thus bears a mighty grudge. Act 3, scene 1, is the setting for Shylock's "Hath not a Jew?" speech, one of the touchstones of any performance. Finlay executes the passage perfectly with passion and meaning.

Early on, we meet Portia, played by the comedienne Maggie Smith. Smith lacks the physical beauty one might expect of Portia but exudes a sweetness and charm that overwhelms the viewer. Her repartee with Nerissa, her handmaiden, is delightful and funny, and we are immediately swept off our feet by the graceful heroine.

In Act 3, scene 2, Bassanio (Christopher Gable) arrives in Belmont to make his casket choice. One of the primary

Table 1: Summary of Five Film Productions of *The Merchant of Venice*

Year Produced	1972	1973	1980	2001	2004
Director	Cedric Messina	John Sichel	Jack Gold	Trevor Nunn	Michael Radford
Casting: Antonio Portia Shylock	Charles Gray Maggie Smith Frank Finlay	Anthony Nicolls Joan Plowright Laurence Olivier	John Robbins Gemma Jones Warren Mitchell	David Bamber Derbhle Crotty Henry Goodman	Jeremy Irons Lynn Collins Al Pacino
Act 1, Scene 1: Meeting Antonio	Antonio unlikable, sinister, seems to have ulterior motives	Antonio elderly but likable	Antonio adequate but more timid than sad	Antonio owlish, expressionless, too bland to be interesting	Antonio appropriately sullen and tired
Act 3, Scene 1: "Hath not a Jew?"	Finlay executes perfectly with passion and meaning	Olivier as Shylock forceful and dynamic, a commanding presence	Mitchell a vibrant Shylock, but incompetent staging undercuts potency	Goodman fine as Shylock, full of passion and pain; high point of production	Pacino out of his depth as Shylock, vocally monotone and expressionless; further, staging incompetent
Act 3, Scene 2: Portia and Bassanio	Smith as Portia delightful and funny; her verve makes up for lifeless Bassanio	Plowright as Portia solid and professional, possesses grace and femininity	Portia too plain; producers should have switched actresses with Nerissa	Portia sleazy, a grating presence	Collins inept as Portia, no range, poor delivery
Act 4, Scene 1: Trial Scene	Audience unable to empathize with Antonio; scene works, though, due to good work by Smith and Finlay	Olivier commands attention but is undercut by prissy setting; Antonio bland but Plowright convincing; Shylock's primal scream off-putting	Antonio cold and distant but Shylock menacing and purposeful; Portia fine, cool, and logical	Setting ridiculous; Goodman effective but players portraying Portia and Antonio amateurish	Film's shortcomings all in evidence, scene falls like a punctured soufflé; Shylock not menacing, Portia overacts, Antonio unsuitably cowardly
Overall Grade	A-	C-	B	F	D-

drawbacks of this BBC production is that Bassanio is an effeminate, wimpy character. It is hard to imagine someone as wise as Portia falling for such a fop. Nevertheless, Smith's enthusiasm and verve make up for Bassanio's shortcomings, and the scene works overall.

Next comes the epic court scene in Act 4, scene 1. As noted, this production's Antonio is a rather unsympathetic actor, and thus it is difficult for the audience to empathize with his plight. Nevertheless, the climactic scene works well here, mainly on the efforts of the old pros, Smith and Finlay. Smith makes a convincing Balthazar and allows the words of the magnificent "quality of mercy" speech to carry the moment. She does not embellish or overemphasize but simply enunciates clearly and with dignity, and that is all that is needed with words so fine.

This scene is also Shylock's big one, and Finlay takes full advantage of the great lines Shakespeare gives him. Going from a confident—even brash—prosecutor of his bond to a crushed, defeated shell of a man within a few dozen lines is a taxing effort for anyone. But Finlay accomplishes this with wonderful verbal and physical virtuosity. By the end, we recognize Shylock's humanity even while we rejoice that his evil intentions were thwarted. It is to Finlay's credit that we feel both emotions deeply, as Shakespeare doubtlessly intended.

Importantly, this production ends as a comedy with laughter and lightness all around. Of the five filmed versions of the play we will discuss, this is the only one that preserves the play's essential nature as a comedy.

Associated Television (1973)

In 1973, Associated Television aired a version of *The Merchant of Venice* directed by John Sichel and starring Laurence Olivier and Joan Plowright. Olivier is, of course, a legendary Shakespearean actor, and any production in which he appears is worth seeing. Likewise, Plowright is a gifted and respected actress.

Sichel's production moves the setting to the early 1900s with the cast costumed in English Edwardian garb. In Act 1, Anthony Nichols makes an elderly Antonio, but this does not undercut the mood as he lends a fatherly presence to the middle–aged Bassanio (Jeremy Brett). Certainly, Antonio's generosity and care for his friend are quite evident here.

In Act 3, scene 1, Olivier's "Hath not a Jew?" speech is forceful and dynamic, as one would expect. We see Olivier's talent in all its glory—he is a commanding presence, and our eyes cannot leave him. He works not only through his words but with his entire physical being—no actor has ever gotten as much out of an arched eyebrow as Olivier. In his big scenes, one forgets there are other actors on the stage.

The veteran Plowright gives a solid, professional performance as Portia. What she lacks in beauty, she makes up for in grace and femininity. While older than many stage Portias, she fits her character here, given the rest of the cast's advanced age. When Bassanio shows up in Act 3, scene 2, to try his hand, Plowright is fine, as she is clearly rooting for Bassanio without giving away her father's game. Her joy at Bassanio's correct choice of caskets is palpable.

In the trial scene in Act 4, Shylock's villainous presence is undercut by the prissiness of the setting. Nevertheless, Olivier commands attention throughout, even as he is upset and battered by Portia's legal analysis. Plowright is convincing as Balthazar and carries off the "mercy" speech in fine form without overstatement. Her methodical reading of machinery of the law adds the right touch. Antonio's bland presence is nearly lost here, however, as the scene belongs to the big names, Olivier and Plowright.

One flaw with this production is that the courtroom tension never builds to the expected fever pitch, as Shylock's knife is only briefly shown and Antonio's breast is not bared. Because Shylock's barbarous intent to butcher Antonio before the crowd is so foreign to the fancy ruffles and bows of the Edwardian setting, director Sichel wisely underplays the savagery, at the cost of the breathtaking suspense of the original. Such is the cost of "modernizing" the production, one supposes.

Further, the scene ends on a jarring note as we hear Shylock's primal scream offstage after his undoing, which is not hinted at by Shakespeare. This gratuitous addition undermines the premise that the villain has received his just deserts and that evil has been foiled by the very means sought to carry out its barbarism.

Finally, the film's ending is flawed, as the reconciliation of the married couples is eschewed for a mournful scene with Jessica singing the Kaddish, the Jewish song for the dead. As with most modern productions of this play, the happy ending Shakespeare envisioned is missing.

BBC and Time Life (1980)

As part of its series The Complete Dramatic Works of William Shakespeare, the BBC and Time Life filmed a 1980 production, directed by Jack Gold. The cast features John Franklyn-Robbins as Antonio, Warren Mitchell as Shylock, and Gemma Jones as Portia.

In Act 1, scene 1, we are struck by how old the cast seems, as Angelo, Solanio, and Salerio are each well into middle age. Nevertheless, their performance in this scene is adequate, although Antonio comes off more timid than sad, and it is hard to imagine him later holding up against the unbearable tension of nearly having his heart cut out.

The veteran Warren Mitchell makes an expressive, vibrant Shylock, and we immediately sense the role is in capable hands. However, the important "Hath not a Jew?" speech in Act 3, scene 1, loses its potency through incompetent staging, as Salerio and Solanio laugh through most of it, an irritating and unnecessary distraction.

In Act 3, scene 2, as Portia and Nerissa prepare for the arrival of Bassanio (John Nettles), we become aware of this production's major flaw. Gemma Jones (playing Portia) is plain, almost homely. Her wan, pasty complexion and bug eyes make her considerably less than the desirable maiden for whom princes would risk all. On the other hand, Nerissa (Susan Jameson) is beautiful, intelligent, and witty, just the attributes Portia should have. One wishes the producers had the foresight to switch actresses playing these roles. Portia's bantering with Bassanio is strained, and the couple seems an ill and uncomfortable match.

The trial scene in Act 4 comes off well, despite Antonio being cold and distant. Mitchell carries off his role admirably, in turn menacing and purposeful, strong and funny, crushed and humiliated. Portia, posing as Balthazar, is fine. She gives a good "mercy" speech and is otherwise cool and logical, as the role demands.

It should be noted that, despite this being a comedy, *The Merchant* here ends on a melancholy, almost sad, note, as the final scene shows Antonio looking mournfully after the lovers, an ending very different from the joyous marriage celebration the author intended.

Royal National Theatre (2001)

In 2001, Britain's Royal National Theatre released a "modernized" version of *The Merchant of Venice*, directed by the renowned Trevor Nunn. The play's setting is moved to 1930s Venice amidst the jazz culture to make the play more "relevant", one presumes.

The truth is, this production is a hideous and ghastly mess. As the credits roll, we see newsreels of 1930s Germany, with sad, evocative music each time a Jewish person appears in case we miss the point. Act 1, scene 1, opens in a Roaring Twenties–type speakeasy jazz club, complete with "Smart Young Men" in suits and ties and painfully thin women with wild hair. Antonio (David Bamber) is an owlish, expressionless figure, too mild and too bland to be interesting. His relationship with Bassanio (Alexander Hanson) is robotic, and their exchanges are flat and superficial.

In scene 2, we meet Shylock (Henry Goodman). Goodman is the film's sole saving grace, as he gives the play's villain a concrete, human presence otherwise lacking in the film. In Act 3, scene 1, Goodman delivers a fine "Hath not a Jew?" speech, full of passion and pain. It is the high point of this production.

Belmont too is (surprise!) a jazz nightclub, and Portia (Derhle Crotty) is a slinky, sleazy flapper in an evening dress. In Act 2, she obviously falls instantly for the Prince of Morocco, so antithetical to Shakespeare's aims. Morocco is a gangsterlike ham who overplays his role, but this is passable as it is consistent with the author's intent. By the time Bassanio arrives to make his casket choice in Act 3, scene 2, Portia has begun to grate on the audience. It would have been better had she flown off with the Prince of Morocco and spared us her smarmy presence over the final three acts.

The big courtroom scene takes place in what looks like a schoolroom with the Duke a priggish teacher. The actors, all in business suits, look like bankers waiting for the opening of the stock exchange. Goodman makes an effective Shylock, menacing and formidable as the action begins. However, the amateurishness of the players portraying Antonio and Portia gives the scene the feel of a high school production. Portia overacts during the "mercy" speech, with awkward pausing and overexaggerated hand movements. At the farewell between Antonio and Bassanio, Antonio cries and collapses in fear, completely undercutting the courageous words he speaks.

As if the natural tension of the scene weren't enough, Shylock makes two runs at Antonio with his knife. He is stopped at a dead run with his blade by Portia's scream of "Tarry!" a jarring and overstated moment. Shylock's collapse is compelling and complete, but the pathos is severely undermined by the spectacle of all the razor-cut, pinstriped young men watching in mock dismay.

Another shortcoming is that Nunn's production completely lacks any comedic element. The final scene, which should be about reconciliation and romance, is ruined by Jessica breaking into a Kaddish, presumably in memory of her now-dead father. The production ends with the sound of thunder breaking in the background, Nunn's none-too-subtle reminder that World War II was just around the corner for these high-living folks.

Sony Film Classics (2004)

In 2004, Sony Film Classics released a production of *The Merchant of Venice* directed by Michael Radford and starring Al Pacino and Jeremy Irons. The movie was rated "R" for nudity, an immediate signal that something is amiss here.

Sure enough, this production reveals all the wrongheaded-ness of the modern artistic mind and shows that Hollywood can take a piece of art that is beautiful and delicate and oaf-ishly turn it into something dark, ugly, and vile.

All of the comedic elements of the story are gone—this is *The Tragedy of Shylock* with a vengeance. The first discordant note comes in the film's opening minutes. The screen's text tells us that in 1596 Venice, "intolerance of the Jews was a fact of life." The city was ruled by "religious fanatics" who looked down upon the lending of money, and the burning of Jewish holy books is shown. Subtlety is not director Radford's strong suit.

In Act 1, scene 1, Antonio (capably played by the old veteran Irons) is seen spitting on Shylock (Pacino). Shortly thereafter, Salerio and Solanio question a morose Antonio about his melancholy. Irons is fine in this scene, appropriately sullen and tired.

In the next scene, a sober Shylock looks on as Christians engage in a variety of revelries, including heavy drinking and cavorting with nearly nude prostitutes. Incredibly, when in Act 3, scene 1, Shylock delivers his important and profound "Hath not a Jew?" speech, not only do Salerio and Solanio listen with mouths agape, but bare-breasted women stand by watching in the background. Such gigantic ineptitude in the film's staging nearly turn what the producers clearly mean to be a "statement" film into a campy farce.

Pacino is clearly out of his depth here. While he has delivered some fine performances (*The Godfather*, *Dog Day Afternoon*, *Serpico*), they came early in his career. Over the years, he has not improved his acting talents and now appears to be coasting. His Shylock is vocally monotone and expressionless, and the actor misses the rhythm and richness of Shakespeare's words. In Pacino's unsteady hands, Shylock becomes so much the victim that both the menace and humor embedded in the role disappear. His comeuppance is less the fall of a villain than just one more instance of discrimination. The great strength of the character is gone, and only the pathos remains. The play's main premise is greatly compromised as a result.

Act 3, scene 2, brings us to Belmont and Portia, woodenly played by Lynn Collins, an actress who is quite lovely but terribly inept. Her Portia has no range, and her delivery is as flat as week-old ale. The character's intended spark and wit are nearly entirely lacking, and one of Shakespeare's great female characters comes across as shallow and one-dimensional. Bassanio, as played by Joseph Fiennes, is an arrogant, smirking young man, and between his cockiness and Portia's mugging for the camera, the casket scene lingers uncomfortably as too bad to be credible and not bad enough to be campy.

All these shortcomings come into play in the big trial scene, which deflates like a punctured soufflé. Shylock never seems menacing, which is the key to the play's climax. He is morose and monotonous, even when delivering his funny lines. Making things worse, Portia overacts in her big scene, bludgeoning several crucial phrases. At the turning point of the drama, when Shylock's knife is poised to enter Antonio's breast, she screams "Tarry!" at the top of her lungs, obliterating the nuance needed to hold the suspense. Further, as the moment of his murder approaches, Antonio collapses in fear, in complete contradiction to the courage Shakespeare clearly instilled in him.

As with most modern productions of the play, the happy ending is killed here. The final scene shows Shylock in sad isolation, then cuts to Jessica's mournful and regretful visage. We are left staring at the consequences of the mean and wretched place in which we live. Belmont cannot exist in such a cruel world.

A Final Thought on *The Merchant* and Modernity

Many (if not most) of Shakespeare's plays do not lend themselves to "updating", and this is certainly true of *The Merchant of Venice*. Because of its treatment of usury, religious differences, and even marriage, attempts to place *The Merchant* in modern settings are inevitably artistically futile. Thus, the key to grasping the play's depth and profundity is to understand the play as Shakespeare wrote it and ignore those who would manipulate the play to conform to a narrow political agenda. The former will provide an exhilarating and intellectually gratifying exploration into the mind of one of history's most creative geniuses, while the latter, to paraphrase G. K. Chesterton, subjects us to "the degrading slavery of being a child of his own age".

The Family in *The Merchant of Venice*

Raimund Borgmeier
University of Giessen, Germany

In Shakespeare's happy comedies, also known as his mature comedies—a group of central plays to which *The Merchant of Venice* (1596–1597) belongs—there are two passages where a prototypical biography is given. A commentator figure sketches, in general terms or with reference to his own *vita*, a survey of the stages a man goes through in the course of his life. And it is noticeable that in both cases the phase of life that has to do with marriage and parenthood, i.e., particularly with the family, is passed over or left out.

In his frequently quoted speech "All the world's a stage" in *As You Like It* (2.7.139ff.), Jaques enumerates seven different ages.[1] The ascending line begins with "the infant", then follows "the whining schoolboy", and finally "the lover,/Sighing like furnace, with a woeful ballad/Made to his mistress' eyebrow". The descending line starts with "the justice,/In fair round belly", continues with "the lean and slipper'd pantaloon [i.e., foolish old man]", and ends in "second childishness". In between, representing the middle of human life, stands "the soldier", and it becomes perfectly evident that the speaker is not metaphorically referring to the role of the paterfamilias with its inevitable battles when he goes on: "Seeking the bubble reputation/Even in the cannon's mouth." With regard to family, therefore, it is a clear case of nil report.

Something similar happens in Feste's song "When that I was and a little tine boy" that concludes *Twelfth Night*. After the

---

[1] All quotations from plays other than *The Merchant of Venice* are from *The Riverside Shakespeare*, ed. G. Blakemore Evans et al., 2nd ed. (Boston: Houghton Mifflin, 1997). All quotations from *The Merchant of Venice* are from the edition published by Ignatius Press: *The Merchant of Venice*, ed. Joseph Pearce (San Francisco: Ignatius, 2009).

third stanza, where the fool reports that he came to take a wife, he immediately proceeds to old age. About a family, even in the form of a wish, there is no mention.

This may be taken as symptomatic for the seemingly small importance of the family in Shakespeare's comedies. In *The Merchant of Venice*, the word "family" does not occur at all. As one might expect, this aspect is taken up by feminist Shakespeare criticism. In an article with the significant title, obviously intended as a rhetorical question, "Where Are the Mothers in Shakespeare?" the critic observes, "[I]n the six most celebrated romantic comedies … no mothers appear at all."[2]

The absence of mothers in the comedies is certainly an unquestionable fact. But the explanation given by the critic suggests that the situation is perhaps not quite as simple as it appears at first glance and that possibly also the importance of the family is not quite as negligible as it seems. What she says about the legal situation of women is certainly true: "In the realm of the legal, we can observe that a married woman in Renaissance England forfeited both agency and identity".[3] And "[t]he silencing of women in the patriarchal culture of Renaissance England"[4] can hardly be disputed as a general cultural phenomenon. Yet these aspects are not decisive for the absence of mothers, and we must take other factors into account.

Precisely because Shakespeare in his comedies places women in the center of dramatic presentation—one critic somewhat grandiosely, but not incorrectly, talks of "Shakespeare's enthronement of woman as queen of comedy"[5]—he must be economical with the use of female figures. For in his company, we can assume, there were only a few boy actors available who still had high-pitched voices, enabling them to play

[2] Mary Beth Rose, "Where Are the Mothers in Shakespeare? Options for Gender Representation in the English Renaissance", *Shakespeare Quarterly* 42 (1991): 291–314, at p. 292.

[3] Ibid.

[4] Ibid., p. 294.

[5] H. B. Charlton, *Shakespearian Comedy* (London: Methuen, 1988). Quoted in *Shakespearean Criticism*, ed. Laurie Lanzen Harris (Detroit, Mich.: Gale Research, 1984–1987), 4:574.

female parts, and who were old enough to learn Shakespeare's demanding texts and convincingly represent grown-up women. And in *The Merchant of Venice*, Shakespeare understandably employs these boy actors to play attractive young women and not mothers.

Furthermore, dramatic and fictional aspects have priority for an Elizabethan playwright. Shakespeare does not in the first place intend to portray cultural reality but to bring interesting figures and their stories onto the stage. Like in the novels of the eighteenth and nineteenth centuries (where, of course, no principal limitations concerning the arsenal of figures to be used existed), incomplete family constellations and gaps in the familial reference system provide more dynamics and a greater potential for the development of conflicts and problems than do complete families. Strictly speaking, the comedy is, according to contemporary and traditional conception, eminently predestined for the presentation of the family. Shakespeare's famous contemporary Ben Jonson quotes in one of his comedies the definition attributed to Cicero that the comedy is "Imitatio vitae, Speculum consuetudimis, Imago veritatis".[6] If we really have here an imitation of life, a mirror of custom, a picture of reality, then the family ought to be a subject of high priority. In this way, for example, in Jonson's comedy *Volpone*, the relationship between father and son and the relation of husband and wife in marriage are treated with satirical criticism.

Shakespeare's comedies, however, are, as everyone knows, different. They are not satirical plays but have been termed, with some justification, romantic comedies. Young love is the dominant theme, and what matters most is the beginning of a love relationship, falling in love and being in love, wooing and courtship. In *The Merchant of Venice*, three couples of young lovers find each other.

The important action, moreover, frequently takes place in a special world, as one critic, with reference to *The Merchant*

---

[6] *Every Man out of His Humour*, 3.6.204–9, from Ben Jonson, *Works*, ed. C. H. Herford and Percy Simpson, vol. 3 (1927, repr. Oxford, 1954), 515.

of Venice, states: "Most of Shakespeare's comedies involve, at some point, a journey to a place where life is heightened, of an extraordinary quality."[7] Belmont in *The Merchant of Venice*, like the forest of Arden in *As You Like It* or Prospero's island in *The Tempest*, is such a special place with specific, almost magical qualities. So we cannot expect to find here an imitation of real life, a mirror of everyday customs, a picture of empirically verifiable reality. This, of course, would seem to confirm the assumption that in such a context the family, with its connections to a regular everyday world, is being rather neglected. At the end of Shakespeare comedies—a sharp-tongued person has remarked—the wedding bells are ringing; what happens afterward (that is, regular marriage and family life) is no longer suitable subject matter for a comedy.

Yet this is only superficially true. At a closer look, it turns out that Shakespeare, also in his comedies, fundamentally takes into account social relations and contexts. Young love is—as recent research has found out[8]—basically presented as *rite de passage*, as an essential social transition. The young person—in the comedies, particularly the young woman—passes to a new phase. There is a change from one social frame of reference to another. Through love and courtship, the young person breaks away, to some extent, from the original family, forms the nucleus of a new family, and also becomes a member of a target family. In general, one can observe that Shakespeare, in the comedies, like other Elizabethan playwrights and later on the authors of novels, makes a decisive plea for a love match, as opposed to the practice of a marriage arranged by parents, which was still prevalent at the time in higher classes.

In *The Merchant of Venice*, three father-child relationships occur. Shakespeare has a different emphasis in each case, yet always the basic attitude is definitely critical. The family connection is not presented as harmonious but as clearly

---

[7] Anne Barton, introduction to *The Merchant of Venice*, in *Riverside Shakespeare*.
[8] See particularly Marjorie Garber, *Coming of Age in Shakespeare* (London and New York: Methuen, 1981).

deficient, and one could almost feel tempted to make the cynical statement that only a dead father is a good father.

This, at least, seems to be the maxim confirmed by the main plot. Portia's father, the only positive father figure in the play, is no longer among the living when the action of the play takes place. He has, as we hear in the second scene, decreed in his testament that his daughter cannot choose a husband she likes but has to follow the results of a lottery; the suitor who chooses the right one of the three caskets of gold, silver, and lead, which her father has prepared, must be accepted by her. Portia is far from happy about this settlement, and when she talks with her waiting-woman Nerissa about "the fashion to choose me a husband", she grumbles: "O me, the word choose! I may neither choose who I would, nor refuse who I dislike; so is the will of a living daughter curb'd by the will of a dead father. Is it not hard, Nerissa, that I cannot choose one, nor refuse none?" (1.2.22–27).

However, she complies. Later on, she declares that she has sworn to adhere to the rules of the game, and she protests that if she should not strictly follow this procedure, "I am then forsworn./So will I never be" (3.2.11–12). In this controversy, "The Right of Choice against the Will of the Parent", as an early critic termed it,[9] Shakespeare for once seems to opt against the right of choice of the daughter and her entitlement to a marriage based on love.

As early as the nineteenth century, this brought Shakespearean critics under pressure to justify the Bard. Denton J. Snider, for example, argued:

> Both sides [father and daughter] have their validity, and it is just this validity of both sides which makes it a genuine collision. None will deny the right of the parent over the child, and this right was less circumscribed in former times than at present [1890?]. But, though the parent may no longer have

[9] Denton J. Snider, *The Shakespearean Drama, a Commentary: The Comedies* (Sigma, 1890?), quoted in Harris, *Shakespearean Criticism,* 4:218.

any legal right, he has still the right of respect; and no child with a truly ethical feeling, such as Portia undoubtedly possessed, would withhold obedience.[10]

Such an attempt at justification is probably suggested in Shakespeare's text by Portia's servant Nerissa, who tries to encourage her mistress to be obedient by emphasizing the impeccable character of the deceased father:

> Your father was ever virtuous, and holy men at their death have good inspirations; therefore the lott'ry that he hath devis'd in these three chests of gold, silver, and lead, whereof who chooses his meaning chooses you, will no doubt never be chosen by any rightly but one who you shall rightly love.
>
> (1.2.27–33)

As a realistic, true-to-life justification, as one tried to give in the nineteenth century, this is hardly convincing. It occurs only in legends and fairy tales that "holy men at their death" are endowed with supernatural faculties, and Nerissa's "no doubt" is, at the most, valid only in the exceptional world of Belmont, where special, fairy-tale laws prevail. And in this fairy-tale world, it is completely unnecessary that Portia—as one can see in some stage productions—cheats and gives her favored Bassanio a (forbidden) tip for the right choice. Instead, she can rely on her father's wise provision that it will lead to the right decision, which will also be favorable to her. But such a procedure—and Shakespeare leaves no doubt—cannot be transferred to real life.

This mystic, one could almost say magic, nature of the world of Belmont is also emphasized in the second scene of the third act when Bassanio finally comes to make the important decision. Portia orders, "Let music sound while he doth make his choice" (3.2.43), and in a beautiful passage, she compares Bassanio's decisive action with the heroic figure of Hercules in battle with the sea monster:

---

[10] Snider, ibid.

> Now he goes,
> With no less presence, but with much more love,
> Than young Alcides, when he did redeem
> The virgin tribute paid by howling Troy
> To the sea-monster. I stand for sacrifice;
> The rest aloof are the Dardanian wives,
> With bleared visages, come forth to view
> The issue of th' exploit. Go, Hercules,
> Live thou, I live; with much, much more dismay
> I view the fight than thou that mak'st the fray.
>
> (3.2.53–62)

In spite of the ironic overtones of this passage, it is manifest that the world of Belmont is different from real life and also that the parent-child relationship of Portia and her deceased father has no direct correspondence with our world.

The second father-daughter relationship of *The Merchant of Venice* is that of Shylock and his daughter, Jessica. She leaves the rich Jew to be united with her beloved Lorenzo and at the same time also lifts her father's ducats and jewels in order to spread them abroad later open-handedly in a kind of jet-set manner, as Tubal reports to the consternate father: "Your daughter spent in Genoa, as I heard, one night fourscore ducats" (3.1.108–9).

Not only in the nineteenth century but up to our own time, the critics have been boiling with indignation at this way of acting, and they talk, for example, about "a breach of elementary filial piety" and "an act of plain theft" [11] or "a monstrous inversion of filial piety, a relationship lacking utterly in both Law and Love". [12] The couple is condemned: "Their love is

---

[11] J. W. Lever, "Shylock, Portia and the Values of Shakespearean Comedy", *Shakespeare Quarterly* 3 (1952): 383–86. Quoted in Harris, *Shakespearean Criticism*, 4:265.

[12] René E. Fortin, "Launcelot and the Uses of Allegory in *The Merchant of Venice*", *Studies in English Literature, 1500–1900*, 14 (1974): 259–70. Quoted in Harris, *Shakespearean Criticism*, 4:325.

lawless, financed by theft and engineered through a gross breach of trust".[13]

Such an attitude appears also to be too realistic and too modern. An Elizabethan audience would certainly take a different view. They would, above all, value the aspect of the true, Christian belief higher. Significantly this aspect is stressed in Jessica's soliloquy before she leaves her father:

> Alack, what heinous sin is it in me
> To be ashamed to be my father's child!
> But though I am a daughter to his blood,
> I am not to his manners. O Lorenzo,
> If thou keep promise, I shall end this strife,
> Become a Christian and thy loving wife.
> (2.3.16–21)

Jessica is aware that she is in a difficult predicament. She should be loyal to and proud of her father, but at the same time she is also an independent moral agent, responsible for her own actions and her position in life. By making her fall in love with Lorenzo and give priority to this love against filial obligations, Shakespeare expresses once more, as in the other comedies, his plea for a marriage of love. And in this case, the marriage is ennobled by the fact that it entails a conversion to the true belief. So Jessica is only partly joking when in a comic dispute with Launcelot, who discloses to her the dire biblical prospect that "the sins of the father are to be laid upon the children" (3.5.1–2), she answers, "I shall be sav'd by my husband, he hath made me a Christian!" (19–20).

To prevent us from viewing Jessica as an unprincipled thief and a degenerate daughter, Shakespeare has Lorenzo not only declare his love exactly when she is leaving her father's house but also give her an extremely good character with the words:

---

[13] Sigurd Burckhardt, *Shakespearean Meanings* (Princeton: Princeton University Press, 1968). Quoted in Harris, *Shakespearean Criticism*, 4:297.

> Beshrow me but I love her heartily,
> For she is wise, if I can judge of her,
> And fair she is, if that mine eyes be true,
> And true she is, as she hath prov'd herself;
> And therefore, like herself, wise, fair, and true,
> Shall she be placed in my constant soul.
>
> (2.6.52–57)

This praise and the unconditionally affirmative evaluation Jessica receives in Belmont make her appear as a clearly positive figure.

She is also, to some extent, rehabilitated by Shylock's reaction after he has discovered her flight. In one breath he complains both about his personal and his material loss: "My daughter! O my ducats! O my daughter!" (2.8.15). The comical alliteration underlines that the child and the money for Shylock have basically the same rank: he regards her merely as a possession. So he must be seen, like Egeus in *A Midsummer Night's Dream*, first and foremost, as a high-handed, self-centered old father who wants only to lock in and suppress his daughter.

On the other hand, Shakespeare rarely presents things and characters in a simple one-sided form; he uses Shylock later on in the court scene also as a comical commentator figure to criticize the potentially lax morals of Christian husbands in an aside:

> These be the Christian husbands. I have a daughter—
> Would any of the stock of Barrabas
> Had been her husband rather than a Christian!
>
> (4.1.295–97)

The third parent-child relationship of the play brings a comic variation of the motif, putting on a confrontation between the figures of Clown Launcelot and Old Gobbo, this time father and son. The two Gobbos appear only in one scene (Act 2, scene 2) on the stage. Launcelot, who has left his master Shylock and is about to become a servant of Bassanio, meets his old father in the street, and he tells the audience: "[T]his is my true-begotten father, who being more than sand-blind, high gravel-blind, knows me not" (2.2.35–37). The fact that Old Gobbo is almost blind is not only the source of comical misunderstanding and facetious entertainment; at the same time, it can also be understood in a figurative manner: fathers very frequently do not know their offspring well. This is the comic lesson that the clown tries to teach when he says to the old man: "Nay, indeed if you had your eyes you might fail of the knowing me; it is a wise father that knows his own child" (2.2.75–77). Here the communication problem between father and son is quite literally pointed out, contributing another facet to the depiction of the family in this comedy.

Critics have furthermore attempted to point out a fourth comparable family relationship in _The Merchant of Venice_. Antonio, the title character, who generously and disinterestedly helps Bassanio to get the necessary financial means for his formal courtship, has been viewed as a "father surrogate".[14] But this attempt seems to be misguided and not supported by Shakespeare's text. If one wanted to interpret the male friendship of Antonio and Bassanio in family terms, then the analogy of an elder brother would be more appropriate for Antonio.

However, in the three existing family relationships, it has become evident that the family in _The Merchant of Venice_, similar to in the other happy comedies, and in contrast to first impressions, has considerable importance. Though Portia's marriage, arranged by her deceased father's lottery, seems to speak a different language, Jessica's choice quite clearly supports the love match, the "romantic-love ideology", as one social historian terms it,[15] and thus Shakespeare opts against the arranged marriage as it was widely practiced then. Love and the choice

[14] Fortin, "Launcelot and Allegory", and Alice Benston, "Portia, the Law and the Tripartite Structure of _The Merchant of Venice_", _Shakespeare Quarterly_ 30 (1979): 367–85. Quoted in Harris, _Shakespearean Criticism_, 4:341.

[15] Alan Macfarlane, _Marriage and Love in England: Modes of Reproduction, 1300–1840_ (London: Blackwell, 1986), p. 120.

of a spouse constitute an important stage in the lives of young people, and this is accompanied by individuation and a change of loyalty in the constellation of family relations. The family appears as a social system with an analogous significance; as a social historian puts it in general terms for Shakespeare's time: "[T]he family may be considered as a small body politic".[16] In spite of the special world of Belmont, this is also the case in *The Merchant of Venice*.

[16] Carroll Camden, *The Elizabethan Woman* (Mamaroneck, N.Y.: Paul P. Appel, 1975), p. 110.

Shakespeare's Italian Stages: Venice and Belmont in *The Merchant of Venice*

Michael G. Brennan
University of Leeds

Shakespeare's Use of Place

The earliest known titles of Shakespeare's two Venetian plays, *The Most Excellent History of the Merchant of Venice* (1600 quarto text) and *The Tragedy of Othello, the Moor of Venice* (1622 quarto text), are deceptive in terms of their titular locations since much of their dramatic action takes place well away from Venice. In *Othello* this geographical contrast in its two major settings is clear-cut, in that only the first act is situated within Venice while the rest of the play's descent into tragic action is enacted on the politically liminal and seductive island of Cyprus, traditionally dedicated to the goddess of love, Venus Aphrodite. But throughout *The Merchant of Venice*, a division of the action between two contrasting environments is more subtly interwoven and dramatically sustained. Shakespeare sets up a constant oscillation between the public, commercial, and male world of Venice and the private, domestic, and female world of Belmont. It is worth mapping out just how consistently the play's action exploits these dramatically progressive switches between Venice (a dominant historical and geographical fixity in the political, religious, and cultural history of western Europe) and Belmont (an elusively nonspecific pastoral locale borrowed from Shakespeare's major source, a late fourteenth-century collection of Italian stories called *Il pecorone* by Ser Giovanni of Florence, and vaguely situated in the play across the sea from Venice).

The exclusively masculine first scene of Act 1 of *The Merchant of Venice* opens in a public street in Venice. Its dialogues rapidly establish the close bonds of emotional and financial dependency between Antonio and Bassanio and their

friendship with a group of other Venetian Christian gentlemen. The second scene then shifts across the sea and indoors
to a room in Portia's house at Belmont where she discusses
with her intimate waiting-woman, Nerissa, her deceased father's
"lott'ry ... devis'd in these three chests of gold, silver, and lead"
(1.2.29–30), by which stratagem he hoped to select post-
humously a suitable husband for her.[1] The rich and intellectually precocious Portia seems to remain willing to acknowledge
the love and authority of her "ever virtuous" (1.2.27) father,
but she resentfully dismisses all other males who come to Belmont as unwanted interlopers:

> If I live to be as old as Sibylla, I will die as chaste as Diana,
> unless I be obtain'd by the manner of my father's will. I am
> glad this parcel of wooers are so reasonable, for there is not
> one among them but I dote on his very absence, and I pray
> God grant them a fair departure.
>
> (1.2.106–11)

The third and final scene of Act 1 returns to a public place at
Venice, this time to establish the vituperative commercial and
racial enmity between the "Christian" Antonio (1.3.42) and
the "gentle Jew" Shylock (1.3.177).

Act 2 follows a similarly oscillating pattern as its first scene
returns to a room in Portia's house at Belmont for the commencement of the caskets' challenge. The next five scenes rapidly move the audience around Venice, beginning with a public
street (scene 2), then moving indoors to a room in Shylock's
house (scene 3), then outdoors again into another street (scene
4), and then there are two slightly longer scenes specifically
located in the street before Shylock's house (scenes 5 and 6).
The familiar and by now anticipated shift from Venice to Belmont is resumed in scene 7, which is set in a room in Portia's

---

[1] All quotations from *The Merchant of Venice* are from the edition published by
Ignatius Press: *The Merchant of Venice*, ed. Joseph Pearce (San Francisco: Ignatius,
2009). The 1600 and 1619 quartos and the 1623 folio of the play provide no references to locations for specific scenes. All quotations from other plays are from
the Arden Shakespeare series, ed. John Russell Brown (London: Methuen, 1981).

house for the continuation of the caskets' challenge. Scene 8 reverts to another Venetian street, and, predictably, scene 9 returns to the room in Portia's house where the caskets are deposited.

In Act 3, scenes 1 and 3 are located in Venetian streets, while scenes 2 and 4 take place in Portia's house at Belmont. Significantly, however, the fifth and final scene of this act does not return to Venice but, underlining the growing significance of Belmont to the potential resolution of the play, is located in a garden there. In Act 4 the culmination of the potentially tragic dispute between Antonio and Shylock, which had been fostered by their financial squabbles in the Rialto before the play begins ("Signior Antonio, many a time and oft / In the Rialto you have rated me / About my moneys and my usances", 1.3.106–8), takes place in the Venetian court of justice (scene 1) and in a nearby street (scene 2). In contrast, since Shakespeare ultimately allows his audience to escape from what seems at the beginning of Act 4 to be the potential tribulations of a tragic Venetian ending (or, at least, so it seems until the cross-dressing Portia—a woman, it seems, can be empowered at Venice only when disguised as male—carries the day for Antonio and Bassanio), the comic romance resolution of the play in Act 5 is facilitated entirely within the cultivated gardens around Portia's house at Belmont.

Once we are fully aware of this tightly interwoven geographical structuring of *The Merchant of Venice*, we may begin to explore exactly what is achieved through this sustained contrasting of the commercial, male urban world of Venice with the domestically feminized and pastoral landscapes of Belmont. Also, how does the insistent presence of Belmont in the play inform our understanding of Venetian society, and are there any significant social and moral continuities between life in Venice and Belmont? Finally, while we readily appreciate the commercial and racial failings of male Venetian society as the enmity between Antonio and Shylock unfolds, does Belmont remain quite such an idealized female and pastoral location as we might at first surmise?

Shakespeare's Venice

While there has been much discussion over the possibility of Shakespeare having traveled on the Continent during his so-called lost years, neither his plays nor the surviving fragmentary details of his life offer any conclusive evidence one way or the other. Much of the enduring popularity of the theory that he had firsthand knowledge of various Italian cities sprang from an early nineteenth-century desire to draw the national playwright into an English love affair with all things Italian. Two early Victorian works were especially influential in this respect. Charles Armitage Brown, a close friend of John Keats, argued in his *Shakespeare's Autobiographical Poems* (1838) that the plays provided documentary evidence of Shakespeare's travels through Venice, Padua, Bologna, Florence, Pisa, Rome, and Verona; these ideas were enthusiastically adopted by Charles Knight in his influential *William Shakespeare: A Biography* (1842–1843). A resurgence of interest in an Italianate Shakespeare during the twentieth century was led by the distinguished editor John Dover Wilson, whose *Essential Shakespeare* (1932) proposed that Shakespeare had been employed by the Earl of Southampton during the early 1590s. Shakespeare supposedly thereby met another of the Earl's employees, the Italian scholar John Florio, who later compiled an English-Italian dictionary, *A World of Words* (1598), and to whom Ben Jonson personally dedicated a copy of the 1607 quarto of his own Venetian play, *Volpone* (now British Library copy C.12.e.17). But, sadly, the contemporary letters, documents, or other historical references to support such alluring theories about Shakespeare's possible travels on the Continent are entirely missing.[2]

---

[2] Michael G. Brennan, "English Contact with Europe", in *Shakespeare and Renaissance Europe*, ed. Andrew Hadfield and Paul Hammond, the Arden Critical Companions (London: Thomson Learning, 2005), pp. 53–97. See also David C. McPherson, *Shakespeare, Jonson and the Myth of Venice* (Newark, Del.: University of Delaware Press; London: Associated University Presses, 1990), and the range of essays in *Shakespeare's Italy: Functions of Italian Locations in Renaissance Drama*, ed. Michele Marrapodi, A. J. Hoenselaars, Marcello Cappuzzo, and L. Falxon Santucci (Manchester: Manchester University Press, 1997).

Instead, it is entirely feasible that Shakespeare could have obtained all the information necessary for his use of Venice as a dramatic location from either printed sources or from conversations in London with actors, musicians, merchants, diplomats, or other travelers who had personally visited Venice.[3] Shakespeare is consistently nonspecific in his use of Italian locales, and he rarely pays any significant attention to the most notable visible facets of his continental locations. In *The Two Gentlemen of Verona*, for example, Shakespeare transports his audience to Verona, Milan, and a forest near Mantua, but no specific details of these three locations are ever provided. Pointedly, the opening scene of this play offers no salient details of Verona, and we know only from the title of the play that it is supposed to be located there. Similarly, Milan merely appears to offer a somewhat distant location from where Valentine will hopefully correspond about his love affairs. Even more confusingly, in the earliest surviving version of the play (the 1623 folio text), the Duke of Milan appears to think that he rules over Verona (3.1.81), and, when clearly in Milan, Speed welcomes Launce to Padua (2.5.1). As already noted, *The Merchant of Venice* does indeed make passing reference to the city's famous Rialto (1.3.107), as well as to its gondolas and synagogues and the renowned civil law school at nearby Padua. But Shakespeare seems generally uninterested in Venice's most renowned and picturesque attributes—its canals, grandiose *palazzi*, and spectacular ecclesiastical buildings (none of which, of course, could have been readily represented on the late Elizabethan stage).

Hence, rather than making any serious attempt to re-create for his audiences some specific visual or geographical details of the continental settings utilized in his plays, Shakespeare seems to have been far more focused upon exploiting, often with the lightest of touch, contemporary popular opinion about the moral and political associations of his various Italian locales.

---

[3] *The Merchant of Venice*, ed. M. M. Mahood, rev. ed., the New Cambridge Shakespeare (Cambridge: Cambridge University Press, 2003), pp. 12–15.

The history, culture, and society of early modern Venice was a familiar subject in a variety of later Tudor publications, and it seems likely that Shakespeare may have read, or at least browsed through, some of these printed works. One of the earliest and most influential during the latter half of the sixteenth century was *The History of Italy* (1549) by William Thomas, which provided its English readers with detailed comparative considerations of Italy's city-states, including Venice, Naples, Florence, Genoa, and Milan. Thomas depicted Venice as a kind of cosmopolitan and commercial utopia, offering to London an example of productive mercantile and interracial functioning. In contrast to the increasingly problematic English monarchy of the 1590s (burdened by the constitutional dilemma over the succession to the aged Queen Elizabeth), Venice's constitution—with its sophisticated system of elections, ballots, and councils—offered an intriguing alternative model of government and political power. Most of all, Thomas celebrated the Venetian commitment to an upholding of the ideal of the absolute liberty of the individual in both spiritual and personal matters:

> He that dwelleth in Venice may reckon himself exempt from subjection. For no man there marketh another's doings, or that meddleth with another man's living. If thou be a papist, there shalt thou want no kind of superstition to feed upon. If thou be a gospeller, no man shall ask why thou comest not to church. If thou be a Jew, a Turk or believest in the devil (so thou spread not thine opinions abroad), thou are free from all controlment. To live married or unmarried, no man shall ask them why.[4]

Given Thomas' explicit reference to Venetian toleration for the "Jew" and the "Turk"—presumably, many members of the first audiences of *The Merchant of Venice* would have been aware that Jews had been prohibited in 1290 by the Edict of Expulsion from living in England (finally repealed only in 1656)—it is interesting to see how Shakespeare's play systematically undermines

[4] *The History of Italy* (London, 1549, 1561), ed. George B. Parks (Ithaca, N.Y.: Cornell University Press for the Folger Shakespeare Library, 1963), p. 83.

this idealistically cast image of racial toleration in sixteenth-century Venice. At the heart of this tension lies the playwright's awareness that although Venice was often viewed as an exotic and alien landscape in comparison with London, there were many similarities between these two great European cities. By 1600 both had comparable populations (around 150,000) and a rich mixture of both resident and transient foreigners. Both were busy, long-established ports, the focus of naval and maritime power, and internationally outward looking. They were both commercially thriving and were recently linked to each other through a charter of 1592 (renewed in December 1600), granting to London's Venice Company a twelve-year monopoly on trading rights between England and Venice.[5] Even though one was a monarchy, ruled by a queen and a parliament, and the other was a republic, presided over by a doge and a senate, the sense that many of the preoccupations of Shakespeare's Venetians were also those of his fellow Londoners comes more clearly into focus when we analyze how our view of the exclusively male world of Venice in the play is consistently informed by the interventions of Belmont and its most prominent female resident, Portia.

Shakespeare's Belmont

On one level, the lush environs of Belmont offer an alluring contrast to the harsh mercantile landscape of Venice. Most famously, in Act 5, scene 1, Lorenzo and Jessica sit lovingly in a grove before Portia's house listening to the sound of gentle music and gazing up into the stars, almost as though Belmont's pastoral perfection is enabling them to aspire to a fleeting vision of heavenly harmony:

> *Lorenzo.* How sweet the moonlight sleeps upon this bank!
>   Here will we sit, and let the sounds of music
>   Creep in our ears. Soft stillness and the night

[5] *Othello*, ed. E. A. J. Honigmann, the Arden Shakespeare (London: Thomson Learning, 2001), pp. 8–9.

Become the touches of sweet harmony.
Sit, Jessica. Look how the floor of heaven
Is thick inlaid with patens of bright gold.
There's not the smallest orb which thou behold'st
But in his motion like an angel sings,
Still quiring to the young-ey'd cherubins;
Such harmony is in immortal souls,
But whilst this muddy vesture of decay
Doth grossly close it in, we cannot hear it.

(5.1.54–65)

However, just as Lorenzo's lyrical rhapsody on "sweet harmony", "the floor of heaven", and "immortal souls" seems to reach its culmination, it is abruptly terminated by his realization that our earthbound bodies, trapped in "this muddy vesture of decay", can never hope even at Belmont to attain a true appreciation of immortal perfection. Poignant as this moment may be, it is usefully representative of how Belmont tends to be utilized in *The Merchant of Venice*. Although it is certainly an attractive and sensually pleasing locale, Belmont can never be entirely viewed as an unproblematic Edenlike environment. Rather, Belmont seems consistently to share and reflect various key concerns of mercantile Venice, but at the same time, it offers a more desirable and holistic way of dealing with the key issues of urban relationships.

Nowhere is this element of the contrast between Belmont and Venice more apparent than in their respective treatment of financial affairs. At Venice, Shylock's sharply focused approach to money is entirely geared to generating more wealth for himself ("For I did dream of money-bags to-night", 2.5.18). The same attitude motivates Venice's Christian traders, including Antonio, who readily exploit Shylock's financial services and are constantly awaiting the safe arrival of their profit-laden merchant ships ("all my fortunes are at sea", 1.1.177). Inevitably, this relentless preoccupation with material goods breeds a kind of moral and spiritual myopia, in which Shylock ultimately can no longer differentiate between the ultimate value of his money and his own flesh and blood ("My daughter!

O my ducats! O my daughter!" 2.8.15). Similarly, Antonio is a supposedly shrewd and experienced Venetian trader who is tempted into a foolishly lethal financial bond with Shylock, even though his usually sound commercial instincts are suppressed in this instance only by his worthy desire to assist his beloved friend, Bassanio.

More surprisingly perhaps, the world of Belmont is no less focused on money, not least in that the first description we have of Portia is provided in Bassanio's typically Venetian characterizing of her as "a lady richly left" (1.1.161). But, unlike the majority of the male characters in the play, Portia views her inherited wealth merely as a useful means of enhancing the quality of her own lifestyle and her reputation for generous hospitality by providing music, entertainment, and good companionship for her guests at Belmont. Her healthy non-Venetian attitude toward money is established early in the play. Immediately following Bassanio's choice of the apparently worthless leaden casket, Portia calculates her true wealth only in terms of the value of their love and intended marital relationship:

> You see me, Lord Bassanio, where I stand,
> Such as I am. Though for myself alone
> I would not be ambitious in my wish
> To wish myself much better, yet for you,
> I would be trebled twenty times myself,
> A thousand times more fair, ten thousand
>   times more rich,
> That only to stand high in your account,
> I might in virtues, beauties, livings, friends,
> Exceed account. But the full sum of me
> Is sum of something . . .
>
> (3.2.149–58)

When, in the same scene, she learns of Antonio's debt of three thousand ducats to the "Jew", Portia readily computes love and friendship to be above base financial calculations:

> What, no more?
> Pay him six thousand, and deface the bond;
> Double six thousand, and then treble that,
> Before a friend of this description
> Shall lose a hair through Bassanio's fault.
> . . . .
> You shall have gold
> To pay the petty debt twenty times over.
> When it is paid, bring your true friend along.
> 						(3.2.298–302, 306–8)

At the very heart of Portia's social values at Belmont lies the ideal of reciprocal love, friendship, and loyalty, in sharp contrast to the competitive and relentless pursuit of individuality and personal wealth in Venice. In this respect, Antonio's apparently foolish generosity toward Bassanio at the beginning of the play implicitly identifies him with the more nourishing social standards of Belmont. Portia herself denotes him as a kindred spirit who, through his loving relationship with Bassanio, has sustained the ideals of Belmont within the harsh confines of Venice. Of all the Venetian gentlemen in the play, only Antonio seems to comprehend that true wealth lies in the life-sustaining warmth of personal and reciprocated relationships rather than merely in the cold rewards of material goods. As Portia explains to Lorenzo:

> I never did repent for doing good,
> Nor shall not now: for in companions
> That do converse and waste the time together,
> Whose souls do bear an egall yoke of love,
> There must be needs a like proportion
> Of lineaments, of manners, and of spirit;
> Which makes me think that this Antonio,
> Being the bosom lover of my lord,
> Must needs be like my lord.
> 						(3.4.10–17)

Despite the evident moral superiority of Belmont over Venice in terms of financial considerations, there still remains (at least for modern audiences) one potentially discordant element in Shakespeare's delineation of its social values. Although Belmont is generally viewed as a charming environment in which love, friendship, and personal loyalties are valued far above mere material considerations, it also seems a place where only a select and deserving few may hope to reside permanently. Even more pointedly, the ideals of Belmont seem especially intolerant of either racial or religious difference—and Shakespeare tends to focus these excluding attitudes specifically upon Portia herself. When her various suitors begin to arrive at Belmont, she and Nerissa have great fun discussing the men's respective limitations. The "Neapolitan prince" (1.2.39) is dismissed as a horse-mad youth; the "County Palentine" (1.2.45) as an unsmiling bore; the "French lord, Monsieur Le Bon" (1.2.54–55) as a foppish fool; and "Falconbridge, the young baron of England" (1.2.66–67) as an unsophisticated bumpkin. These scenes may be regarded as gently comic in intent, since they merely seem to mock the popular racial stereotypes of the time. But Portia's treatment of the Prince of Morocco, "a tawny Moor, all in white" (2.1, stage direction), in Act 2, scenes 1 and 7, is rather more challenging and, ultimately, disturbing.

Like Othello, an accomplished and princely military commander hired by Venice to defend the city from the impending threat of the Turkish infidel, the Prince of Morocco is presented in these two scenes of *The Merchant of Venice* as a courteous, well-spoken, and attractive figure. But, as in *Othello*, white Christian Venice simply cannot allow him to remain unaware of his racial difference. As though responding to this sense of inescapable alienation, Morocco's first words to Portia earnestly plead for her racial toleration:

> Mislike me not for my complexion,
> The shadowed livery of the burnish'd sun,
> To whom I am a neighbor and near bred.

Bring me the fairest creature northward born,
Where Phoebus' fire scarce thaws the icicles,
And let us make incision for your love,
To prove whose blood is reddest, his or mine.
                                   (2.1.1–7)

Although Portia dutifully assures him that her father's will has
ensured that her own choice of spouse cannot be "soly led/By
nice direction of a maiden's eyes" (2.1.13–14), when Morocco
fails the test, Portia's curt words of dismissal unambiguously
expose her own personal distaste for the color of his skin:

A gentle riddance. Draw the curtains, go.
Let all of his complexion choose me so.
                                   (2.7.78–79)

It could even be argued that Portia's clear racial hostility toward
the color of the Prince of Morocco's skin is more disturbing
than Iago's vituperative dismissal of Othello's sensual love for
his wife Desdemona ("an old black ram/Is tupping your white
ewe", 1.1.88–89) since Iago is an unwaveringly malevolent villain, while Portia is meant to be the worthy heroine of Belmont and the ideal spouse of Bassanio.

Nor does Portia hesitate to carry over this form of racial
stereotyping into her treatment of Shylock in Act 4 during
the trial scene. Simply by disguising herself as Balthazar, "a
young doctor of Rome" (4.1.153), she seems immediately to
adopt both the physical and racist identity of a typical male
Venetian lawyer, as her opening words to the court confirm:
"Which is the merchant here? and which the Jew?" (4.1.174).
This abruptly discriminatory commencement of her legal brief
becomes all the more pointed when it is immediately fol-
lowed by her famously lyrical speech on the "quality of mercy"
as "an attribute to God himself" (4.1.184, 195). But she then
thwarts Shylock's pursuit of his "pound of flesh" by remind-
ing him of his status as an "alien" (4.1.349), and her stratagem exploits the law, which allows a Venetian whose life "by
direct or indirect attempts" (350) has been threatened by an

"alien", to seize "one half his goods" with the other half being taken by "the privy coffer of the state" (353–54). Antonio then steps in to give the final vengeful twist to the legalistic knife plunged into Shylock by Portia by demanding that Shylock "presently become a Christian" (387). In this concluding scene of the play, the audience is offered a final, confirming reminder of the ruthless racial and financial exclusivity of both Venice and Belmont when Nerissa explains to Lorenzo (whose beloved Jessica has given up her Jewish faith to marry him) that Portia and Antonio have secured for him in the law court an unexpected bonus:

Portia.   How now Lorenzo?
    My clerk hath some good comforts too for you.

Nerissa. Ay, and I'll give them him without a fee.
    There do I give to you and Jessica,
    From the rich Jew, a special deed of gift,
    After his death, of all he dies possess'd of.

Lorenzo. Fair ladies, you drop manna in the way
    Of starved people.

                   (5.1.288–295)

While Portia was earlier delighted to ensure that the tawny Prince of Morocco was not able to reside with her in Belmont, and Jessica is able to be there only because she has renounced her Jewish faith, there seems to be no problem in these closing lines of the play for Jewish money to be transferred to Belmont for the personal benefit of its Christian residents.

Text as Test: Reading *The Merchant of Venice*

Crystal Downing
Messiah College

Many people approach Shakespeare the way suitors approach
Portia in *The Merchant of Venice*: seeking relationship through
reading. To get the hand of Portia, potential husbands must
interpret various caskets; to get a handle on Shakespeare, potential Shakespeareans must interpret various plays, doing their
best to assess the deeper meanings inside. And what both types
of readers end up getting depends upon which casket, or text,
they choose to open. The first of Portia's suitors, Morocco,
discovers "carrion Death"—a skull—inside the gold casket,
while the second, Arragon, receives "a fool's head" from the
silver. Similarly, those who open the text of *Hamlet* behold
"carrion Death" when corpses litter the stage at its close. In
contrast, those who choose *Twelfth Night* end up with a "fool's
head", the play closing with the words of Feste, the play's "fool"
or "clown".

This easy distinction between Shakespearean tragedy and
comedy does not work as well with the text of *The Merchant
of Venice*. As Mary E. Cregan notes, the title page of the first
published version, in 1600, presents *The Merchant of Venice* as
a "most excellent history" about the "extreme cruelty of Shylock the Jew toward the said merchant in cutting a just pound
of his flesh": not typically the stuff of comedy.[1] Nevertheless,
those who published the first collection of Shakespeare's plays
(in 1623) put *The Merchant of Venice* with the comedies, most
likely regarding Shylock as "the portrait of a blinking idiot"
(to use the words of Arragon upon opening the silver casket).
By 1709, however, dramatist Nicholas Rowe was to write in

---

[1] Mary E. Cregan, *William Shakespeare's The Merchant of Venice: Official Teacher's
Guide*, http://www.sonypictures.com/merchantofvenice.

his edited edition of Shakespeare's plays, "tho' we have seen ... the Part of the Jew perform'd by the Excellent Comedian, yet I cannot but think it was design'd Tragically by the Author."[2] It took another century, however, until Shylock could be portrayed on stage with tragic force. In the early nineteenth century, Edmund Kean, an actor admired by the likes of Keats, Byron, Shelley, and Coleridge, portrayed Shylock with unprecedented dignity, eliminating the conventional red wig that former actors had employed to enhance Shylock's comical villainy. By the middle of the Victorian era, as John Gross notes, "the idea of an impressive, half-sympathetic Shylock was well established", people often reading the play "as a plea for tolerance".[3] *The Merchant of Venice*, then, has become a casket test, offering meanings inside that depend on the agendas of the readers who open it.

Parallels between the *The Merchant of Venice* as casket test and the actual casket test within the play are striking. Just as the latter depends upon three containers established by Portia's predecessor, her father, the play itself depends upon three stories established by predecessors of Shakespeare: the casket device, the bond-of-flesh story, and the ring test.[4] The choice among three caskets to win a lover's hand was a well-known tale even before Boccaccio made use of it in the fourteenth century. The story of a vicious Jew demanding a pound of human flesh, also well known in medieval Europe, was appropriated by the fourteenth-century Italian Ser Giovanni Fiorentino for a prose collection called *Il pecorone*. Not published until 1558, the year Queen Elizabeth came to the throne, Fiorentino's anthology also contained a ring story like that with which Shakespeare ends his play. What we get out of *The Merchant of Venice*, then, depends on which story—which

[2] Quoted in Brents Stirling, introduction to *The Merchant of Venice* (New York: Penguin, 1987), pp. 14–15.

[3] John Gross, *Shylock: A Legend and Its Legacy* (New York: Simon and Schuster, 1992), pp. 128, 133.

[4] Harold C. Goddard, *The Meaning of Shakespeare* (Chicago: University of Chicago Press, 1951), p. 82.

narrative casket—we select as most fully capturing the intentions of Shakespeare.

Readers of the Golden Casket: The Bond-of-Flesh Story

"Who chooseth me shall gain what many men desire", states the golden casket (2.7.5).[5] The desire of many who approach *The Merchant of Venice* is to read the famous story about the Jew of Venice, even though the play's title refers to someone besides Shylock: if not to the mercantile Bassanio, who regards Portia as valuable merchandise (1.1.161–75), then to the merchant Antonio, who borrows money from Shylock in order to help Bassanio "get clear of all the debts" (1.1.134).

Despite these eponymous merchants, the title *Merchant of Venice* usually raises thoughts of Shylock. Indeed, as early as 1598—only two years after the play's presumed premiere—a stationers' register listed the play as *The Marchaunt of Venyce or otherwise called the Jewe of Venyce.* As Harold Goddard notes, "Here is testimony that already in Shakespeare's own day the public was puzzled by the title of the play and had substituted for, or added to, the author's another title more expressive of what seemed to be its leading interest and central figure."[6] And ever since Kean's dignified portrayal of Shylock two centuries later, readers have approached the bond-of-flesh story with sympathy, pointing out that Shylock has reason to act the way he does. Christians repeatedly spit upon him and slur him with canine metaphors: "cut-throat dog" (1.3.111), "impenetrable cur" (3.3.18), "inexecrable dog" (4.1.128). It seems only natural for the dehumanized Shylock to propose a financial arrangement that will literally dehumanize Antonio by killing him.[7]

[5] All quotations from *The Merchant of Venice* are from the edition published by Ignatius Press: *The Merchant of Venice*, ed. Joseph Pearce (San Francisco: Ignatius, 2009).

[6] Goddard, *Meaning of Shakespeare*, p. 90.

[7] I make this same point in Crystal Downing, "Close(d) Readings of Shakespeare: Recovering Self-Reflexivity in the Classroom", *College Literature* 29 (Spring 2002): 117.

Significantly, Antonio readily agrees to Shylock's proposal, willing to offer a pound of his flesh if he cannot repay the loan—"I'll seal to such a bond,/And say there is much kindness in the Jew" (1.3.152–53)—apparently seeing it as a bit of whimsy on Shylock's part. We have no evidence that Shylock plans to follow through on what he calls "this merry bond" of flesh (1.3.173)—until, at least, Christians deprive him of his own flesh and blood: his daughter. When Jessica elopes with a Christian, it cuts Shylock like a knife—"Thou stick'st a dagger in me" (3.1.110)—hardening his heart enough to insist on cutting Antonio's flesh with a dagger.

If someone were to protest that Shylock despairs as much over his lost ducats as over the daughter who stole them, golden-casket readers would point out that we never hear Shylock utter the words attributed to him: "My daughter! O my ducats! O my daughter!/Fled with a Christian! O my Christian ducats!/Justice! the law! my ducats, and my daughter!" (2.8.15–17). Solanio reports these words, recognizing in Shylock the same obsession with wealth that he himself displays in the first scene of the play. After Antonio opens the play with "I know not why I am so sad", Solanio comments that if he were Antonio, "every object that might make me fear/Misfortune to my [financial] ventures, out of doubt/Would make me sad" (1.1.20–22). So perhaps he projects onto Shylock what he himself would feel.

We are, in fact, given no reason to consider Solanio a trustworthy reporter. Indeed, when Shylock later converses with Solanio, he makes no mention of his ducats, focusing only on his daughter: "My own flesh and blood to rebel! ... I say, my daughter is my flesh and my blood" (3.1.34, 37–38). And it is to Solanio and Salerio that Shylock makes his stirring speech about ethnic equality: "Hath not a Jew eyes? ... If you prick us, do we not bleed? ... The villainy you teach me, I will execute" (3.1.59, 64, 71–72).

This is not to say that Shylock does not despair over the items that Jessica stole from him. But Shakespeare has Shylock rave to Tubal, a fellow Jew, who would understand that the ducats and jewels are the "flesh and blood" of his livelihood. In Shakespeare's day, European Jews were still not allowed to own property or hold public office, making usury one of the few ways they might earn a living. This explains Shylock's agony when the Duke appropriates all of his wealth during the courtroom scene: "You take my house when you do take the prop / That doth sustain my house; you take my life / When you do take the means whereby I live" (4.1.375–77). It is quite easy to see why Shylock dreams of money bags: he needs his ducats and jewels to survive!

Like Morocco, then, who is sorely grieved after reading the contents of the golden casket, those who read *The Merchant of Venice* as a play primarily about Shylock's pound of flesh cannot help feeling disappointed at its end. What started out as an apparently golden portrayal of a dignified Jew "perplexed in the extreme" (to borrow words from *Othello*) offers, at its end, only an image of decay. In Act 4 Shylock disappears soon after uttering "I am content" (1.394)—an unsettling statement for anyone bothered by what has happened to him during the courtroom scene, where he loses his dignity. By legalistically demanding a pound of the Christlike Antonio's flesh, Shylock has fulfilled the racist cliché of a Christ-killing Jew. Then, after he refuses to exercise mercy, Shylock is manipulated out of his faith—as though a forced conversion will magically transform him. It is no wonder twentieth-century readers like Harold Bloom regard Shylock as "Shakespeare's anti-Semitic creation".[8]

Such Morocco-like readers therefore regard *The Merchant of Venice* in terms similar to those that appear inside the golden casket:

> All that glisters is not gold,
> Often have you heard that told;
> Many a man his life hath sold
> But my outside to behold.
>
> (2.7.65–68)

---

[8] Quoted in E. A. J. Honigmann, "Playing the Unplayable", *New York Review of Books*, June 10, 1993, p. 46.

These golden-casket readers see "a man his life hath sold" when they see Shylock renounce his faith in order to keep some gold. Like Morocco, who leaves the golden casket with "too griev'd a heart / To take a tedious leave" (2.7.76–77), they exit the play too grieved to enjoy what comes after Shylock's "I am content": 425 lines of silly, sometimes tedious, antics among married lovers. Not surprisingly, Act 5 was eliminated altogether in many nineteenth-century productions, golden-casket readers having decided to end the play with the tragic death of Shylock's soul.[9]

Readers of the Silver Casket: The Casket Story

In contrast to those who read the play as anti-Semitic tragedy are readers who choose the "casket test" as the story through which the play must be interpreted. Such readers parallel Arragon, who understands the danger of appearances. Repudiating "the fool multitude that choose by show, / Not learning more than the fond eye doth teach, / Which pries not to th' interior" (2.9.26–28), Arragon bypasses the golden casket the way his like-minded readers refuse to denounce the play as anti-Semitic. He, instead, chooses the silver after reading on its surface, "Who chooseth me shall get as much as he deserves" (2.9.50).

Those readers who foreground the casket test therefore choose what they believe they deserve: a Shakespeare worthy of assiduous study because he transcends the petty prejudices of his day. Rather than the golden "show" of a noble Jew destroyed by anti-Semitism, these readers choose a silver play that is as much about Christian hypocrisy as it is about Jewish vindictiveness. As early as 1838, a popular Shakespeare scholar argued that, in *The Merchant of Venice*, "Shakespeare . . . draws so philosophical a picture of the energetic Jewish character, that he traces the blame of its faults to the iniquity of the

[9] Gross, *Shylock*, p. 153. See also Linda Rozmovits, *Shakespeare and the Politics of Culture in Late Victorian England* (Baltimore: John Hopkins University Press, 1999).

Christian world." And in 1884, celebrated actor and theater manager Sir Henry Irving, who played Shylock as a "martyred saint", remarked, "I look upon Shylock as the type of a persecuted race; almost the only gentleman in the play, and the most ill-used." [10]

Silver-casket readers note that Shylock, unlike Christians in the play, disguises neither his body nor his faith. He fulfills Arragon's ideal of "the true seed of honor .../Pick'd from the chaff and ruin of the times" in contrast to those Christians who "go about/To cozen fortune, and be honorable/Without the stamp of merit" (2.9.47–48, 37–39). Indeed, Bassanio readily admits to cozening fortune, going after Portia because her wealth can solve his financial woes. As he tells Antonio, "I have disabled mine estate,/By something showing a more swelling port/Than my faint means would grant continuance" (1.1.123–25).

While Bassanio puts on a show of financial solvency, his friend Gratiano extends the pretense to spiritual hypocrisy. Instructed to act with "modesty" during the visit to Portia, Gratiano responds that he will put on a false front of Christian piety:

[I will] Wear prayer-books in my pocket, look demurely,
Nay more, while grace is saying hood mine eyes
Thus with my hat, and sigh and say amen ...
                                        (2.2.192–94)

Even if Gratiano is being facetious here, Shakespeare paints him as the most vicious character in the play. Not only does he wish the worst for Shylock (4.1.379, 398–400), he has a cynical attitude toward love—"All things that are,/Are with more spirit chased than enjoy'd" (2.6.12–13)—making us uncomfortable about his copycat marriage to Portia's attendant, Nerissa.

It is no wonder, then, that Shylock expresses disgust at the Venetian Christians and their love of masques, warning his daughter, Jessica, not to "gaze on Christian fools with varnish'd

[10] Gross, *Shylock*, pp. 133, 159, 147.

faces" (2.5.33). "Varnish'd faces" refers, of course, not only to the gloss put on masks for indulgent masquerades but also to the false fronts displayed by Christians in their everyday affairs. Ironically, Jessica, pretending to respect Shylock's warning against Christian masks, puts on a false front to her father—literalized in the next scene when she puts on male clothing in order to elope with Lorenzo on his way to a masque.

Silver-casket readers play up this masking. A 1984 Royal Shakespeare Company production had the characters in the elopement scene wear pig masks, thus fulfilling Shylock's vision of Christians' piggish indulgence, which is everything orthodox Jews, with their proscriptions against pork, repudiate. The production also had Solanio don "the caricature mask of a Jew" while delivering his parody of Shylock—"My daughter! O my ducats!"—thus reinforcing the idea that Solanio merely puts on an act while he quotes the Jew.[11] These 1984 readers perhaps noted that Shakespeare has Solanio swear "by two-headed Janus" in the first scene of the play (50). Conventionally aligned with hypocrisy, Janus is the god by whom another two-faced Venetian will swear in a play written eight years after *The Merchant of Venice*: Shakespeare's Iago, the master of false fronts.[12]

Jessica's false front is intensified by sixteenth-century sumptuary laws. In Shakespeare's day, it was illegal to dress in clothing not appropriate for one's economic status, profession, or gender. Significantly, Arragon alludes to sumptuary laws as he contemplates the silver casket:

> Let none presume
> To *wear* an undeserved dignity.
> O that estates, degrees, and offices
> Were not deriv'd corruptly, and that clear honor
> Were purchas'd by the merit of the *wearer*!
>   (2.9.39–43, my emphasis)

[11] Ibid., p. 329.
[12] See *Othello*, 1.2.30.

Sumptuary laws explain why females in Shakespeare plays are completely unrecognizable when dressed as males: it is a much more subversive activity than in our own day. Portia, then, can pretend to be a doctor of law and fool even her husband. In Portia's case, however, "clear honor" is indeed "purchas'd by the merit of the wearer": she wears a disguise to save the life of her husband's friend.

Jessica, in contrast, dresses as a male in order to become a Christian and thereby serve her own interests. She begins her elopement with a Christian by throwing a "casket" of stolen goods out the window (2.6.33), thus reinforcing the casket test as key to understanding the play. For, unlike Portia, who honors the caskets set up by her father, Jessica breaks two of the commandments required of Christians and Jews alike: "Honor your father" and "You shall not steal" (Exodus 20:12, 15).

Shakespeare actually puns on the word "steal" in the last act of the play, implying that the contents of Jessica's stolen casket are not worth her choice of a husband: "In such a night / Did Jessica steal from the wealthy Jew, / And with an unthrift love did run from Venice" (5.1.14–16). This is part of a supposedly romantic, moonlit dialogue between Jessica and Lorenzo: a litany of famous lovers who took action "in such a night". However, the dialogue is like the gold and silver caskets: pretty on the outside until one studies the contents. For all the famous lovers named by Jessica and Lorenzo exemplify unfaithful, betrayed, or impeded love. As stated by the "schedule" inside the silver casket, "Some there be that shadows kiss, / Such have but a shadow's bliss" (2.9.55, 66–67). And we sense from the final statement Jessica makes in the play that hers is a shadow's bliss: "I am never merry when I hear sweet music" (5.1.69). The 2004 film version of *The Merchant of Venice* starring Al Pacino demonstrates this silver-casket reading. The last time we see Jessica on screen, she walks alone to the shores of Belmont, where she sadly watches a fisherman ineffectually shoot arrows into the sea.[13] We sense

[13] *The Merchant of Venice*, directed by Michael Radford (MGM, 2004).

that Jessica mournfully reflects on the ineffectuality of her stolen casket.

Significantly, the Jew from whom Jessica steals explicitly indicts unfaithful, betrayed love during the trial scene. When Bassanio and Gratiano proclaim that they would gladly sacrifice their wives to save Antonio's life, Shylock wryly comments, "These be the Christian husbands. I have a daughter—/Would any of the stock of Barabbas/Had been her husband rather than a Christian!" (4.1.295–97). In contrast to the glib dismissal of marriage vows by Christian husbands, Shylock displays genuine honor for his wife, even after her death. Upon hearing that Jessica bought a monkey—an Elizabethan symbol for lechery—in exchange for a stolen ring,[14] Shylock moans, "It was my turkis [turquoise], I had it of [my wife] Leah when I was a bachelor. I would not have given it for a wilderness of monkeys" (3.1.121–23).

In this same scene, Shakespeare offers the most cutting condemnation of Christian hypocrisy in the whole play. When the Duke asks him to exercise mercy, Shylock responds:

> You have among you many a purchas'd slave,
> Which like your asses, and your dogs and mules,
> You use in abject and in slavish parts,
> Because you bought them. Shall I say to you,
> "Let them be free! Marry them to your heirs!"
> . . . .
> You will answer,
> "The slaves are ours." So do I answer you:
> The pound of flesh which I demand of him
> Is dearly bought as mine, and I will have it.
> (4.1.90–94, 97–100)

Shylock's demand for one pound of flesh is slight compared to the many pounds of flesh Christians have forcibly taken, and killed, through the institution of slavery.

---

[14] Gross, *Shylock*, p. 69.

Like Arragon, then, those who read *The Merchant of Venice* as an indictment of hypocritical Christians "assume desert" (2.9.51). They "deserve" a Shakespeare who undermines the play's anti-Semitism through his presentation of Christian hypocrisy: a Shakespeare who warrants their respect because he challenges sexism and racism the way they do; a Shakespeare as enlightened as they.

However, anyone who assumes Shakespeare interpreted life exactly like people centuries later deserves exactly what Arragon got: "the portrait of a blinking idiot". Though breathtakingly brilliant in both word and thought, Shakespeare was nevertheless molded by the assumptions and values of his own culture—as are we all. Living in an England that had banned Jews for three hundred years, he was surely influenced by a scandal several years before he wrote *The Merchant of Venice*. In 1593 a Portuguese Jew named Roderigo Lopez was implicated in a conspiracy to poison Queen Elizabeth. Claiming to be a Christian while serving as the queen's personal physician, Lopez was convicted and executed—even though evidence was inconclusive. He may well have been a victim of anti-Semitism, and, if not that, accusations against him certainly rekindled anti-Semitism. Performances of Marlowe's *Jew of Malta* (c. 1589) were revived in 1594 to "capitalize on the public interest aroused by the Lopez case."[15] Marlowe's Jew kills seven people, poisons a whole convent, and kills his daughter after she elopes with a Christian. In comparison, Shakespeare's Shylock seems to exercise considerable restraint. Nevertheless, we cannot ignore the anti-Semitic clichés with which Shakespeare colors the play: Shylock's obsession with money and his repudiation of Christian mercy while legalistically demanding a pound of Antonio's flesh.

[15] Anne Barton, introduction to *The Merchant of Venice*, in *The Riverside Shakespeare*, ed. G. Blakemore Evans (Boston: Houghton Mifflin, 1974), p. 250.

Readers of the Lead Casket: The Ring Test Story

Just as Bassanio gets Portia by choosing the lead casket, so readers get Portia when they choose the ring test as the story through which *The Merchant of Venice* might best be interpreted. For it is Portia who initiates the ring test while dressed as the young lawyer Balthazar.

Notice how little Portia has figured in the casket readings above, except implicitly as the prize of the casket test and explicitly as a contrast to Jessica. In the lead-casket reading, however, Portia is the prize of the whole play: the example of selfless love through which all the rest of the characters must be judged. Unlike Jessica, who throws her father's casket out the window after choosing her own husband, Portia honors the caskets set up by her father, willing to submit to a test that determines whom she will marry. She thus combines the best of both Jew and Christian: she follows the law laid down by her father while also practicing the mercy she preaches during the court scene.[16]

Shakespeare reinforces the difference between the two cross-dressing women through their common references to candlelight. When Portia returns home after saving Antonio's life, she notices a light burning in her hall: "How far that little candle throws his beams!/So shines a good deed in a naughty world" (5.1.90–91). Jessica, however, thinks not of good deeds but only of her embarrassment in male clothing: "What, must I hold a candle to my shames?/They in themselves, good sooth, are too too light" (2.6.41–42).

Disguised as Balthazar, Portia seems to have learned from the caskets that appearances often belie reality. Hence, she wisely starts the court case by asking, "Which is the merchant here? and which the Jew?" (4.1.174). In Shakespeare's day, the answer would have been quite obvious; actors portraying Jewish males dressed in a conventional costume of

---

[16]Of course, people who choose a different casket story as key to the play regard Portia as simply another Christian hypocrite. See, for example, Goddard, *Meaning of Shakespeare*, pp. 102, 110–11, and Gross, *Shylock*, p. 154.

gabardine cloak, red wig, and yellow or red hat. But for Portia, justice is blind, and she treats Christian and Jew as the same before the law. Shylock, in fact, recognizes her fairness with exuberance, enthusiastically calling her "[a] Daniel come to judgment!" (4.1.223). It is only when Portia holds him to his own punctilious standards that Shylock loses the case in disgrace.

Though Portia's manipulation of Shylock seems anti-Semitic to golden-casket readers and hypocritical to silver-casket readers, it must be noted that Portia treats the Christian Bassanio similarly: holding him to his own proclaimed standards. This, of course, becomes evident through the ring story. Immediately after Bassanio chooses the lead casket, Portia generously endows him with "[t]his house, these servants, and this same myself". But then she adds, "I give them with this ring,/ Which when you part from, lose, or give away,/ Let it presage the ruin of your love" (3.2.171–73). But Bassanio is not intimidated. Like Shylock, who assuredly proclaims, "I stand here for law" (4.1.142), Bassanio assumes his own invincibility and self-confidently proclaims, "But when this ring/ Parts from this finger, then parts life from hence;/ O then be bold to say Bassanio's dead!" (3.2.183–85). And like Shylock, who must eventually sacrifice faith in his own law, Bassanio must eventually sacrifice faith in his own love.

Hence, rather than reading *The Merchant of Venice* as either anti-Semitic (according to gold-casket readings) or anti-Christian (according to silver-casket readings), we might read Portia's leaden story as indicting arrogance of any kind: not only arrogance reflected in rigid legalism but also that manifest by glib proclamations of love. Thus Bassanio and Shylock reflect each other even as they stand on either side of Antonio, who operates as the mirror between them: for Antonio agrees to Shylock's bond of flesh in order to help Bassanio make his way to Belmont for the casket test. The mirroring of Shylock and Bassanio might explain why Shakespeare puts the ring test immediately after Shylock's exit from the play.

After Shylock leaves the stage, Bassanio and Antonio approach Portia, still disguised as Balthazar, with gratitude. When Balthazar refuses payment for saving Antonio's life, Bassanio insists on "some remembrance", and Portia requests his ring (4.1.422, 427). After Bassanio deflects Balthasar's request, calling the ring a "trifle" (430), Portia uses the language of desire that has been identified with the gold casket: "I *will have* nothing else but *only this*,/And now methinks I have a mind to it." Then, when that does not work, she employs the tactic of the silver casket, making reference to "how well I have *deserv'd* this ring" (4.1.432–33, 446, emphasis mine). But Bassanio holds out, refusing the tactics of desire and deserts just as he refused to fall for the gold and silver caskets.

The ring test—the last casket story of *The Merchant of Venice*—thus encompasses and supersedes the statements of the other two caskets. And like the lead casket, it is about the need to "give and hazard all [one] hath" (2.7.9). Antonio, who hazarded all he had for Bassanio, asks Bassanio to hazard all he hath—the love and wealth of Portia—by sacrificing the ring. And only for this reason—rather than for desire or deserts—does Bassanio send the ring to Balthasar.

Back at Belmont, Portia, now undisguised, acknowledges that Antonio hazarded much for her husband, telling Bassanio, "You should in all sense be much bound to him,/For as I hear he was much bound for you" (5.1.136–37): it has been a bond of flesh. But she also realizes that marriage—represented by a wedding ring—is a bond of flesh that must encompass and supersede bonds of friendship. Portia therefore continues the ring test. First she scolds Gratiano, who gave Nerissa's ring to Balthazar's clerk:

> You were to blame, I must be plain with you,
> To part so slightly with your wive's first gift,
> A thing stuck on with oaths upon your finger,
> And so riveted with faith unto *your flesh*.
> (5.1.166–69, emphasis mine)

Marriage as a bond of flesh is reinforced by the sexual puns that follow, Portia and Nerissa returning the rings while stating that they have slept with Balthazar and his clerk. But, since "the quality of mercy is not strain'd", they alleviate their husbands' despair quickly. By the end of the play, all is resolved and the characters are rewarded with more than they desired or deserved. Bassanio discovers his wife to be not only beautiful, wealthy, and loving, but also very smart; Portia gets a husband whose faithfulness is guaranteed by his best friend (5.1.251–53); Jessica and Lorenzo get assurance they will inherit Shylock's possessions (291–93); and, most extraordinary of all, Antonio is told his "ships / Are safely come to road" (287–88): an ending hyperbolic in its comedic joy.

But what about Shylock? How can we tolerate this happy ending when he left the stage moaning, "I am not well" (4.1.396)? Perhaps, like all lead-casket readers, we need to "give and hazard all [we] hath", refusing to impose on Shakespeare's text either what we desire or what we deserve. We need to acknowledge that for Shakespeare's Christian audience, Shylock's forced conversion is perhaps a happy ending: upon his death, Shylock will now attain the golden streets of Heaven rather than burn in the fires of Hell.

This, of course, is little comfort to most readers today— Christian and non-Christian alike. For the idea of forced conversion defies religious tolerance on the one hand and belief in salvation through heartfelt, willing repentance on the other. Nevertheless, as lead-casket readers we must give to the text its context, and hazard all our own ideologies and expectations in the process. As Julian Wolfreys notes in his book on close readings,

> There is always the chance of coming face to face with that which, in the event of reading, will disarm all protocols, all programmes, all methodologies, all self-circumscribing modes of exegesis *finding in the text something one does not expect* we cannot account for this, nor can we anticipate it, and it is

precisely this inconceivable encounter which we hazard every
time we read.[17]

Though Wolfreys is not talking about *The Merchant of Venice*
here, his diction endorses lead-casket reading: by refusing to
impose our own agendas, "we hazard every time we read."[18]
Portia makes this clear to each one of her casket readers. To
Morocco she states, "[A]fter dinner / Your *hazard* shall be made"
(2.1.44–45); she reminds Arragon, "To these injunctions every
one doth swear / That comes to *hazard* for my worthless self"
(2.9.17–18); and she implores Bassanio, "I pray you tarry, pause
a day or two / Before you *hazard*" (3.2.1–2).

Only Bassanio realizes that the hazard encompasses reading
itself. As he stands before the caskets and reflects on the decep-
tions of "ornament", he gives the example of "law" and "religion": two arenas dependent upon faithful reading (3.2.74–80).
Willing to hazard his own desires and his sense of deserts,
Bassanio—despite his many flaws—avoids "[t]he seeming truth
which cunning times put on / To entrap the wisest" (3.2.100–101).

As we read *The Merchant of Venice*, perhaps we can learn
from his example. What are the seeming truths of our own
cunning times that entrap the wisest as they impose their own
ideologies on the text? Feminist truths? Marxist truths? Post-
colonial truths? Gay and lesbian truths? Though all these ideologies have insights to offer, *The Merchant of Venice* suggests
that we, as readers, may never "get" the text until we pass the
test, willing to give and hazard all we have.

[17] Julian Wolfreys, *Readings: Acts of Close Reading in Literary Theory* (Edinburgh: Edinburgh University Press, 2000), p. 57. The odd grammar is the author's,
emphasizing his italicized quotation of Shoshana Felman.
  [18] I make this same point in Downing, "Close(d) Readings of Shakespeare",
p. 122.

The Hazard of Love

Anthony Esolen
Providence College

"Greater love than this hath no man", says Jesus, prophesying his death, "than to lay down his life for his friends." In *The Merchant of Venice*, the merchant Antonio, apparently bankrupt, is willing to die for his friend Bassanio yet wins no credit from the modern audience. Why so?

I concede that, after our recent miserable century, the most tolerant Jewish reader might not stomach the final conversion of Shylock, not to mention the rough words he takes from Antonio. Yet Shakespeare knew little about Jewish piety, perhaps as little as the typical secular theatergoer today. There were, basically, no Jews in his England. But there were loan sharks; wherever there are cities and idle young men, you are going to find that predator prowling about, seeking whom to devour. And there were Puritans. If the Jew reminded Shakespeare's audience of anyone they might meet as they stumbled home after the show, it was the sober, circumspect, thrifty, self-righteous Puritan.

That too is liable to be misunderstood by the modern audience. For us, a Puritan is anyone who advocates the morals of a creature slightly nobler than a dog in heat. The Puritans of old often mistook innocent merriment for lust. We have advanced beyond that. We no longer know "innocent merriment". All is lust, and lust is good. A glance at our mass entertainment will show that we have combined the vices of the precise, scheming, bet-hedging prig with the dissipation of the debauched. We do not know what is wrong with Shylock, because what is wrong with Shylock is wrong with us; nor do we know what is *right* with all the adventurous lovers in the play, including the adventurous friend and merchant, Antonio.

183

Those words of Jesus lance open our infection. Love *must* make one vulnerable. You cannot love if you are not willing to be wounded. That is in the first instance an acknowledgment of frailty. The streets of Shakespeare's Venice are crowded with men and women whose love is shown most nobly through embarrassed circumstances: Bassanio overspends himself; Portia obeys the terms of her deceased father's lottery; Nerissa ties her fate to Portia's; Jessica steals from her father's house dressed as a boy. Her blushing modesty is as winning as her courage:

> I am glad 'tis night, you do not look on me,
> For I am much asham'd of my exchange.
> But love is blind, and lovers cannot see
> The pretty follies that themselves commit,
> For if they could, Cupid himself would blush
> To see me thus transformed to a boy.
>
> (2.6.34–39)*

To come down, to be vulnerable, to admit embarrassment, is to open oneself to the grand *comedy* of love. Both hazard and forgiveness—hazard of body and soul, forgiveness of debts and follies and sin—are essential to the comic vision of this play. It is not simply that we are frail but that our strength lies in openness to the wound. He who would gain his life must lose it. He must cast his bread upon the waters. Hazard is his security, and freeheartedness his bond. "Who chooseth me", says the message on the leaden casket, "must give and hazard all he hath" (2.7.16).

The Adventurers

If so, we see why the play is called *The Merchant of Venice* and not *The Moneylender of Venice*. Shakespeare does not wish to celebrate, as did his predecessor Christopher Marlowe in *The Jew of Malta*, the boisterous malignity of a hate-filled Jewish

---

*All quotations from *The Merchant of Venice* are from the edition published by Ignatius Press: *The Merchant of Venice*, ed. Joseph Pearce (San Francisco: Ignatius, 2009).

merchant. Instead, against the moneylender, he gives us a *Christian* merchant whose life is one of hazardous business. If there is romance in trade, Antonio has known it. Consider his risks. One had to trust one's wealth to a mere hull, in danger of storm, or pirate, or the dishonesty of men; one might pledge, as collateral, capital sent forth in trade; the ship bearing spices from India might cover for the ship bringing cloth from Holland. Nor could one monitor their progress by radio or telegraph or oversee one's agents from afar.

The hazards are too great for Antonio's friends to fathom. Salerio and Solanio, trying to cheer him by poking fun at their own weakness, introduce us to this shy yet extraordinary merchant by flights of comic imagination:

> *Salerio.*   My wind cooling my broth
> Would blow me to an ague when I thought
> What harm a wind too great might do at sea.
> I should not see the sandy hour-glass run
> But I should think of shallows and of flats,
> And see my wealthy *Andrew* [dock'd] in sand,
> Vailing her high top lower than her ribs
> To kiss her burial.
>
> (1.1.22–29)

It is interesting that these two pleasant worldlings would *therefore* shy away from the risk. Their association of worldliness with care is seconded by the merry Gratiano:

> You look not well, Signor Antonio,
> You have too much respect upon the world.
> They lose it that do buy it with much care.
>
> (73–75)

But we never do see Antonio preoccupied with the profit that gains the world and loses the soul. He can afford the risk of trade, because his hopes do not hang upon *that* merchandise. His "ventures are not in one bottom trusted" (42), he says, with an unintended double meaning. He does not trust all his ventures to the world. So we learn from his manly reply to Gratiano:

> I hold the world but as the world, Gratiano,
> A stage, where every man must play a part,
> And mine a sad one.
>
> (77–79)

His sadness, more likely, springs from another venture: his friendship with Bassanio. Here again modern audiences are in difficult straits. The ancients viewed the bond between man and man as the noblest form of love; and outside the Greek cult of pederasty, it had nothing to do with sexual intercourse. Roman soldiers sometimes swore oaths of blood brotherhood with one another; and even now, when "friend" designates someone of either sex whom I happen to know a little, soldiers at least still understand how powerfully one may love the comrade, the brother, the one for whom they might lay down their lives.

Now, Antonio has invested a great deal in this friendship, as Bassanio confesses. To him, he says, he owes "the most in money and in love" (1.1.131). Bassanio is no greedy man. Instead, he suffers the most natural of the young man's vices: a taste for a "swelling port" or high style (124), mingled with an appealing ease in giving money away. He is a soft touch for a suitor, whether the shiftless and big-eating Launcelot, or Gratiano, who, of all people, wants to accompany him on his quest to woo Portia:

Gratiano. Signior Bassanio!

Bassanio. Gratiano!

Gratiano. I have a suit to you.

Bassanio.   You have obtain'd it.
                             (2.2.175–78)

The generous Bassanio is a match for the older Antonio, though the younger man's grace will win him friends wherever he goes, while Antonio must mainly be content with those who wish him well from a reverent distance: "A kinder gentleman treads not the earth", says Salerio (2.8.35). To befriend a young prodigal seems a losing enterprise, and in fact Bassanio is about to ask Antonio to do something that might rob the older man of his company and friendship—might, if Bassanio were not both noble and true. He first assures Antonio, with a playful allusion to boyhood, that the venture will be worth the risk:

> In my school-days, when I had lost one shaft,
> I shot his fellow of the self-same flight
> The self-same way with more advised watch
> To find the other forth, and by adventuring both
> I oft found both.
>
> (1.1.140–44)

But Antonio needs no assurance, even if the calculation of it is half in fun. He has already left himself open and vulnerable to Bassanio's need:

> My purse, my person, my extremest means,
> Lie all unlock'd to your occasions.
>
> (138–39)

So Bassanio begs Antonio for the means to travel to Belmont to woo the fair and virtuous Portia, heiress of a great fortune. He has a hunch he will thrive. He is already in love and guesses that Portia loves him too. It is little to build on. Why should a rich heiress wed a gentleman of no means? Antonio must know this, and yet, in the romantic hope that his friend will win the lady (and not expecting that he will see his money again), he agrees. The agreement places him in danger, expressed in bodily terms; he will have to rack his credit "even to the uttermost" (181). But loan or gift, it makes no difference to Antonio.

We should not underestimate the redeeming power of such friendship, nor should we see Antonio's generosity as compelled by emotional needs. He does not "buy" Bassanio but will spend much to speed him on his way. Such liberality is common for him. When the two friends meet on the Rialto to secure the money—when we first learn of the existence of Shylock—we hear that Antonio has snatched many a prodigal from the jaws of the shark. *Before* any confrontation between merchant and moneylender, Shylock sneers at him aside:

> How like a fawning publican he looks!
> I hate him for he is a Christian;
> But more, for that in low simplicity
> He lends out money gratis, and brings down
> The rate of usance here with us in Venice.
>
> (1.3.41–45)

Antonio undercuts Shylock's business, in what the Jew calls "low simplicity", folly. Why give without the expectation of material gain? Christ teaches that we gain only by giving, and yet we do not give in order to gain, as if love were a business deal. On some level Shylock understands this, so he pretends to engage in a merry sport to gain Antonio's love, giving him the use of the money Bassanio needs, for nothing in return, except, should Antonio fail to repay on the specified date, a pound of flesh

> to be cut off and taken
> In what part of your body pleaseth me.
>
> (150–51)

to which Antonio binds himself, though he had never taken such a bond before, and lays his body open to the knife:

> Content, in faith, I'll seal to such a bond,
> And say there is much kindness in the Jew.
>
> (152–53)

Bassanio, careful of his friend's safety, urges against it, but Antonio trusts he will meet the payment, and Shylock actually persuades him that the deal is meant in friendship. Such a trick could be played upon a man only as generous and plain-dealing as Antonio, as Shylock knows.

The cynic might say that in wooing Portia, Bassanio risks only his friend's money, as if Bassanio could calmly endure his friend's loss. But the wooing itself is a splendid venture. Bassanio compares it, justly, to the sailing of Jason and his men to take the golden fleece (1.1.167–72). For when we meet Portia, we first learn that her father has not left her marriage up to her. He has instead set up a kind of magic lottery that reveals the character of her suitors. He did so not by calculation but by the inspiration that comes to holy men at the point of their last sailing forth. "[T]herefore", says the maid Nerissa, "the lott'ry that he hath devis'd in these three chests of gold, silver, and lead, whereof who chooses his meaning chooses you, will no doubt never be chosen by any rightly but one who you shall rightly love" (1.2.29–33).

Is Portia's father a controller, leaving nothing to chance? The terms of the lottery suggest otherwise. Desiring for Portia the security of an adventurer, he has placed her picture in the leaden casket, the one that demands most and promises least: "Who chooseth me must give and hazard all he hath" (2.7.16). But the other caskets encourage the chooser to rely upon some surety that the world provides. He who chooses the gold will "gain what many men desire" (37); the silver, "as much as he deserves" (23). Nor is the choice free of consequences. Choosers swear that if they lose, they will never marry at all. To understand that this lottery is more than the whim of an old man, you must understand that Portia is a pearl of great price; to gain her, you would sell all you have. But if you understand that, you will know the romance of the hazard. You will see that the world's stock exchange brings nothing but losses, and the true winnings are gained by the folly of exuberant love. "A golden mind stoops not to shows of dross", says one of the failed wooers, Morocco, as he bypasses the casket that might have provided him a world of love, had he been capable of receiving it (2.7.20). We might reverse his wisdom, thinking of the risk-all Incarnation, and affirm that stooping is *exactly* what the golden mind does.

So Bassanio risks a life of happiness in this venture, which he will win only if he knows that winning depends upon his willingness to throw cautious reckoning to the winds. He will win Portia's love only by love. A lottery is a lottery, and though we know that Bassanio *has* to choose correctly, he and Portia are apprehensive. If she were a shrew, she would ignore her father's will and dispense with the game. If he were a cad, he would take the oath in bad faith, intending to break it should he lose. The game is no game unless the players are noble and accept the hazard, obeying the rules, come what may. They really are vulnerable. That is clear from Portia's sweet attempt to delay Bassanio's choice. She would detain him for a month, she says, adding that she could teach him how to choose right but that she will not, lest she be forsworn. Loyally, fully, unsparingly is the only way Portia knows to love:

> Beshrow your eyes,
> They have o'erlook'd me and divided me:
> One half of me is yours, the other half yours—
> Mine own, I would say; but if mine, then yours,
> And so all yours.
>
> (3.2.14–18)

But Bassanio insists, for he too is suffering:

> Let me choose,
> For as I am, I live upon the rack.
>
> (24–25)

Critics note that Portia slyly (I'd say girlishly) gives Bassanio a clue at the beginning of the song that accompanies his viewing of the caskets:

> Tell me where is fancy *bred*,
> Or in the heart or in the *head*?
> How begot, how nourish*ed*?
> (63–65; italics mine)

That rhyme on "lead" is not much of a hint, though. And Portia is still not sure Bassanio will choose correctly. She compares herself to Hesione, whom young Hercules saved from the sea monster that was to devour her as a sacrifice to the gods. Portia too stands "for sacrifice" (57), exposed to the chances of her suitor's reasoning, risking all at this moment that she might risk all forever.

Bassanio seems engrossed in the task, missing the rhyme but interpreting the song as shrewd criticism of the world's values. The old, proud, superserious world seasons illegal pleas with the smoothness of a lawyer, gilds heresy with a "sober brow" (78), hides the coward under a Herculean beard, and even buys the beauty of borrowed hairs, "the skull that bred them in the sepulchre" (96). The gold, the safest bet, he thus rejects, and similarly the silver, that metal for common business, "thou pale and common drudge/'Tween man and man" (103–4). Instead, moved by the paleness of the lead, without a single reason to choose it *other than* that it makes no assurances, Bassanio chooses right.

Shakespeare knew what we have forgotten, that the hazard is essential to love. It does not cease with a betrothal. Rather, the betrothal is when it really begins. Portia's love, described in a shy aside as Bassanio opens the casket, shakes the frame of her being:

> O love, be moderate, allay thy ecstasy,
> In measure rain thy joy, scant this excess!
> I feel too much thy blessing; make it less,
> For fear I surfeit.
>
> (111–14)

And after Bassanio gazes upon the beauty of Portia's picture, and reads the scroll that declares his chance fair and his choice true, he turns to the woman he has won and, with courtly humility, with a sense of his own frailty, begs a kiss. Even that does not seal the matter. His head swims with happiness—he half believes he is dreaming—but without Portia's full consent, he will not take her. He will not insist upon some inviolable legal bond. He gives Portia the chance to wound him forever by rejecting him—or by loving him truly:

So, thrice-fair lady, stand I, even so,
As doubtful whether what I see be true,
Until confirm'd, sign'd, ratified by you.
                                    (146–48)

Portia, the prize, could now use her position to wield authority over Bassanio forever. Instead, her authority is to surren-
der; her self-regard is to know how little she is, and to beg
forgiveness; her love is to entrust everything to the vessel of
her husband, now her lord:

You see me, Lord Bassanio, where I stand,
Such as I am. Though for myself alone
I would not be ambitious in my wish
To wish myself much better, yet for you,
I would be trebled twenty times myself,
A thousand times more fair, ten thousand times more rich,
That only to stand high in your account,
I might in virtues, beauties, livings, friends,
Exceed account. But the full sum of me
Is sum of something; which, to term in gross,
Is an unlesson'd girl, unschool'd, unpractic'd,
Happy in this, she is not yet so old
But she may learn; happier than this,
She is not bred so dull but she can learn;
Happiest of all, is that her gentle spirit
Commits itself to yours to be directed,
As from her lord, her governor, her king.

                                    (149–65)

In the light of the brave risk of these young, delightful,
generous lovers, we interpret the rest of the play: the game-
some and musical Lorenzo and his Jessica; the clown Launcelot, who gives up Shylock to follow Bassanio; the submission
of Gratiano and Nerissa to the fortunes of their friends; Portia's insistence that Bassanio defer the joys of the wedding
night to assist his friend in need; and most of all, Portia's

gambit, playing not only for Antonio's life but for Shylock's soul.

Now let us turn to that talented and tormented man.

The Bonds of Law

As soon as we meet Shylock, we see he is out of place. He is not garrulous, like Gratiano, though when he gets going he can rail enough. He is not amiable and witty, like Lorenzo, though he can crack a dry pun or two. He is wary, his speech clipped, as of a man revolving stratagems:

Shylock. Three thousand ducats, well.

Bassanio. Ay, sir, for three months.

Shylock. For three months, well.

Bassanio. For the which, as I told you, Antonio shall be bound.

Shylock. Antonio shall become bound, well.

(1.3.1–5)

Though Bassanio always treats Shylock with respect, he is understandably eager for an answer here. But Shylock knows how to play upon such eagerness. He evaluates Antonio not by his honor but by his means; Antonio is "a good man" (12) because his credit is good. Bassanio does not think in such terms:

Shylock. Three thousand ducats: I think I may take his bond.

Bassanio. Be assur'd you may.

Shylock. I will be assur'd I may; and that I may be assur'd, I will bethink me.

(26–30)

Shylock insists upon security; a man who lends to profligates at high rates of interest does not favor great risks. Yet perhaps for the first time in his life, he prepares to roll the dice, aiming for Antonio's destruction while pretending to risk his three thousand ducats at no charge.

Granted, Shylock's circumspection stems in part from his enmity with the society that spurns him for being a Jew. But we cannot rest content with that cause. Shylock is too powerful and dangerous to be reduced to a token. His devotion to his business dealings, upright in his own eyes, is too strong; long before the trial, he stands, like Chesterton's madman who has lost every faculty *but* his reason, for law. To live in Shylock's house is to be armed, always, against the follies of humanity and life. It is to be steeped in the sin of believing oneself sinless, in no one's debt; of owing no gratitude; and of begging no forgiveness. Says Jessica, as Launcelot prepares to leave:

> I am sorry thou wilt leave my father so.
> Our house is hell, and thou, a merry devil,
> Didst rob it of some taste of tediousness.
>
> (2.3.1–3)

At this point she hands him a letter to give to Lorenzo. There is no wariness in the daughter, who appeals to us by her candor. She loves her father but reaches for a salvation and a love not inherited but given freely and dangerously:

> Alack, what heinous sin is it in me
> To be ashamed to be my father's child!
> But though I am a daughter to his blood,
> I am not to his manners. O Lorenzo,
> If thou keep promise, I shall end this strife,
> Become a Christian and thy loving wife.
>
> (16–21)

Typical of self-involved fathers everywhere, Shylock misses the threat in his own home. He gives Jessica his keys, ordering her to look after his house, "for I did dream of money-bags to-night" (2.5.18). He wants her not only to lock the doors but to shut up the windows—stopping the house's ears, he says—against the music of revelry below. "Let not the sound of shallow fopp'ry enter/My sober house" (35–36). The saying

with which he leaves, his last words to Jessica in the play, suggests a man averse to the risks of faith and love: "Fast bind,
fast find—/A proverb never stale in thrifty mind" (54–55).

There we find the spiritual meaning of Shylock's devotion
to binding, to law. At the trial, he is urged to admit his frailty,
for, as Portia says, "in the course of justice, none of us/Should
see salvation" (4.1.199–200). He admits none: "My deeds upon
my head! I crave the law,/The penalty and forfeit of my bond"
(206–7). Portia pleads that by its nature mercy is "not strain'd"
(184), but Shylock will admit nothing but compulsion, from
without or from within, comparing his pursuit of Antonio's
life with the neural tics of a man who cannot stand cats or
who cannot contain his urine "when the bagpipe sings i' th'
nose" (49). He whets his knife on the sole of his shoe and,
like a devotee of all things signed, straight, legal, and just, even
suggests that he would sin if he took anything but the terms
of the bond. No surgeon will he have near as he cuts Antonio's
flesh, asking, "Is it so nominated in the bond?" (259). This is
more than a Pauline criticism of the insufficiency of the Old
Law, condemning us because we sinners can never fulfill it. It
is Shakespeare's examination of the type of man who could
love the bonds of the law, not understanding that they bind
hard, and do not set free.

For by that staid, sober, unforgiving letter of the law, we all
must be hanged somehow or other. It matters little how.
Shylock's bond grants him a pound of flesh but, as Portia notes
with devastating literalism, "no jot of blood" (4.1.306). If he
sheds one drop of that blood, his lands and goods may be seized
by the state. Shylock retreats and says he will take the offer of
thrice the principal, at which Bassanio holds forth the money.
That will not do. You play the game of justice, you take your
chances; *that* is where the most terrible risk lies. Portia will
not even grant him the bare principal, though Bassanio again
offers it. "He shall have merely justice and his bond", says she
(339). When Shylock attempts to leave in disgust, the law
plays its last trump, convicting him of conspiracy against the
life of a Venetian citizen. It is a capital crime.

Forgive Us Our Debts

Before we look at Shylock's last words, accepting the terms offered him by the Duke and Antonio, we should remember that the trial is *not* the play's final scene, just as Shylock is not the title character. In the final scene, Portia and Nerissa forgive their new husbands an offense that they themselves, in disguise as the young lawyer and his clerk, encouraged them to commit. The raillery that ends the play brings to completeness the comic world of the play.

In that world, to love is to tease and be teased, to poke fun at a friend's weakness, and to laugh at one's own to boot. It is a world of self-depreciation, buffoonery, a touch of the bawdy, and all the silly laughter without which human society is impossible or intolerable. Such comedy is a kissing cousin to forgiveness, since it is the merriment of creatures who acknowledge their follies. We have seen it in the affable teasing of Antonio that begins the play. Then, when Gratiano assumes the task of cheering Antonio, he half joshes him into humor. "I tell thee what, Antonio", he says, with his best attempt at wisdom, "I love thee, and 'tis my love that speaks" (1.1.86–87), giving us a delightful parody of Antonio, a stupidly sober "Sir Oracle" (93), considered wise only because he never says anything. Lorenzo straightaway makes fun of both himself and Gratiano:

> Well, we will leave you then till dinner-time.
> I must be one of these same dumb wise men,
> For Gratiano never lets me speak.
>
> (105–7)

The banter between the two young men fairly brings a smile to Antonio's lips:

> Fare you well! I'll grow a talker for this gear.
>
> (110)

Gratiano has a ready common sense but is no deep thinker, as his good friend Bassanio, still laughing, will acknowledge:

"Gratiano speaks an infinite deal of nothing, more than any man in all Venice" (114–15). Yet, as we have seen, when Gratiano comes blustering into Bassanio's delicate plans, his noble friend is not too embarrassed to welcome him along to Belmont, though he begs him, without hurting his feelings, to watch his manners a little. Gratiano takes the advice freely, making himself (*and* those who cannot laugh at themselves) the butt of humor. He'll "swear but now and then", he says, wear prayer books in his pocket, "sigh and say amen" when grace is said at table, and in general be the model of a prissy gentleman fit to please his grandmother (2.2.191, 194–97).

The fact is, though, that Bassanio enjoys Gratiano's grains of reason in all that chaff of silly talk, and Gratiano the scapegrace knows himself well enough to play the gentleman at Belmont. But he also trusts Bassanio's friendship and the goodwill of Portia and Nerissa well enough to venture a volley of bawdy jokes once the ladies have been won. Announcing to Bassanio that he too will be marrying, he gives us a parody of himself and the supposedly sluggish Nerissa a-courting:

> For wooing here until I sweat again,
> And swearing till my very [roof] was dry
> With oaths of love, at last, if promise last,
> I got a promise of this fair one here
> To have her love—provided that your fortune
> Achiev'd her mistress.
>
> (3.2.203–8)

And when Portia and Bassanio welcome the addition of another couple—"Our feast shall be much honored in your marriage", says the gracious and manly Bassanio (212)—Gratiano announces a new and pleasant game:

Gratiano. We'll play with them the first boy for a thousand ducats.

Nerissa. What, and stake down?

> *Gratiano.* No, we shall ne'er win at that sport, and stake down.
>
> (213–17)

But Gratiano is hardly the only character to combine love, humility, a silly swagger, and friendly fun. Lorenzo and Jessica do almost nothing but tease one another—or touch one another with wonder. When Lorenzo asks his new bride what she thinks of Portia, Jessica, without embarrassment, replies almost in a rapture of youthful admiration. She sets herself up for humor, and Lorenzo takes the opportunity, setting himself up in turn:

> *Jessica.* Why, if two gods should play some heavenly match,
>   And on the wager lay two earthly women,
>   And Portia one, there must be something else
>   Pawn'd with the other, for the poor rude world
>   Hath not her fellow.
>
> *Lorenzo.*   Even such a husband
>   Hast thou of me as she is for [a] wife.
>
> *Jessica.* Nay, but ask my opinion too of that.
>
> (3.5.79–85)

When we meet the lovers again, they are waiting for Portia and Bassanio to return to Belmont, looking upon the starry sky, singing a veritable hymn to fabled young men and women who risked all for love. Then Lorenzo turns the hymn to teasing, and Jessica takes him up on it too, in loving humor and forgiveness:

> *Lorenzo.*   In such a night
>   Did Jessica steal from the wealthy Jew,
>   And with an unthrift love did run from Venice,
>   As far as Belmont.
>
> *Jessica.*   In such a night
>   Did young Lorenzo swear he lov'd her well,
>   Stealing her soul with many vows of faith,
>   And ne'er a true one.

Lorenzo.   In such a night
          Did pretty Jessica (like a little shrow)
          Slander her love, and he forgave it her.

(5.1.14–22)

Even Portia and Nerissa indulge the playfulness, and in the final scene, "learning" that Bassanio and Gratiano have given their rings to a young lawyer and his clerk, they pretend to have lain with those men to get the rings back—all of which sets up the final revelation that it was Portia who prosecuted the trial, Portia who demanded the ring, and Portia who gives it to Bassanio again, not holding her husband to the letter of his promise but grateful for her husband's gratitude for his friend.

And in all this frothy, foolish, racy world, where does Shylock fit, he of the closed doors? He who would wound is struck to the heart when he loses his daughter and the money and the two jewels she took with her. It is a blow to his self-sufficiency. By report we hear—Shakespeare will not reduce the Jew to miserable ridiculousness in our sight—that he races through the streets, crying,

> My daughter! O my ducats! O my daughter!
> Fled with a Christian! O my Christian ducats!
> . . . .
> And jewels, two stones, two rich and precious stones,
> Stol'n by my daughter! Justice! find the girl,
> She hath the stones upon her, and the ducats.

(2.8.15–16, 20–22)

At this point, those creatures that ever have an ear for the bawdy and the absurd pick up the refrain:

> Why, all the boys in Venice follow him,
> Crying, his stones, his daughter, and his ducats.

(23–24)

Shylock is unconscious of the absurdity. Whether he ever will become a man who could jest at his own expense, we do not know. We do know that the end of the play does more

than convict him of attempted murder. It embarrasses him.
He has been worse than evil. He has been silly, more foolish
than the taunting Gratiano. He who has lived by the law has
felt the edge of the law turned against him, and his private
temple of belief, built upon his righteousness, is destroyed. With
the same words whereby Antonio agreed to sign the original
bond, as in sport, Shylock now agrees to let Antonio use half
of his wealth in business for Lorenzo and Jessica and to grant
them all of his wealth at his death. That, and to become Christian. He is, we may say, now truly invited to a dinner. He will
sign a *deed of gift* that witnesses his giving up all trust in deeds.
He will assure the court that he no longer stands surety for
himself. "I am content", he says (4.1.394). His last words in
the play are those of a man of penetrating mind struggling to
live in a new world:

> I pray you give me leave to go from hence,
> I am not well. Send the deed after me,
> And I will sign it.

> (395–97)

What will happen then? Shakespeare leaves it as a mystery
of providence, beyond the bounds of the fairy tale. There are
many who cannot believe that the man's soul may be reclaimed
from its alienation, its bonds of selfishness. Such will find it
hard to believe in the nobility of Portia and Bassanio, and the
childlike love of Lorenzo and Jessica. If they cannot believe in
love, the play is not for them. But then, this world is not for
them, either. Not unless they someday meet a young lady dressed
up as a lawyer in a Venetian court. Let us hope they do.

Breeding Barren Metal:
Usury and *The Merchant of Venice*

James E. Hartley
Mount Holyoke College

"What indeed has Athens to do with Jerusalem? What concord is there between the Academy and the Church? What between heretics and Christians?"[1] Since Tertullian asked that question sometime in the second or third century, the history of Western civilization has been the search for an answer. Athens placed its emphasis on reason: we discover what is morally right and wrong by reasoning it out. Jerusalem placed its emphasis on faith and revelation: we discover moral truth by divine revelation. For the last two thousand years, these traditions have been in an uneasy synthesis; at times, the predominant thought drifted toward one axis or the other, but there has always been a reversion, preserving the inherent tension between the two. Shakespeare has long been a fascinating figure in the development of the West for this among many other reasons; Shakespeare, perhaps more than any other author, captures the inherent tensions in the mind of the West.

And yet, when we turn to *The Merchant of Venice*, we find at its heart one issue on which there was complete agreement between Athens and Jerusalem. This issue is crystallized in the nature of Shylock. Shylock is a villain in the play, and we know this not because he was a Jew but rather because he habitually commits a wrong so egregious that it was condemned in no uncertain terms by every writer from both the Athenian and the Jerusalem traditions. Shylock practices usury, he charges interest to those to whom he lends money, and that act marks Shylock as a villain worthy of great condemnation.

[1] Tertullian, *The Prescription against Heretics* 7.

201

This observation about the role of usury in *The Merchant of Venice* is often overlooked in modern readings of the play, which have portrayed Shylock in a more sympathetic light. In the wake of the Holocaust, readers focus on the fact that Shylock is a Jew and have pitied Shylock; such a reading would have been rather surprising to Shakespeare and his audience. It is thus useful to step back and look again at the reasons why usury was universally condemned.

The starting place for any discussion of Athenian thought on usury is Aristotle. We begin with an observation: nobody really wants money for its own sake. Money is useful only because it enables us to purchase the things we actually desire. Consider the following offer: you may have one million dollars in currency, but you are never allowed to spend it, give it away, or do anything other than simply hold onto it. Do you still want it? Is the money of any use whatsoever?

> [C]oined money is a mere sham, a thing not natural, but conventional only, which would have no value or use for any of the purposes of daily life if another commodity were substituted by the users ... But how can that be wealth of which a man may have a great abundance and yet perish with hunger, like Midas in the fable, whose insatiable prayer turned everything that was set before him into gold?[2]

Money was created by society as people began trading. In bartering goods, sometimes you will want to sell something now and purchase something later, or sell something to one person and purchase something from another person. Money arose as a means of arranging barter more efficiently; we all agree to take a useless good, money, in exchange for the valuable goods we actually want. Bassiano captures this feature of money when he describes silver as "thou pale and common drudge/'Tween man and man" (3.2.103–4).[3] Silver, or money,

[2] Aristotle, *Politics* 1.9.11.

[3] All quotations from *The Merchant of Venice* are from the edition published by Ignatius Press: *The Merchant of Venice*, ed. Joseph Pearce (San Francisco: Ignatius, 2009).

is a drudge, doing the dull, routine work of arranging transactions between two people.

Money is thus properly used to arrange exchanges of goods. The practice of lending money out at interest is a violation of this natural purpose. Lending at interest, or usury, is a sort of money-making that is "justly censored".[4]

> The most hated [means of earning income], and with the greatest reason, is usury, which makes a gain out of money itself, and not from the natural use of it. For money was intended to be used in exchange, but not to increase at interest. And the term usury which means the birth of money from money is applied to the breeding of money because the offspring resembles the parent. Wherefore of all modes of making money this is the most unnatural.[5]

Usury is condemned by Aristotle because it is "unnatural", using money for purposes for which it was not intended, generating income from something that was never intended to generate income, and violating the ethical principles of exchange. Aristotle argues that exchanges are moral only if things of equal value are being exchanged.[6] If one gives up gold in exchange for gold, then 100 gold coins would necessarily be equal to 100 gold coins. To give up 100 gold coins and demand 110 gold coins in return is an inherently unequal trade and an unnatural way of earning income.

Aristotle is not the only one of the ancient classical philosophers to condemn the practice of charging interest. Plato, for example, forbids the practice in his *Laws*: "[N]o one shall deposit money with another whom he does not trust as a friend, nor shall he lend upon interest; and he who borrows shall not be required to pay either capital or interest."[7] The Romans similarly condemned the practice. Cicero, for example, approvingly relates the following anecdote about Cato the Elder: "His

---

[4] Aristotle, *Politics*, 1.10.5.
[5] Ibid.
[6] Aristotle, *Nichomachean Ethics* 5.5.
[7] Plato, *Laws* 5.742.

questioner asked him what he thought of money-lending. But then he replied: 'You might as well ask me what I think about murder.'"[8] A money lender and a murderer are much the same; compare Shylock.

The Jerusalem tradition gets its start with the Pentateuch, the first five books of the Bible. Unlike the Athenian tradition, in which all truth needed to be determined by reasoning it out, the Jerusalem tradition begins by finding truth literally written on stone tablets. Moses then elaborates on the Ten Commandments by delivering the Law straight from God himself. And the Law leaves little doubt about whether it is proper to charge interest on loans. "If you lend money to any of my people with you who is poor, you shall not be to him as a creditor, and you shall not exact interest from him" (Exodus 22:25).[9]

This unambiguous message is repeated elsewhere in the Old Testament. In the Psalms, we read, "O LORD, who shall sojourn in your tent? Who shall dwell on your holy mountain? He ... who does not put out his money at interest" (Psalm 15:1–2, 5). The rather clear conclusion is that he who lends his money with usury will not dwell in the sanctuary of the Lord. The prophet Ezekiel adds similar warnings, contrasting the one who does not take usury—"[H]e is righteous, he shall surely live"—with the one who does take usury: "[S]hall he then live? He shall not live. He has done all these abominable things; he shall surely die; his blood shall be upon himself" (Ezekiel 18:9, 13). And, just to make sure that we do not miss the point of how vile it is to take usury, Ezekiel provides a litany of the sins of Israel.

> Behold, the princes of Israel in you, every one according to his power, have been bent on shedding blood. Father and mother are treated with contempt in you; the sojourner suffers extortion in your midst; the fatherless and the widow are wronged in you. You have despised my holy things, and profaned my

[8] Cicero, *On Duties* 2.25.88.

[9] All biblical quotations are from the Revised Standard Version, Second Catholic Edition.

sabbaths. There are men in you who slander to shed blood, and men in you who eat upon the mountains; men commit lewdness in your midst. In you men uncover their fathers' nakedness; in you they humble women who are unclean in their impurity. One commits abomination with his neighbor's wife; another lewdly defiles his daughter-in-law; another in you defiles his sister, his father's daughter. In you men take bribes to shed blood; you take interest and increase and make gain of your neighbors by extortion; and you have forgotten me, says the Lord GOD. (Ezekiel 22:6–12)

Note the other sins in that list. Usury is *that* wrong.

There is, however, a very important exception to these blanket prohibitions on charging interest. In the retelling of the Law, we find the following: "You shall not lend upon interest to your brother, interest on money, interest on victuals, interest on anything that is lent for interest. To a foreigner you may lend upon interest, but to your brother you shall not lend upon interest; that the LORD your God may bless you in all that you undertake in the land which you are entering to take possession of it" (Deuteronomy 23:19–20). It is on this passage that the drama of *The Merchant of Venice* hangs.

Shylock, a Jew, interprets that passage to mean exactly what it says. While he is forbidden to charge interest to another Jew, he is perfectly free to charge interest on all loans to non-Jews. Antonio, a Christian, has a different reading of that same passage. It is this difference between Jewish and Christian theology that explains why Jews became so associated with the practice of usury in the history of Europe. As we will see, the prohibition on charging interest becomes a blanket prohibition for Christians but not for Jews.

The early Church began the process of synthesizing the traditions of Athens and Jerusalem, and the first place they turned for guidance was, of course, the writings that would eventually form the New Testament. The most obvious reference was Christ's admonition "[L]ove your enemies, and do good, and lend, expecting nothing in return" (Luke 6:35). Christ himself enjoined people from charging interest, even to enemies.

But what about the accepted allowance in the Old Testament for charging interest to foreigners? The early Church Fathers noted that in the New Testament age, God's chosen people had been expanded to include people other than biological descendants of Abraham, fundamentally altering the Old Testament distinction between God's chosen people and their enemies. In the Old Testament age, the Jews were allowed to charge interest to foreigners because foreigners were *enemies* of the people of God. Now, in the New Testament age, everyone is potentially a member of the Church; the brotherhood of man is universal.[10] So, when Christ notes that we should lend without expecting anything in return, he is noting that there are no longer exceptions to that rule for charity. Usury is theft, and it violates the command to love your neighbor as yourself.

The matter was important enough to the early Church that it shows up in the seventeenth canon of the First Council of Nicaea (325):

> Forasmuch as many enrolled among the Clergy, following covetousness and lust of gain, have forgotten the divine Scripture, which says, He has not given his money upon usury, and in lending money ask the hundredth of the sum [as monthly interest], the holy and great Synod thinks it just that if after this decree any one be found to receive usury, whether he accomplish it by secret transaction or otherwise, as by demanding the whole and one half, or by using any other contrivance whatever for filthy lucre's sake, he shall be deposed from the clergy and his name stricken from the list.[11]

The prohibitions in the Council of Nicaea are extended to laymen and repeated numerous times by subsequent councils and in the canonical law of the Middle Ages.

---

[10] See discussion in Benjamin Nelson, *The Idea of Usury: From Tribal Brotherhood to Universal Otherhood*, 2nd ed. (Chicago: University of Chicago Press, 1969).

[11] "First Council of Nicæa (A.D. 325)", trans. Henry Percival, in *Nicene and Post-Nicene Fathers*, ed. Philip Schaff, 2nd ser., vol. 14 (Buffalo, N.Y.: Christian Literature, 1900). Online edition at New Advent, rev. and ed. by Kevin Knight, http://www.newadvent.org/fathers/3801.htm.

As theology developed during the Middle Ages, the Scholastic tradition reached its zenith with the work of Thomas Aquinas in the thirteenth century. In his mammoth work, the *Summa theologica*, Aquinas devotes a section to the question "Of the Sin of Usury". The first article of that question is "Whether It Is a Sin to Take Usury for Money Lent?" to which the answer is an unambiguous yes.[12]

In characteristic fashion, Aquinas explains his answer as being derived from the two impeccable sources: the Bible and the Philosopher (Aristotle). After quoting the aforementioned Exodus 22:25, Aquinas argues that usury is unjust because it is selling that which does not exist. He explains this point by comparing wine and houses. Consider wine. It would be perfectly just to sell wine to another. However, if someone were to try to sell the wine to one person and meanwhile sell the right to drink the wine to another person, then he would be acting unjustly. The purpose of wine is to be drunk, and thus there is no difference between ownership of the wine and ownership of the right to drink the wine. Housing is a quite different matter. Since using a house is not the same thing as consuming a house (the house is not destroyed in its use), there is no injustice in separating the ownership of a house from the use of a house. Thus a house may justly be rented or lent to another while ownership is retained. There is no equivalent ability with wine; one cannot lend a glass of wine to another to be used and later expect it to be returned intact.

Is money akin to wine or housing? As noted above, Aristotle argues that money's purpose is to aid exchange. In using money for this purpose, it is inherently consumed; after using money for its proper purpose, there is no way to return it intact to another. Now, it is perfectly just to lend wine to a person today and expect that he will repay you with an equivalent amount of wine in the future; exchanging one bottle of wine for another bottle of wine is simply exchanging things of equal value. But it is unjust to demand in addition to this repayment

---

[12] Aquinas, *Summa theologica* IIa IIae, q. 78, art. 1.

a fee for the use of the wine since the use of wine is insepa-rable from its ownership. The same is true of money; to lend one sum and expect both a repayment of the sum and a pay-ment for the use of the money is unjust. Since the purpose of money is in effect to consume it, to ask for a payment both for the loan itself and for the use of the lent money is selling some-thing that does not exist.

There are a couple of other matters that arise in Aquinas relevant to the drama in *The Merchant of Venice*. First, while Shylock generally takes usury on loans he makes, does he vio-late any ethical principles in the loan he makes with Antonio? After all, there is no interest charged on that particular loan. Aquinas, however, forestalls that line of argument by also inquir-ing "Whether It Is Lawful to Ask for Any Other Kind of Con-sideration for Money Lent?"[13] Aquinas answers that it is not, using much the same reasoning as above. Aristotle had noted that a thing can be considered to be money if it can be valued in monetary terms. In this case, the general rule that all exchanges must be equivalent applies, and as long as Antonio's heart has greater value than the amount lent, then asking for the pound of flesh is demanding more in repayment than the amount lent.

Another possible objection to the course of the play is the observation that there were two parties to the transaction. If the lender Shylock is guilty of being a usurer, then should we not also condemn Antonio for being a party to the same loan contract? Aquinas also asks "Whether It Is Lawful to Borrow Money under a Condition of Usury", and he answers yes.[14] Again citing Aristotle, Aquinas notes that suffering injury is no sin, and since usury inflicts injury on borrowers, there is no sin in being so injured. Antonio is blameless in agreeing to the loan.

Dante's *Divine Comedy* is both the culmination of the Mid-dle Ages and the inauguration of the remarkable explosion of

[13] Ibid., art. 2.
[14] Ibid., art. 4.

artistic achievement in the Renaissance. In his work, there is no question at all about the status of usurers. Dante meets the usurers in the seventh circle of Hell, and their location tells us quite a bit about the universal view on usury.

The seventh circle contains all those who committed sins of violence, with three regions for violence against others, self, and God. In the portion of the circle housing those whose sin is violence against God, we find the blasphemers, homosexuals, and usurers. Note again: usury is punished in the same circle as *blasphemy*. To the modern student, these three classes of sin seem to have nothing to do with one another, but Dante would insist that the problem is that the modern student simply does not recognize the true nature of the sins in this circle. As Virgil, Dante's guide in Hell, explains:

> Violence may be committed against God
> When we deny and curse him in our hearts,
> Or when we scorn nature and her bounty.
>
> And so the smallest ring stamps with its seal
> Both Sodom and Cahors and those
> Who scorn Him with their tongues and hearts.[15]

(As Sodom was the town most associated with homosexuality, Cahors was the city most associated with usury.) Virgil goes on to note that both Genesis and Aristotle's *Physics* show that it is proper for man to toil to gain what he wants. The usurer, on the other hand, tries to earn his living in a different manner, scorning the natural order.

As a result, the usurers find themselves on a desert plain with the blasphemers, who wished for a world without the God who gives life, and the homosexuals, whose love is inherently barren. The usurers spend eternity sitting in a circle in a desert with flames of fire descending upon them, with "restless" hands trying to beat off the fire from the sky and sand, and doing nothing other than staring longingly at the money purses

---

[15] Dante, *Inferno* 11.46–51.

hanging around the others' necks. Just as in life, they do no work, they make no effort to gain anything, but they desire to gain the contents of another's purse without offering anything in exchange for it. Usury is violence against God's creation; it is attempting to create profit from what is naturally barren.

From its very beginning, English law incorporated prohibitions on usury. While the Scholastics were working out the theology of usury, the nobility in England were engaged in a conflict with King John, resulting in the Magna Carta, the first great document presaging the rise of individual rights by limiting the power of the Crown. At a time when the prevailing interest rates available from Jewish moneylenders in England were between 50 and 120 percent per year, the Magna Carta prohibited the king from accepting any interest on certain types of loans.[16] Subsequently, canonical law prohibited usury. Eventually, King Henry VIII altered the law to allow for loans charging up to 10 percent; Edward VI abolished that allowance, prohibiting all interest; and Elizabeth reinstated the legal limit of 10 percent.[17] While interest was legally allowed in Elizabethan England, there was little change in the perceived morality of usury. It was, in this respect, much like modern laws on adultery; while it is not a crime, there are few who think the act is morally acceptable.

With the onset of the Renaissance and the invention of the printing press, there was an explosion of writing on every subject imaginable, and usury elicited its share of books and pamphlets. Unlike with most subjects, however, the pamphlets do not contain a debate on the merits of usury; there was not a single pamphlet published defending usury until after 1600.[18] The English pamphlets on usury are much alike, containing rousing denouncements of usury and refutation of any

[16] Sidney Homer, *A History of Interest Rates*, 2nd ed. (New Brunswick, N.J.: Rutgers University Press, 1977), p. 91.

[17] "The Death of Usury, or The Disgrace of Usurers" ([Cambridge]: John Legatt, Printer to the University of Cambridge, 1594).

[18] John W. Draper, "Usury in *The Merchant of Venice*", *Modern Philology* 33, no. 1 (1935): 43.

conceivable argument in favor of allowing for the practice. These pamphlets are wide-ranging; Mosse, for example, cites 157 authorities in his *Arraignment and Conviction of Usury.*[19] To give one example of the flavor of these pamphlets, Smith provides the following *definition*: "Usury is that gain which is gotten by lending for the use of the thing which a man lendeth, covenanting before with the borrower to receive more than was borrowed and therefore one calls the usurer a legal thief, because before he steals, he tells the party how much he will steal, as though he stole by law."[20] He goes on to provide four reasons for the sinfulness of usury. First, it is against the law of charity because it demands of another more than one's own. Second, it violates the law of nations because every country has laws against the practice. Third, it violates the law of nature; man should have a natural compassion, and just as a river fills every spot it meets before moving on to another place, so man ought to fill every household with wealth before amassing in one place. Fourth, usury violates the law of God; in addition to referring to the passages from the Law and the Gospel of Luke, Smith elaborates on the creation account: "When God had finished his creation, he said unto man and unto beasts and unto fishes *increase and multiply*, but he never said unto money, increase and multiply because it is a dead thing which hath no seed and therefore is not fit to engender."[21] Throughout these pamphlets, there is an understanding of lending as a means of charity in which the rich can help the poor meet their needs. To refuse to lend if one cannot charge usury is every bit as bad as to be a usurer.[22]

Shakespeare wades into this world with a portrait of a usurer. That Shylock is Jewish is convenient to the purpose. Being Jewish, Shylock is not bound by Christian readings of the Law;

[19] Miles Mosse, *The Arraignment and Conuiction of Vsurie* (London: Printed by the Widdow Orwin, for John Porter, 1595).

[20] Henry Smith, *The Examination of Vsvry, in Two Sermons* (London: R. Field for Thomas Man, 1591), pp. 4–5.

[21] Ibid., p. 15.

[22] Ibid., pp. 27–28.

rather, he is free to charge interest to the gentiles of Venice. And indeed, when we first hear Shylock speak of his grievances against Antonio, it is not Antonio's habitual insults to which Shylock first refers.

> I hate him for he is a Christian;
> But more, for that in low simplicity
> He lends out money gratis, and brings down
> The rate of usance here with us in Venice.
>
> (1.3.42–45)

Antonio is a rival in moneylending, but whereas Shylock seeks to profit from lending money, Antonio does the proper Christian thing of lending money as to a friend and charges no interest. Yet when Antonio goes to Shylock, he demands:

> If thou wilt lend this money, lend it not
> As to thy friends, for when did friendship take
> A breed for barren metal of his friend?
> But lend it rather to thine enemy,
> Who if he break, thou mayst with better face
> Exact the penalty.
>
> (1.3.132–37)

Antonio asks to be charged interest as an enemy, which was the only way that Shylock, a Jew, would be allowed to charge him. Shylock calls Antonio "the fool that lent out money gratis" (3.3.2), but Shakespeare's audience would know who was in the wrong here.

Indeed, Shylock is a perfect characterization of the image of a usurer. As Bell in his tract on usury notes, "[U]surers are unmerciful and very cruel men" who "take pleasure in the misery of the poor and will have no compassion on them."[23] That Shylock has no pity on Antonio in Act 4 is exactly what Shakespeare's audience would expect. Moreover, Bell also observes, "[H]owsoever usurers protest and swear that they have no money; yet so soon as excessive filthy gain is promised by their

---

[23] Thomas Bell, *The Speculation of Vsurie* (London: Valentine Symmes, 1596).

needy neighbors, they grant they have enough in store; nevertheless to hide their guilefully painted hypocrisy, they say it is their friends, and not their own."[24] This tendency of the usurer explains the seemingly odd aside by Shylock:

> I am debating of my present store,
> And by the near guess of my memory,
> I cannot instantly raise up the gross
> Of full three thousand ducats. What of that?
> Tubal, a wealthy Hebrew of my tribe,
> Will furnish me.
>
> (1.3.53–58)

Shylock is not without a defense of his practice. Immediately after Antonio declares that he never charges or pays interest, Shylock launches into a retelling of the story of Jacob and Laban. The story seems rather beside the point, for as Antonio notes twice, nowhere in the story is interest charged, but rather the story is simply a case of a business transaction.

> This was a venture, sir, that Jacob serv'd for,
> A thing not in his power to bring to pass,
> But sway'd and fashion'd by the hand of heaven.
> Was this inserted to make interest good?
> Or is your gold and silver ewes and rams?
>
> (1.3.91–95)

To this, Shylock replies, "I cannot tell, I make it breed as fast" (1.3.96). That reply contains the condemnation of Shylock, for of course Shylock does no such thing. He cannot breed money; it, unlike sheep, is barren. Breeding ewes and usury are not morally equivalent activities, and Shylock's failure to see the difference is a sign of his villainy, his lack of any ability to tell right from wrong. If he is willing to extract interest from barren metal, is it really any wonder that he is willing to tear out Antonio's heart?

[24] Ibid.

Although many of the arguments above about the injustice of usury will strike the modern student as rather foolish or nonsensical, it is important to keep in mind that not only did they not seem foolish to the authors; they were accepted as true by every philosopher and theologian of note until the sixteenth century. We should not be too quick to dismiss these arguments, even if we ultimately find them unpersuasive. So, why the change in beliefs about usury?

This revolution in thought was inaugurated by John Calvin. In a letter to Claude de Sachinus, Calvin outlines his thoughts on usury, noting that it was an error to prohibit charging interest on loans.[25] First, Calvin notes, while there is clear biblical warrant to prohibit charging interest on loans to the poor, who need funds for daily necessities (see, for example, Leviticus 25:35–36), this does not mean that there is a similar prohibition on charging interest on loans to the wealthy. Moreover, the Old Testament prohibition on usury in the nation of Israel no longer automatically holds in the modern age. Unless usury violates some principles of justice or charity, there is no reason to continue banning the practice. And there is no violation of either one if someone charges interest on a loan to another who plans to use the funds for a profitable venture. If one is allowed to charge rent on land that another will use for the profitable venture of farming, then how is it any different to charge interest on a loan that one will use to complete a profitable business opportunity?

While it would take some time before defenses of usury became the norm, Calvin's argument was the seed of a rethinking of the whole matter. In a time when society was largely nomadic and agricultural, those needing loans would primarily be the poor, who otherwise lack the means of surviving. But, by the seventeenth century, the demand for loans was beginning to be of a fundamentally different nature. As England headed toward

---

[25] John Calvin, "De usuris responsum", found in Calvin Elliott (1902), *Usury: A Scriptural, Ethical, and Economic View* (Millersburg, Ohio: The Anti-Usury League), pp. 70–71. Calvin also discusses the matter in his commentaries on the biblical passages commonly used to attack usury.

the Industrial Revolution, those demanding loans were becoming more likely to want them for profitable ventures. To say that one should lend to the needy for food and not charge them interest is a rather different matter than saying one should not charge interest to the capitalist who wants money to build a factory. The changing nature of society rather quickly brought about a complete rethinking of the nature of usury.

In 1601, Francis Bacon published an essay, "Of Usury", arguing at the outset: "Many have made witty invectives against usury.... But few have spoken of usury usefully."[26] The short essay outlines the costs and *benefits* of usury. Today, the modern student sees only the benefits, and *The Merchant of Venice* now seems to lack a villain. If Shylock does no wrong in lending at interest, then why is he condemned? And if Shylock does not stand condemned, then is there any virtue in his conversion to Christianity at the end of Act 4? To see this play as a comedy, a story with a happy ending, it is essential to see usury the way that Shakespeare's audience would have seen it.

Bibliography

Aquinas, Thomas. *Summa theologica*. Translated by the Fathers of the English Dominican Province. 1948; repr., Allen, Tex.: Christian Classics, 1991.

Aristotle. *Nichomachean Ethics*. Translated by Terence Irwin. Indianapolis: Hackett, 1999.

Aristotle. *Politics*. Translated by Benjamin Jowett. 1885; repr., Mineola, N.Y.: Dover, 2000.

Bacon, Francis. "Of Usury". In *Francis Bacon: The Major Works*, edited by Brian Vickers. Oxford: Oxford University Press, 1996.

Bell, Thomas. *The Speculation of Vsurie*. London: Valentine Symmes, 1596.

[26] Francis Bacon, "Of Usury", in *Francis Bacon: The Major Works*, ed. Brian Vickers (Oxford: Oxford University Press, 1996), p. 421. Draper, "Usury in *The Merchant of Venice*", p. 43, cites this as the "first fully reasoned defense of interest", though it is not much more tilted in favor of interest than Calvin's similarly nuanced discussions.

Calvin, John. "De usuris responsum". Found in Calvin Elliott (1902), *Usury: A Scriptural, Ethical, and Economic View* (Millersburg, Ohio: The Anti-Usury League), pp. 70–71.

Cicero. *On Duties (II)*. In *Cicero: On the Good Life*, translated by Michael Grant. London: Penguin Books, 1971.

Dante Alighieri. *Inferno*. Translated by Robert and Jean Hollander. New York: Doubleday, 2000.

"The Death of Usury, or The Disgrace of Usurers". [Cambridge]: John Legatt, Printer to the University of Cambridge, 1594.

Draper, John W. "Usury in *The Merchant of Venice*". *Modern Philology* 33, no. 1 (1935): 37–47.

"First Council of Nicæa (A.D. 325)". Translated by Henry Percival. In *Nicene and Post-Nicene Fathers*, edited by Philip Schaff. 2nd ser. Vol. 14. Buffalo, N.Y.: Christian Literature, 1900. Online edition at New Advent, revised and edited by Kevin Knight. http://www.newadvent.org/fathers/3801.htm.

Homer, Sidney. *A History of Interest Rates*. 2nd ed. New Brunswick, N.J.: Rutgers University Press, 1977.

Mosse, Miles. *The Arraignment and Conuiction of Vsurie*. London: Printed by the Widdow Orwin, for John Porter, 1595.

Nelson, Benjamin. *The Idea of Usury: From Tribal Brotherhood to Universal Otherhood*. 2nd ed. Chicago: University of Chicago Press, 1969.

Plato. *Laws*. In *The Dialogues of Plato*, translated by Benjamin Jowett. Vol. 4. New York: Scribner, Armstrong, 1876.

Shakespeare, William. *The Merchant of Venice*. Edited by Joseph Pearce. San Francisco: Ignatius, 2009.

Smith, Henry. *The Examination of Vsvry, in Two Sermons*. London: R. Field for Thomas Man, 1591.

Tertullian. *The Prescription against Heretics*. Translated by Peter Holmes. In *Latin Christianity: Its Founder Tertullian*, edited by A. Cleveland Coxe. Vol. 3 of *The Ante-Nicene Fathers: Translations of the Writings of the Fathers down to A.D. 325*, edited by Alexander Roberts and James Donaldson. 1869; repr., Grand Rapids: Wm. B. Eerdmans, 1968.

Law and Mercy in *The Merchant of Venice*

Daniel H. Lowenstein
University of California, Los Angeles

Many of Shakespeare's plays reflect the playwright's interest in law, or at least his sense that he could use law as an element in the construction of good plays. Many of his plays also reflect a similar interest in mercy, forgiveness, and reconciliation. The tension between impartial justice, which is the aim of law, and mercy, a basic human need central to Christianity, has always been recognized. The tension is widely supposed to be close to the core of *The Merchant of Venice*.

I shall argue that this common view of *The Merchant of Venice* is incorrect. The contest between Shylock and Portia is not between law and mercy but between two competing conceptions of law. From early in the play to its ending, Portia stands firmly and consistently for law. Although her most famous speech is an eloquent plea for mercy, in its context that speech emerges from Portia's understanding of Shylock's true situation in relation to the law. This by no means implies that the play is unconcerned with mercy. Portia tries hard to extend mercy to Shylock, though in a manner often overlooked, but their conflict is not one of mercy versus law. Portia stands for law every bit as much as Shylock does.

Two Conceptions of Law

Although *The Merchant of Venice* has long been subject to sharply varying interpretations, most interpreters understand the conflict between Shylock and Portia as a conflict between law and mercy. What I shall call the conventional view of the play usually sees Shylock's effort to enforce his bond as evil but as apparently sanctioned by the law of Venice. Portia, in this view, saves Antonio by a delightful bit of legal trickery.

But the true justification for saving Antonio is not in her verbal dexterity but in the principle of mercy, which is superior to law. The conventional view has been challenged for two centuries by actors, directors, and critics who see Shylock as a maligned and mistreated victim or who regard Portia and the other Christian characters as hypocrites at least as bad as Shylock, assuming that Shylock is bad at all. No doubt the rejection of the conventional view has many causes, probably including all or many of the following: the attraction of leading male actors in the late eighteenth and nineteenth centuries to a tragic interpretation of Shylock's character; a more recent attraction to novel or ironic readings; increased reaction against anti-Semitism, greatly intensified after World War II; and, since about the 1970s, the fashionable moral privileging of the "other" and a sometimes fashionable hostility to Christianity or traditional ethics. As Alan Dessen suggests, contemporary reactions to *The Merchant of Venice* may "tell us more about ourselves than about the comedy."[1]

Unconventional interpretations also gain impetus from certain inadequacies of the conventional approach, as usually presented. Some readers regard Shylock as badly abused by the elopement of his daughter, Jessica, with the Christian Lorenzo and by her making off with some of Shylock's money and jewelry. Indeed, some assert, mistakenly, that Shylock never intends to enforce the bond against Antonio until the elopement gives him the motive of revenge.[2] Most important, however, is the perception that the Christians, especially Portia, hypocritically inflict cruelty on Shylock in the trial scene rather than demonstrate the mercy that they supposedly stand for. A number of critics also suggest that Portia traps Shylock during the

---

[1] Alan C. Dessen, "The Elizabethan Stage Jew and Christian Example: Gerontus, Barabas, and Shylock", *Modern Language Quarterly* 35 (1974): 232. Emphasis removed.

[2] In Belmont, Jessica reports, "When I was with him I have heard him swear / To Tubal and to Chus, his countrymen, / That he would rather have Antonio's flesh / Than twenty times the value of the sum / That he did owe him" (3.2.284–88). Manifestly, Jessica has never been "with" Shylock since the elopement.

trial scene, egging him on by leading him to believe that the law is on his side.

Many of the controversies stem from the widespread assumption, shared by most conventional and unconventional interpreters alike, that Shylock and Portia respectively represent two opposing concepts such as law and mercy, or law and equity, or in the more theological interpretations, the Old Law (of the Old Testament) and the New Law. Typically, conventional interpreters accept on its face what they assume is Portia's claim to speak for mercy, equity, or the New Law, while unconventional interpreters regard this claim as hypocritical.

The play falls into much clearer focus once it is recognized that the conflict between law and mercy is a false one and that Portia demonstrates a strong commitment to law and to honoring obligations from very early on in the play. As Alice Benston has summarized the point:

> [M]any readers conclude that the saving of Antonio represents the triumph of mercy over justice. Portia's beautiful speech on the "quality of mercy" easily leads one to see her as the personification of that virtue. Hence the confusion when she shows no mercy toward Shylock. As long as we fail to see that Portia does not represent mercy, this confusion will remain. We must observe that it is justice—law—not mercy that prevails under Portia's direction at the trial. This is not to say that the nature and value of mercy are of no thematic importance. On the contrary, because Portia does not argue that it become a state policy displacing the law, mercy is all the more protected as the higher virtue. Mercy must not function until after adjudication is made and justice is dispensed.[3]

Portia stands for law, but her conception of law is altogether different from Shylock's. If we wish to treat these two characters as representative of competing principles, the principles are not Portia's mercy against Shylock's law but Portia's

[3] Alice N. Benston, "Portia, the Law, and the Tripartite Structure of *The Merchant of Venice*", in *"The Merchant of Venice": Critical Essays*, ed. Thomas Wheeler (Oxford: Taylor and Francis, 1991), pp. 173–74.

law as a purposeful institution serving human ends against Shylock's law as a set of words divorced from human purposes and subject to manipulation by those who are clever enough to seize the advantage.

Portia's Law

In her first scene in the play, Portia chafes under her father's will, which requires her to marry whichever suitor solves the riddle of the three caskets:

> O me, the word *choose*! I may neither choose who I would, nor refuse who I dislike; so is the will of a living daughter curb'd by the will of a dead father. Is it not hard, Nerissa, that I cannot choose one, nor refuse none?
>
> (1.2.22–27).[4]

She and Nerissa then discuss the many suitors who have already arrived, from all over Europe. For apparently good reasons, Portia regards each one as worse than the one before. At this point, Nerissa informs her that all of these suitors have withdrawn from the contest, unwilling to court her,

> unless you may be won by some other sort than your father's imposition depending on the caskets.
>
> *Portia.* If I live to be as old as Sibylla, I will die as chaste as Diana, unless I be obtain'd by the manner of my father's will. I am glad this parcel of wooers are so reasonable, for there is not one among them but I dote on his very absence.
>
> (1.2.103–110)

These lines express the serious change in Portia's outlook. At the beginning of the scene, she felt her father's will merely as a restraint. Now she recognizes that the obligation imposed by the will can protect as well as restrict her. Her acceptance

---

[4] All quotations from *The Merchant of Venice* are from the edition published by Ignatius Press: *The Merchant of Venice*, ed. Joseph Pearce (San Francisco: Ignatius, 2009).

of the beneficence of this obligation is strengthened when Morocco and Arragon choose the wrong caskets. It has become a full conversion by the time Bassanio, whom she loves, chooses the right one. It is important to recognize that the authority that Portia accepts is not presented as arbitrary. The correctness (within the play) of Nerissa's earlier statement has become clear: "Your father was ever virtuous, and holy men at their death have good inspirations; therefore the lott'ry that he hath devis'd … will no doubt never be chosen by any rightly but one who you shall rightly love" (1.2.27–29, 31–33). Thus, by the time Bassanio is about to select, Portia has fully internalized the value of the casket test: "Away then! I am lock'd in one of them;/If you do love me, you will find me out" (3.2.40–41). The test, then, is not an arbitrary restriction but a device that will filter out those who lack courage and therefore are unwilling to take the casket test as well as those whose supposed love for Portia reflects self-love (causing them to select the silver casket) or regard for the opinion of the world (drawing them to the gold casket). Portia accepts her obligation because she understands its purpose. She is rewarded with the husband she truly loves and whose love for her is unselfish and courageous.

Of course, the casket scene will not convey this meaning if it is staged, as directors sometimes do, with Portia cheating by signaling to Bassanio which is the correct casket. There are many textual indications that she does not cheat, including, most persuasively, the usually poised and self-assured Portia's manifest nervousness in her long speech to Bassanio immediately before he chooses (3.2.1–24). Why should she be so nervous if she is planning to cheat? The textual basis for her cheating consists primarily of words such as "bred" and "head" that rhyme with "lead" in the song that is sung while Bassanio is deliberating (3.2.63–65). As Joan Ozark Holmer points out, Portia says to Morocco, "First, forward to the temple;/after dinner/Your *hazard* shall be made" (2.1.44–45, emphasis added), and to Arragon, "To these injunctions every one doth swear/That comes to *hazard* for my worthless self" (2.9.17–18, emphasis added).[5] If either of these had been the lucky suitor, critics would have had a stronger case for Portia cheating than they have with respect to Bassanio.[6]

The Portia who intervenes in the trial is the Portia who has come to see the importance of laws and obligations for the fulfillment of legitimate human purposes. The play underlines the specific importance of consistent and rigorous enforcement of contracts for the commercial life of Venice, which is an international trade center whose economy depends on the assurance of merchants around the world that their contracts will be enforced in Venice. Antonio himself has affirmed,

> The Duke cannot deny the course of law;
> For the commodity that strangers have
> With us in Venice, if it be denied,
> Will much impeach the justice of the state,
> Since that the trade and profit of the city
> Consisteth of all nations.
>
> (3.3.26–31)

During the trial scene, Portia will endorse a similar idea:

> [T]here is no power in Venice
> Can alter a decree established.
> 'Twill be recorded for a precedent,
> And many an error by the same example
> Will rush into the state. It cannot be.
>
> (4.1.218–22)

It is true that Portia comes to Venice to save Antonio, but when she enters, Antonio is in less imminent danger than is the law of Venice. Despite the acknowledged importance of upholding the law and enforcing contracts, the Duke, faced with Shylock's intransigence in insisting upon his bond, is on

---

[5] Joan Ozark Holmer, *"The Merchant of Venice": Choice, Hazard and Consequence* (New York: St. Martin's, 1995), p. 100.

[6] The inscription on the lead casket reads, "Who chooseth me must give and hazard all he hath" (2.7.9).

the verge of saving Antonio's life in the only way he can imagine, by overriding the law:

> Upon my power I may dismiss this court,
> Unless Bellario, a learned doctor,
> Whom I have sent for to determine this,
> Come here to-day.

> (4.1.104–7)

It is at this very moment that the arrival of Portia, substituting for Bellario in the guise of Balthazar, is announced. She enters a courtroom in which the sacrifice of Antonio's life to the law is a less likely prospect than the sacrifice of the law to save Antonio's life.

Shylock's Law

Let us leave Portia temporarily and turn to Shylock, who has usually been credited as standing for law and the strict observance of obligations. He himself says, "I stand here for law" (4.1.142), and he certainly does in the sense that he is the plaintiff, seeking the sanction of the law for the enforcement of his bloody bond. But he does not deserve his reputation as a character who is righteous in his observance of obligations, because he is not above violating his oaths outright. The play contains three clear instances. First, Shylock declares that he will neither eat nor drink nor pray with Bassanio and Antonio (1.3.36–38). The next time we see Shylock, he is going out to have dinner with Bassanio and Antonio (2.5.11–15). Second, when he first encounters Antonio in the play, Shylock declares, "Cursed be my tribe / If I forgive him!" (1.3.51–52). Shylock recalls this oath during the trial scene. When Portia urges him to spare Antonio and accept three times the amount of the debt, Shylock responds,

> An oath, an oath, I have an oath in heaven!
> Shall I lay perjury upon my soul?
> [No], not for Venice.

> (4.1.228–30)

Yet, during the trial, in order to save his property from forfeiture, Shylock forgives Antonio by forswearing his bond, thereby laying perjury upon his soul and, presumably, bringing a curse on all Jews (4.1.305–19). Finally, to save his life he renounces his Jewish religion (4.1.386–94), in contrast to his unwillingness to break an oath or commit perjury to save another man's life. Shylock, then, is a man who asserts the sanctity of law and obligation but who presses a claim that he can see threatens to unsettle the rule of law in Venice; who sees obligations as properly subject to manipulation and trickery; and who is quite willing to break his commitments if his self-interest so dictates.

However, let us return to Shylock's statement, "I stand here for law", because for present purposes the kind of "law" he stands for is more important than his inconsistencies. For Shylock, an agreement, a bond, a law, is no more than a set of words. The words have a fixed meaning, independent of their purpose or their context, so that once they have been set down, it is perfectly all right to manipulate events to gain more from the words than was ever intended.

The futility of Shylock's conception of law as neither more nor less than words is foreshadowed in a comic scene at Belmont that immediately precedes the trial scene. Lorenzo asks the servant Launcelot Gobbo to go into the house and have dinner served. In a typical series of Shakespearean puns, Launcelot perversely misinterprets everything Lorenzo says (3.5.46–64). In frustration, Lorenzo exclaims, "I pray thee understand a plain man in his plain meaning" (3.5.57–58). Launcelot walks off punning to the opposite effect, that is, by twisting Lorenzo's later words around to achieve what all along was the obvious meaning of his earlier words (3.5.61–64).

Given Lorenzo's difficulties with Launcelot, we should be well prepared for Shylock's "pound of flesh" being trumped by Portia's "no jot of blood". As Lorenzo has said, "How every fool can play upon the word!" (3.5.43)—and Portia is no fool. Words can be made to mean many things, and if the law and Shylock's bond are divorced from any broader purposes they are intended to serve, one interpretation is as good as another. When Portia says, "This bond doth give thee here no jot of blood" (4.1.306), the dramatic effect is stunning. But despite its dramatic felicity, we miss the point of the trial scene if we assume that "no jot of blood" is Portia's main point.

To understand the trial scene, we must understand it as a whole. The scene—as well as the Shylock-Antonio portion of the play generally—is about an act of attempted murder. Critics tend to write as if the scene is really about the bond, with Portia's invocation of the criminal statute treated as if it were an afterthought. Only by bearing in mind the attempted murder question while reading or watching the scene can we understand Portia's conduct and the richness of Shakespeare's writing.

Repeatedly, before the trial begins, Shylock has publicly declared his intention to enforce the bond and take a pound of Antonio's flesh. Following through on these public statements, he has had Antonio arrested. He has refused in open court to accept twice the sum owed in lieu of his bond and has declared, rhetorically, that he would reject twelve times the amount owed (4.1.84–87). These actions are easily sufficient to constitute "direct or indirect attempts" to take Antonio's life (4.1.350). Therefore, prior to Portia's arrival, Shylock is already guilty of the offense. It is thus mistaken to assume that Portia is trapping Shylock. He has already walked into the trap. Portia's most strenuous endeavor in the trial is to induce him to walk out before the trap springs shut.

"The quality of mercy is not strain'd" (4.1.184) is one of the two most famous speeches in the play,[7] but it is not often noticed that the first line of the speech seems directly to contradict Portia's preceding utterance:

---

[7] The other famous speech, of course, is Shylock's "Hath not a Jew eyes?" (3.1.53–73). Just as the context and therefore the significance of Portia's appeal for mercy is usually ignored, the popular imagination is rarely aware that Shylock's speech is a rationalization for revenge. It is telling that Portia's speech is identified by its first statement, but Shylock's speech is never identified by *its* opening: "To bait fish withal."

> *Portia.*   Then must the Jew be merciful.
>
> *Shylock.* On what compulsion must I? tell me that.
>
> *Portia.* The quality of mercy is not strain'd.
>
>   (4.1.182–84)

If mercy is not strained (compelled), how can it be that the Jew *must* be merciful? Both statements are true, paradoxically, precisely because Shylock has placed himself in a paradoxical position by attempting to kill Antonio. Shylock is guilty of a serious crime and will face a severe punishment, but because Antonio is still alive and unharmed, it is still possible for Shylock to extricate himself by voluntarily sparing his adversary. Thus, he "must" be merciful in the sense that if he is not, he will be punished. Yet the mercy cannot be "strain'd", because once he is informed of his plight, his abandonment of the bond will no longer be voluntary and his guilt will be unexpunged. Far from trapping Shylock, Portia essays some of the most eloquent words ever uttered in the English language to induce him to abandon his fatal course.

Portia lets everyone believe up to the last moment that she will permit Shylock to enforce with impunity the forfeiture set forth in the bond, though of course she knows she will not. She does this to make sure that the test of Shylock's guilt is a fair one. Perhaps Shylock has been bluffing. Perhaps his real goal was to bring embarrassment on the law of Venice, with the damaging consequences for its trade that would be likely to ensue. That would have been a malevolent endeavor, but not murder. Perhaps the suggestion that Shylock provide a surgeon will at least mitigate the offense (4.1.257–62). No. Shylock is resolute. The trap closes in on him. He has himself to blame, not Portia, who has done her best to save him.

If Portia's only goals were to preserve and apply the law and to save Antonio, she could have started with the criminal statute and brought the trial to a quick close. Her true act of mercy in this scene is her strenuous effort to save Shylock by persuading him to relent. That act of mercy is not at all in conflict or tension with her firm adherence to law.

Portia's Judgment

Unlike anyone else in the courtroom, Portia understands the law as a unified institution that serves human ends. She does not favor the letter of the law over the spirit or the spirit over the letter. All must be harmonized. One of the law's highest aims is the protection of human life against violence. To further this aim, Portia must either persuade Shylock to abandon his murderous course or she must impose the punishment established by law. As we have seen, another important aim of the law, especially in Venice, is the promotion of free trade by the strict enforcement of commercial agreements. For this reason, Portia must and does resist steadfastly the repeated suggestion by the Venetians that the law be bent to save Antonio. Antonio will be saved, but he will be saved by enforcing the law that protects his life, not by bending the law that protects his commerce.

There is no conflict between the laws in question or the respective purposes that they serve. Personal bonds are enforced for the promotion of commerce and economic security, not to facilitate private projects of revenge, envy, or malice. The incidents of the trial scene and Shylock's own vicious statements make it clear beyond question that commerce has nothing to do with his enforcement of the bond. No one with a legitimate commercial objective need be deterred from relying on any Venetian contract because of the precedent that Portia sets.

Portia does not engage in wordplay to evade the letter of the bond. But neither is her reading of the bond superior to Shylock's simply on the basis of the words used and their syntax, divorced from the purposes of the bond and of the law, both commercial and criminal. Rather, she finds the meaning of the words used in the bond in the only way anyone can find the meaning of words, by considering them in their context. The purposes of the law, which are to guarantee contract rights and to protect the lives of citizens, cry out against an expansive reading of this bond. So does common sense, which cannot imagine that the bond was actually meant to authorize Shylock to remove the flesh nearest Antonio's heart. Portia is true to the letter of the law as well as to its spirit.

Many people, naturally enough, are troubled by the punishments inflicted on Shylock, especially that he convert to Christianity. I shall make only a couple of points here. First, as we have seen, Shylock agrees to convert to Christianity to save his *own* life despite having previously insisted that he must take *another man's* life to avoid perjury. Portia asks Shylock, "Art thou contented, Jew? what dost thou say?" (4.1.393). He *could* have responded: "When you said I would lose all my property, I said take my life, because 'you take my life / When you do take the means whereby I live' (4.1.376–77). How much more essential is my faith than my wealth! Take my life if you will, but you shall not have my soul." If he had said that, *The Merchant of Venice* would have been a very different play. But he did not, because he is not a tragic hero and because Shakespeare chose to write a comedy.

Second, though we may regard the sentence as cruel, it does not follow that Antonio and the Duke have a cruel purpose in inflicting it. Most of us believe, and some in Shakespeare's audience may have thought, that a forced religious conversion is an oxymoron, in every important sense. But there is no reason for us to imagine that Antonio and the Duke believe this. Antonio, who is still under the impression that he is wiped out financially, is entitled under the law to half of Shylock's wealth. In consideration for Shylock's conversion to Christianity, Antonio either renounces his entitlement entirely or accepts a restriction on it (4.1.381–82). If the sentence is assumed to be cruel, Antonio and the Duke may fairly be charged with insensitivity but not with hypocrisy or malice.

If, these points notwithstanding, it is supposed that the Duke and Antonio act without mercy, then they indeed fall short in their profession of Christianity. But it is only in a caricature of the conventional understanding of *The Merchant of Venice* that all the Christian characters must be paragons. The essential point for present purposes is that Portia is not the one who imposes the sentence. The law, as she describes it, subjects Shylock to the death penalty and gives the power to commute that punishment to the Duke and Antonio. If Portia is what I have claimed—a person committed to law—then there is no inconsistency and no hypocrisy. To the contrary. Her question—"What mercy can you render him, Antonio?" (4.1.378)—surely is an encouragement to act mercifully. In addition, Portia knew earlier where the trial was headed and that the audience for her eloquent words in behalf of mercy included the Duke and Antonio.

Law's Harmony

One reason to understand Portia as committed to law is that doing so solves the problem of Act 5. Far from being an anticlimax, Act 5 is the necessary and logical culmination of many of the play's major themes. Portia has saved the law of Venice in the trial scene, but she has noticed the tendency of her husband and some of his friends to subordinate their obligations to the needs of the moment. Bassanio, before the play began, had borrowed money from Antonio that he could not repay. During the trial scene, it is Bassanio who urges Portia, "Wrest once the law to your authority: / To do a great right, do a little wrong" (4.1.215–16). But Portia has concluded during the first half of the play that great rights are done by adhering to obligations, not by committing little wrongs, and it is important for her to bring this point home to her husband. She tests Bassanio while she is still in the role of Balthazar, by asking for and receiving his wedding ring as a gift of gratitude. Beneath the music, poetry, and comedy of the last act is Portia's serious business of impressing Bassanio with the gravity of the marriage oath and of the ring that symbolizes that oath as well as the more general lesson that she has accepted several acts earlier, of the importance of living up to obligations that protect as well as bind.

Because of the widespread view that Portia stands for mercy in the play, many conventional interpreters characterize her actions in Act 5 as merciful. That characterization is forced and unpersuasive. What is at stake is not remediation of an offense but repair of a character defect that jeopardizes marriage and friendship. Actual punishment would be ludicrous and could never have been contemplated by Portia. Bassanio and Antonio suffer serious discomfiture but not for the sake of punishment. What needs to be and is accomplished in the ring trick is bringing them to see, in a manner they are unlikely to forget or disregard, the binding nature of obligations.

At the climax of Act 5, Bassanio asks for pardon and swears by his soul that he will never again break an oath to Portia (5.1.247–48). At this point, Antonio joins in:

> I once did lend my *body* for his wealth,
> Which but for him that had your husband's ring
> Had quite miscarried. I dare be bound again,
> My *soul* upon the forfeit, that your lord
> Will never more break faith advisedly.
>
> (5.1.249–53, emphasis added)

Antonio's words raise a difficult and important question. Has Antonio learned nothing in these five acts? Or is it possible that Antonio acts more prudently when he stakes his soul on what Bassanio will do than he did when he staked only his life on his ability to repay Shylock? Perhaps so. The nature of the contingency is different. In Act 1, Antonio's ability to repay was contingent on the fate of ships at sea, which no human being can completely control. Here, he is guaranteeing his friend's fidelity. It is an act of faith in his friend and kinsman.[8]

---

[8] That Bassanio is Antonio's "most noble kinsman" (1.1.57) is often overlooked. That oversight may help account for the now widespread view, so common in contemporary productions as to have achieved the status of cliché, that there is a more or less overt homoerotic relationship between Antonio and Bassanio, or at least a homoerotic longing for Bassanio on the part of Antonio. This

Whether we can accept that act as prudent must depend, in particular, on whether we believe Antonio accurately assesses Bassanio's character and, in general, on whether we believe in the possibility of human constancy. In any event, by staking his soul on his friend's steadfastness, Antonio makes the choice that Bassanio made in the casket scene: "Who chooseth me must give and hazard all he hath" (2.7.9).

Portia accepts Antonio's gesture because, however hard-nosed she may be, she is an optimist. In particular, she has faith in Bassanio, and therefore she approves Antonio's faith in him. Her optimism entails a conviction that the important things in this play—the letter of the law, the spirit of the law, the quality of mercy, love in friendship and in marriage, the ultimate hope for redemption—are not forces contending with one another. Properly conceived, they work together like the harmony that is in immortal souls. Though it be true that "whilst this muddy vesture of decay/Doth grossly close it in, we cannot hear it" (5.1.64–65), Portia more nearly hears it than anyone else in the play and, no doubt, than most of us in the audience.

Bibliography

Auden, W. H. "Brothers and Others". In *"The Merchant of Venice": Critical Essays*, edited by Thomas Wheeler, pp. 59–78. Oxford: Taylor and Francis, 1991.

Benston, Alice N. "Portia, the Law, and the Tripartite Structure of *The Merchant of Venice*". In *"The Merchant of Venice": Critical Essays*, edited by Thomas Wheeler, pp. 163–94. Oxford: Taylor and Francis, 1991.

Danson, Lawrence. *The Harmonies of "The Merchant of Venice"*. New Haven: Yale University Press, 1978.

---

is highly implausible, in part because of the kinship relation. In a play filled with fathers living and dead (Portia's, Jessica's, Gobbo's), we hear nothing of Bassanio's father. Antonio is best understood as an uncle or other relative who has assumed the role of surrogate father to Bassanio.

Dessen, Alan C. "The Elizabethan Stage Jew and Christian Example: Gerontus, Barabas, and Shylock". *Modern Language Quarterly* 35 (1974): 231–45.

Girard, René. "'To Entrap the Wisest': A Reading of *The Merchant of Venice*". In *Literature and Society: Selected Papers from the English Institute*, edited by Edward Said, pp. 100–119. Baltimore: Johns Hopkins University Press, 1980.

Goddard, Harold C. *The Meaning of Shakespeare*. Chicago: University of Chicago Press, 1951.

Gross, John. *Shylock: A Legend and Its Legacy*. New York: Simon and Schuster, 1992.

Holmer, Joan Ozark. *"The Merchant of Venice": Choice, Hazard and Consequence*. New York: St. Martin's, 1995.

Hyman, Lawrence W. "The Rival Lovers in *The Merchant of Venice*". *Shakespeare Quarterly* 21 (1970): 109–16.

Lewalski, Barbara. "Biblical Allusion and Allegory in *The Merchant of Venice*". In *The Merchant of Venice*, edited by Leah Marcus, Norton Critical Editions, pp. 169–89. New York: Norton, 2006.

Lowenstein, Daniel H. "The Failure of the Act: Conceptions of Law in *The Merchant of Venice*, *Bleak House*, *Les Misérables*, and Richard Weisberg's *Poethics*". *Cardozo Law Review* 15 (1994): 1139–243.

Moody, A. D. "The Letter of the Law". In *"The Merchant of Venice": Critical Essays*, edited by Thomas Wheeler. Oxford: Taylor and Francis, 1991.

Murry, John Middleton. "Shakespeare's Method: *The Merchant of Venice*". In *"The Merchant of Venice": Critical Essays*, edited by Thomas Wheeler, pp. 37–57. Oxford: Taylor and Francis, 1991.

Short, Hugh. "Shylock Is Content: A Study in Salvation". In *"The Merchant of Venice": New Critical Essays*, edited by John W. Mahon and Ellen M. Macleod Mahon, pp. 199–212. New York: Routledge, 2002.

The Merchant of Venice and the Goods of Friendship

Michael Martin
Marygrove College

for Donald Levin

You thought you'd found a friend to take you out of this place,
Someone you could lend a hand in return for grace. It's a beautiful day.
— U2, "Beautiful Day"

Will Shakespeare was a scavenger. Interested in characters—the attributes of men and women, the personae of a play, as well as the signature qualities of a piece of writing—he was not as keen at developing plots. He put together snatches from other writers, his contemporaries as well as those august figures he knew from his schooldays. He might filch a plot from Plautus, borrow a motif of the alchemists, or outfit a character from the men of parts (or the parts of men) he found at court. After he collected the miscellanea necessary to the business of creation, he set to work.

Shakespeare pulls together many sources for his plays and fashions them into sums often greater than their parts. In *Hamlet*, for instance, he combines contrivances of the Renaissance revenge tragedy, Saxo Grammaticus' tale of Ameleth, and a theological debate on Purgatory into the action of the play. In the English histories, he layers his main source, Holinshead, with philosophical considerations of loyalty, kinship, kingship, and sometimes wry commentary on social stratification.

In *The Merchant of Venice*, Shakespeare likewise combines an otherwise disparate set of materials and frames them in a way that is both innovative and thought provoking. From Christopher Marlowe's *Jew of Malta* (c. 1592) Shakespeare derives the character of Shylock, though he is not nearly so repellent a caricature as Marlowe's Barabbas. The "pound of flesh" motif he could have taken from a few different sources, including the Florentine writer Ser Giovanni's tale "Giannetto

233

of Venice and the Lady of Belmont" and Alexander Silvayn's *Orator* (a French work, translated into English in 1596). The "fairy tale" of the three caskets was available in a variety of formats, from John Gower's *Confessio Amantis*, to Boccaccio's *Decameron*, to the *Gesta Romanorum*.[1]

Shakespeare's philosophical framework for *The Merchant of Venice* has as one of its sources Cicero's *De amicitia* (*On Friendship*), which Shakespeare would have encountered as a schoolboy in Stratford. As Lawrence J. Mills remarks, the use of Cicero as "illustrative material" during the English Renaissance transmitted his ideas of friendship to those learning the language.[2] Furthermore, Mills asserts that *De amicitia* was "the most important single source" for the philosophy of friendship at the time. But becoming conversant with the antique Roman's speculations concerning friendship in Elizabethan culture at large would have been relatively easy—even without having read them in the original.

Indeed, Elizabethan England saw rather an explosion of "friendship literature" in general, most of it bad for both friendship and literature. Relying on classical friendship theory, Richard Edwards' didactic *The Excellent Comedie of the Moste Faithfullest Freendes, Damon and Pithias* (neither excellent, nor comedic) was published in 1571 though probably performed as early as the turning of 1564 to 1565.[3] John Lyly in his *Endimion* (presented 1588; published 1591) likewise utilizes classical models of friendship, as does Marlowe in *Edward II*.[4]

So, why was there such a vogue for friendship literature at this time? Some critics suggest that the proliferation of friendship literature during the English Renaissance was an attempt of authors to mitigate the social distances between patron and

---

[1] Anthony Davies, "*The Merchant of Venice*", in *The Oxford Companion to Shakespeare*, ed. Michael Dobson (Oxford: Oxford University Press, 2001), p. 288.

[2] Lawrence J. Mills, *One Soul in Bodies Twain: Friendship in Tudor Literature and Stuart Drama* (Bloomington: University of Indiana Press, 1937), p. 78.

[3] Ibid., p. 134.

[4] Ibid., pp. 151, 248.

patronized.[5] Certainly, the dynamic between the speaker of Shakespeare's sonnets and the young man to whom they are addressed points to this—while the friendships in his plays do not. Perhaps predictably, feminist critics have seen the so-called friendship literature as evidence of another pathetic attempt by male power structures to secure hegemony and maintain oppression of the female "other".[6] But such criticisms are founded more on postmodern biases than early modern realities. Men, no matter what sociological or political context they might find themselves in, should still be allowed to have friends. It may be that societal structures relaxed in the Renaissance, making the period more conducive to an appreciation of the qualities of friendship.[7]

Indicative of the popularity of friendship literature is the fact that it was parodied by some of the very playwrights who popularized it. Robert Stretter, for his part, speculates that *Edward II*, Lyly's *Old Wives Tale*, Beaumont and Fletcher's *Coxcomb*, and even Shakespeare's *Two Gentlemen of Verona* exploit the idea of friendship by way of parody.[8] To this list we might add Shakespeare's *Timon of Athens*, an *anti*friendship play if ever there was one. And the relationship between Hal and Falstaff in the *Henry IV* plays is an obviously comic, if ultimately cynical, take on the friendship theme. Too popular a topic, it seems, ever invites ridicule—if not outright contempt.

But in *The Merchant of Venice*, Shakespeare avoids both ridicule and contempt. There he treats the subject of friendship in conformity with classical ideals while at the same time expanding the early modern understanding of friendship.

---

[5] Tom Macfaul, *Male Friendships in Shakespeare and His Contemporaries* (Cambridge: Cambridge University Press, 2007), pp. 9–11.

[6] Eve Kosofsky Sedgwick, quoted in Macfaul, *Male Friendships*, p. 3.

[7] Macfaul suggests that feudal notions of allegiance gave way to Renaissance ideas of friendship. See his *Male Friendships*, p. 5.

[8] Robert Stretter, "Cicero on Stage: *Damon and Pithias* and the Fate of Classical Friendship in English Renaissance Drama", *Texas Studies in Literature and Language* 47, no. 4 (2005): 345–65, at p. 345.

The Classical Turn

"[I]n the course of history," writes Cicero, "men can name scarcely three or four pairs of friends; to this category, I venture to hope, men will assign the friendship of Scipio and Laelius."[9] The friendship of these two Romans was indeed legendary. In addition to Cicero, Polybius, in the tenth book of his *Histories*, depicts their association as truly exceptional.[10] Shakespeare, it seems from *Merchant*, would like to make Antonio and Bassanio a fifth pair to this august list.

In *De amicitia*, Cicero's discussion of friendship primarily focuses on the type of friendship that "can exist only between good men."[11] The operative word here, of course, is "good". Cicero asserts that he is not being idealistic about what constitutes the good. Pragmatically, he dismisses those who hold that to be good a man must have attained "perfect wisdom". "Perhaps so," he says, "but they are talking about a kind of wisdom that no man to this day has ever acquired."[12] Cicero's evaluation of goodness is grounded in traditional Roman *virtus*. Good men, the Orator claims, "are men who behave in such a way that they are regarded as models of honor, integrity, justice, and generosity, men who have no vestige of avarice, lustfulness, or insolence, men of unwavering conviction."[13] A good friend is one picked out of a thousand.

Furthermore, Cicero believes *amicitia perfecta* (perfect friendship) to be nearly the greatest gift the gods have given to men:

> Now friendship is just this and nothing else: complete sympathy in all matters of importance, plus good will and affection,

---

[9] Cicero, *De amicitia*, trans. Frank Copley, in *Other Selves: Philosophers on Friendship*, ed. Michael Pakaluk (Indianapolis: Hackett, 1991), 15.

[10] Polybius, *The Histories*, trans. W.R. Paton, vol. 4, Loeb Classical Library (London: Heinemann, 1925), 10.3.

[11] Cicero, *De amicitia* 18.

[12] Ibid.

[13] Ibid., 19.

and I am inclined to think that with the exception of wisdom, the gods have given nothing finer to men than this.[14]

Virtue, according to Cicero, if not a finer thing than friendship, is friendship's antecedent, for "without virtue friendship cannot exist at all."[15] As virtuous men are difficult to find, finding *amicitia perfecta* is doubly rare—which is why Cicero can locate only a handful of examples throughout all of history.

Cicero, though he writes with great eloquence on the subject of friendship, was not the first in classical times to write of its value. Predating as well as inspiring the Roman's discussion of friendship, three centuries earlier Aristotle took up the subject in both his *Nichomachean Ethics* and *The "Art" of Rhetoric*.

Aristotle's *Nichomachean Ethics*, which, in addition to a multitude of Latin translations would have been available to Shakespeare in John Wilkinson's English translation of 1547,[16] includes the Philosopher's most complete discussion of friendship. Friendship, he says, "is a virtue, or involves virtue, and besides is most necessary for our life."[17] Indeed, much of Cicero's thought on the subject derives from Aristotle. However, in the *Ethics*, Aristotle categorizes friendship into three types; these categories and Aristotle's treatment of them bear a significant influence on *The Merchant of Venice*.

Aristotle's first and meanest category in the hierarchy of friendship falls under the title of "utility". A useful friend is someone we may rely on for helping to advance our careers, for giving us an "in" to a nice vacation spot, or for helping us

---

[14] Ibid., 20.

[15] Ibid.

[16] *The Ethiques of Aristotle, that is to saye, precepts of good behauoure and per-fighte honestie, now newly translated into English*, trans. John Wilkinson, from the compendium of Brunetto Latini, 8 vols. (London: Richard Grafton, 1547). For an exhaustive list of Aristotle editions in the late Renaissance, see F. Edward Cranz, *A Bibliography of Aristotle Editions, 1501–1600*, 2nd ed. (Baden: Verlag Valentin Koerner, 1984).

[17] Aristotle, *Nichomachean Ethics*, trans. Terence Irwin, in *Other Selves: Philosophers on Friendship*, ed. Michael Pakaluk (Indianapolis: Hackett, 1991), 1115a.

secure tickets for the World Series. According to Aristotle, "Those who love each other for utility love the other not in himself, but in so far as they gain some good for themselves from him."[18] This type of amiable opportunism, therefore, is not really friendship.

Next on the Aristotelian scale of friendship is the friendship of "pleasure". Pleasurable friends make us laugh, are good for entertainment purposes, render office parties tolerable. According to the Philosopher, those who collect pleasurable friends "like a witty person not because of his character, but because he is pleasant to themselves."[19] Indulging in a pleasurable friendship, then, is not real friendship either.

Aristotle's third category of friendship, and the one most deserving of the name, is that in which the partners esteem each other regardless of the advantages or disadvantages of usefulness or pleasure and their absence. The friend is loved *in himself*, and for no other reason. "Complete friendship", says Aristotle,

> is the friendship of good people similar in virtue; for they wish goods in the same way to each other in so far as they are good, and they are good in themselves. . . . Now those who wish goods to their friend for the friend's own sake are friends most of all; for they have this attitude because of the friend himself, not coincidentally. Hence these people's friendship lasts as long as they are good; and virtue is enduring.[20]

As with Cicero, in Aristotle's thought virtue is antecedent to friendship. Bad men cannot be true friends.

In *The Merchant of Venice*, Shakespeare scavenges the classical friendship corpus in order to fit out his play. The Ciceronean atmosphere of *amicitia* certainly stands as the backdrop to the play, and, indeed, it may be appropriate to name "friendship", or at the very least *philia*, as the central character of the play. The traditional notion of a protagonist is decentralized

[18] Ibid., 1156a.
[19] Ibid.
[20] Ibid., 1156b.

throughout *Merchant*. As J. Middelton Murry notes, the play boasts no "Shakespearean" individuality at its core; rather, "[t]he Berowne-Mercutio-Benedick figure, witty, debonair, natural, is diffused into a group of Venetian noblemen."[21] And these Venetian noblemen are emblematic of the various aspects of friendship directly inspired by Aristotle.

Shakespeare opens the play with a group of young men giving encouragement to a forlorn associate, Antonio. Antonio, his friends Salerio and Solanio think, is troubled by the fortunes of his ships and fortune at sea. "Your mind is tossing on the ocean", says Salerio,

> There where your argosies with portly sail
> Like signiors and rich burghers on the flood,
> Or as it were the pageants of the sea,
> Do overpeer the petty traffickers
> That cur'sy to them, do them reverence,
> As they fly by them with their woven wings.
>
> (1.1.9–14)[22]

But when Antonio brushes aside this conjecture, saying, "[M]y merchandise makes me not sad" (1.1.45), Solanio immediately concludes, "Why then you are in love" (1.1.46). And so the theme of *Merchant* is established, in which Shakespeare contrasts the materialistic goods of merchandise and gold with the transcendental goods of friendship and love. But just as we find three types of chests in Belmont, we find different types of friendships and loves in Venice.

The first and least complicated of friendships involves Gratiano—and, to a less developed degree, Salerio and Solanio. These Aristotle would classify as "friendships of pleasure". On Bassanio's entrance into the play, seeing Salerio and Solanio,

---

[21] J. Middleton Murry, "Shakespeare's Method: *The Merchant of Venice*", in *Shakespeare: The Comedies; A Collection of Critical Essays*, ed. Kenneth Muir (Englewood Cliffs: Prentice Hall, 1965), pp. 32–46, at p. 33.

[22] All quotations from *The Merchant of Venice* are from the edition published by Ignatius Press: *The Merchant of Venice*, ed. Joseph Pearce (San Francisco: Ignatius, 2009).

he asks, "Good signiors both, when shall we laugh?" (1.1.66). Gratiano leaps directly into the role of the pleasurable friend when he boasts,

> Let me play the fool,
> With mirth and laughter let old wrinkles come,
> And let my liver rather heat with wine
> Than my heart cool with mortifying groans.
>
> (1.1.79–82)

Shakespeare, a man who purportedly died after an evening of carousing with chums, certainly does not disparage pleasurable friendships. They are worthy in themselves, though, ultimately, as Bassanio says of Gratiano's banter, "an infinite deal of nothing" (1.1.114). More complicated is the manner in which Shakespeare explores the friendship of utility in the play.

His central examination of this type of friendship is seen foremost in the development of Shylock's character. When Bassanio attempts to secure a loan from Shylock, Shylock is not confident of his ability to supply the young nobleman with three thousand ducats. But he reassures himself when remembering the usefulness of one of his friends: "What of that?/ Tubal, a wealthy Hebrew of my tribe,/Will furnish me" (1.3.56–58). Shylock initiates a utilitarian friendship, albeit an insincere one, even when he speaks to Antonio. "Why, look how you storm!" he says.

> I would be friends with you, and have your love,
> Forget the shames that you have stain'd me with,
> Supply your present wants, and take no doit
> Of usance for my moneys, and you'll not hear me.
> This is kind I offer.
>
> (1.3.137–42)

Shylock wants neither Antonio's friendship nor his love. His interest is exclusively found in the utility (of revenge) located in the pound of flesh. To Shylock, all friendships—and even enmities—are relationships of utility.

Aristotle is rather cautionary when it comes to friendships of utility, even when the partners have no ulterior motives. The motivation for gain is the primary agent in these types of associations and makes them "liable to accusations".[23] This, certainly, is not only what Shylock does in the end; it is also, as we know, his sole intention in entering into negotiations in the first place.

But it is in his treatment of the most important manifestation of Aristotelian friendship, that of loving the friend for his own sake in *amicitia perfecta*, that Shakespeare departs from classical models and explores friendship in a revolutionary context. Obviously, the friendship of question here is that between Antonio and Bassanio, a friendship that Cicero would not deem a bonding of good men, equal in virtue. Although Bassanio describes Antonio, in terms that smell of Cicero, as "one in whom/The ancient Roman honor more appears/Than any that draws breath in Italy" (3.2.294–96), the audience recognizes that Antonio's treatment of Shylock prior to the action of the play has not always been charitable.

On the other hand, Antonio's indulgence of Bassanio has been overly charitable. Antonio has repeatedly loaned money to his friend, even though Bassanio, by his own admission, has "disabled mine estate" (1.1.123). And he is well on his way to ruining Antonio's! Bassanio initially has no claim to Cicero's image of the friend as the man good, virtuous, and noble. As many critics—and many students—have noticed, Antonio could find better friends than Bassanio.

And they are right. Bassanio is a wastrel and a spendthrift who, as he confesses, shows "a more swelling port/Than my faint means would grant continuance" (1.1.124–25). He treats Antonio like an ATM, taking advantage of his friend's generosity as a result of his own profligacy. In Macfaul's opinion, Bassanio is "an insensitive creature, equally incapable of understanding or reciprocating Antonio's goodness. . . . Bassanio has no more affection for Antonio than for the young men of his

---

[23] Aristotle, *Nichomachean Ethics* 1162b.

social group, including Gratiano and Lorenzo." [24] Indeed, looking at the relationship with Bassanio foregrounded, one could
easily call this a friendship of utility. But, viewing the relationship with Antonio in mind, we see something very foreign to the concept of utility, something illustrated in the
classical figure of *asphalia*, making oneself the surety for another.

The Christian Turn

It is evident to even the most cursory eye that Bassanio does
not deserve Antonio's love. It is also evident that the love
Antonio quite literally embodies is more than human, even
divine. Indeed, as have many students of the play, Macfaul
notices "Christ-like *charitas*" in Antonio's self-sacrifice.[25] And
who deserves Christ's love? No one.

The notion of friendship between gods and men was foreign to the classical mind-set, despite the efforts of Renaissance humanists to Christianize it. Though in *Merchant* Lorenzo
describes friendship as "godlike amity" (3.4.3), in the *Nichomachean Ethics* Aristotle considers the possibility of man-god
friendship a logical inconsistency: "Hence there is this puzzle:
do friends really wish their friend to have the greatest good?
For [if he becomes a god], he will no longer have friends, and
hence no longer have goods, since friends are goods." [26]

C. S. Lewis concurs with this point of view in his book *The
Four Loves*. Though he easily identifies friendship among the
ancients, he believes Scripture, for the most part, "ignores"
friendship. The love between God and man, he suggests, can
be described as "affection" when considering God as Father,
or even as *eros* when considering Christ as the Bridegroom—
but friendship is reserved for commerce between men.[27]

---

[24] Macfaul, *Male Friendships*, p. 162.

[25] Ibid.

[26] Aristotle, *Nichomachean Ethics* 1159a.

[27] C. S. Lewis, *The Four Loves* (1960; repr., New York: Harcourt Brace Jovanov-
ich, 1988), p. 78.

Jesus, though, in the fifteenth chapter of Saint John's Gospel absolutely and definitively answers both Aristotle and C. S. Lewis when he says,

> This is my commandment, that you love one another as I have loved you. Greater love has no man than this, that a man lay down his life for his friends. You are my friends if you do what I command you. No longer do I call you servants, for the servant does not know what his master is doing; but I have called you friends, for all that I have heard from my Father I have made known to you.
>
> (15:12–15)

This is the association Shakespeare is trying to make with Antonio's *asphalia*. Antonio, sinner though he is, commits himself to this greatest of loves.

Antonio is no cipher for Christ; but when he makes himself the surety for his friend, he accesses the love Christ embodies. As it did with the martyrs of the Church (I think immediately of the loving-kindness with which Robert Southwell faced his execution), *love* renders Antonio more than what he would be if left to his own nature. It is not so much what quality of personhood Antonio can claim for himself but how the quality of his personhood is transformed by his love for his otherwise undeserving friend. As Shakespeare puts it in *Hamlet*, "Use every man after his desert, and who shall scape whipping?" (2.2.523–25).[28] It is precisely the fact that Bassanio does not deserve Antonio's love that makes Antonio's deed all the more impressive. It is an analog for grace. As a friend of mine puts it, "Mercy is not getting what you deserve; grace is getting what you don't."

Some critics display open hostility to the friendship exemplified by Antonio and, by extension, to that of Christ. Christopher A. Colmo, for one, harshly describes Antonio's love

---

[28] William Shakespeare, *Hamlet*, ed. Joseph Pearce (San Francisco: Ignatius, 2008).

for Bassanio as "pathological".[29] But it is not Antonio's sacrifice that betrays sickness; rather, it is the critic's denigration of love that does. Colmo succumbs to the postmodern relativization of friendship, a move that has replaced the word "friendship" with an altogether meaningless designation: "community". I prefer friendship.

Some critics, anxious to see homoerotic motives in play, view Antonio as in competition with Portia for Bassanio's affections. Macfaul, for one, misses Shakespeare's point when he describes Antonio as "defeated in a way that Hamlet is not, and this is because he has believed too much in the ideal of friendship."[30] He could also argue that Christ failed because, when he most needed them, his disciples abandoned him.

The materialistic scorekeeping of scholars whose ultimate criterion seems to be based on assumptions shaped by a decidedly narrow concept of "success" is symptomatic of a culture that has also rejected beauty in favor of glamor and truth in favor of acceptance. Such thinkers would be abashed by Martin Buber's description of the *I-Thou* relationship, whether between two human beings or between a human being and God, which

> can be effective, helping, healing, educating, raising up, saving. Love is responsibility of an *I* for a *Thou*. In this lies the likeness—impossible in any feeling whatsoever—of all who love, from the smallest to the greatest and from the blessedly protected man, whose life is rounded in that of a loved being, to him who is all his life nailed to the cross of the world, and who ventures to bring him to the dreadful point—to love *all men*.[31]

Antonio assumes responsibility for his irresponsible friend Bassanio. And Antonio's love for his friend initiates a chain

[29] Christopher A. Colmo, "Law and Love in Shakespeare's *The Merchant of Venice*", *Oklahoma City University Law Review* 26, no. 1 (2001): 307–27, at p. 308.

[30] Macfaul, *Male Friendships*, p. 25.

[31] Martin Buber, *I and Thou*, ed. and trans. Ronald Greiger Smith, 2nd ed. (New York: Charles Scribner, 1958), pp. 14–15.

reaction of "helping, healing, educating, raising up, saving" that infects Bassanio, spreads to Portia, and even grazes Gratiano and Nerissa.

The responsibility inherent in friendship can also be seen in terms of the letter and spirit of the law. In Saint Paul's words, "[T]he written code kills, but the Spirit gives life" (2 Corinthians 3:6). This is evident in the contrast of the exercise of friendship exemplified by Shylock and Antonio. But not only in the New Testament do we find such an attitude; we also see it in Aristotle when he writes,

> Friendship dependent on rules is the type that is on explicit conditions. One type of this is entirely mercenary and requires immediate payment. The other is more generous and postpones the time [of repayment], but conforms to an agreement [requiring] one thing in return for another.[32]

Shylock is, without doubt, dependent on rules: he will have his bond. Antonio, by contrast, who lends without interest (or, as far as Bassanio is concerned, without expectation of repayment) is heroically generous. It is hard for us not to sympathize with Antonio, despite our reservations about Bassanio. And this is as Aristotle believes it should be, as he states in *The "Art" of Rhetoric*: "[W]e like those who are ready to help others in the matter of money or personal safety; wherefore men honour those who are liberal and courageous and just."[33]

Extending the Bonds of Friendship

In the English Renaissance, friendship was understood, as it was in classical times, as a relationship between *men*. But, in addition to these notions of amity, in *The Merchant of Venice* (as well as in *Twelfth Night*), Shakespeare also explores the parameters of friendship between men and women.

[32] Aristotle, *Nichomachean Ethics* 1162b.
[33] Aristotle, *The "Art" of Rhetoric*, trans. John Henry Freese, Loeb Classical Library (London: Heinemann, 1926), 1381a.

More than any of his contemporaries, Shakespeare shows women to be on an equal footing with men. In *Twelfth Night*, certainly, Viola, in disguise as the page Caesario, is every bit Orsino's intellectual equal. By unintended subterfuge, she befriends her master before she becomes (or he recognizes her as) his mistress. In *The Merchant of Venice*, Portia's gesture of appearing in court incognito in order to save Antonio's life is not on par with Antonio's valorous *asphalia*; yet, unlike Antonio, she actually achieves her goal. Antonio, though there are a few tense moments during the trial, ends by sacrificing *nothing*. Portia, on the other hand, saves *him*.

Portia's reasons for doing so are consonant with Antonio's reasons for helping others. "I never did repent for doing good," she says, "[n]or shall not now" (3.4.10–11). Furthermore, her intentions also ring of classical *amicitia* of the friend as "second self" (*alter ego*): "[T]his Antonio,/Being the bosom lover of my lord,/Must needs be like my lord" (3.4.16–18). Joan Ozark Holmer believes Shakespeare "ennobles" Portia by illustrating her allegiance to classical notions of friendship, extending to the male-female synergy a previously unappreciated dimension of *amicitia*.[34] But Portia's avowal of the classical model of friendship is not the same thing as her entering into a friendship of classical proportions with a man would be.

It is important, I think, to notice that Shakespeare, though he undoubtedly shows women to be *equal* to men, does not show them to be the *same* as men. The friendship between a man and woman in Shakespeare is very different from the friendships between two men or two women. C. S. Lewis argues that the contemporary tendency to pretend that friendships between men and women are the same as gender-specific friendships has led to the "modern disparagement of friendship" in general and of male friendship in particular.[35] And one might wonder if male friendship is not on the verge of disappearing

---

[34] Joan Ozark Holmer, *"The Merchant of Venice": Choice, Hazard and Consequence* (New York: St. Martin's, 1995), p. 267.

[35] Lewis, *Four Loves*, pp. 75–76.

altogether. However, Portia's charitable gesture is grounded in her love for her husband, Bassanio. Though not required of her, she sees it as an act of duty.

Friendship between men and women in Shakespeare, then, is akin to, but not the same as, marital love. Even in the sonnets, the relationship between the speaker and the Dark Lady is of a palpably different tone than that between the speaker and the young man.

Goods and "the Good"

Aristotle in *Nichomachean Ethics* repeatedly refers to friendship as a "good". Inspired by the Philosopher, Shakespeare throughout *The Merchant of Venice* toys with the denotations and connotations of the word. The characters of the play, so long as they understand the connotations, are safe. Once they confuse them, they run into trouble. As Holmer assesses it, "Those [in the play] who choose love as primarily a motive of gaining and getting what is desired and deserved lose. Those who choose love as primarily a motive and act of giving and hazarding all for the sake of the beloved win." [36] Both money and love entail risk, but the risk is predicated upon what one truly values.

Antonio, for one, has his "goods" in order. Though a businessman, he is not overly concerned with gain. He is not averse to making money, but neither is that the centerpiece of his identity. He lends without interest (or expectation of return). Having money for him is an opportunity for showing his love, as Bassanio affirms: "To you, Antonio, / I owe the most in money and in love" (1.1.130–31). Antonio harbors no self-interest. Rather, his being is permeated with charity and love. And, as it is phrased in the Latin text of the Holy Thursday antiphons, *Ubi caritas et amor, Deus ibi est.* [37] Antonio's relationship to money and to others lives in plasticity; he has not ossified

---

[36] Holmer, *Choice, Hazard and Consequence*, p. 8.
[37] *Liber usualis: Missae et officii pro Dominicis et festis I. vel II classis, cum cantu Gregoriano, ex editione Vaticana adamussim excerpto et rhythmicis signis in subsidium*

through possessiveness or acquisitiveness. He is not compromised, as Shylock is, by what Ovid calls *amor sceleratus habendi*—"this sinful love of having".[38] Antonio's reason for acquiring goods is that they may afford him the opportunity to *do* the good.

By contrast, Shylock's understanding of all varieties of goods is dominated by the concept of gain. At Gratiano's report of Jessica's elopement with Lorenzo, Shylock equates his daughter with filthy lucre:

> My daughter! O my ducats! O my daughter!
> Fled with a Christian! O my Christian ducats!
> Justice! the law! my ducats, and my daughter!
> (2.8.15–17)

Indeed, he does not seem to know the difference between Jessica and his ducats: they are alike possessions to him, items to tally in a ledger. Shylock's insistence on law, contrasted with the mercy Portia urges him to display, evinces his lack of flexibility.

Shakespeare, in his development of Portia's character as foil to Antonio's, limns how the concepts of material goods and transcendental good can be united. Portia's generosity cannot be contested. When she hears of Antonio's plight, she vows "[t]o pay the petty debt twenty times over" (3.2.307). Moreover, Portia's very self is identified with both golden currency and golden virtue. Bassanio describes her value:

> In Belmont is a lady richly left,
> And she is fair and, fairer than that word,
> Of wondrous virtues.
> . . . .

---

cantorum a Solesmensibus monachis (Parisiis: Societatis S. Joannis Evang., 1932), p. 581.

[38] *Ovid's "Metamorphoses", Books 1–5*, ed. William S. Anderson, rev. ed. (Norman: University of Oklahoma Press, 1998), 1.131.

> Nor is the wide world ignorant of her worth,
> For the four winds blow in from every coast
> Renowned suitors, and her sunny locks
> Hang on her temples like a golden fleece.
>
> (1.1.161–63, 167–70)

And though she is wealthy (Shylock also is wealthy), her value is calculated not by her checkbook but by her goodness.

Certainly, the subplot of the three chests also addresses the theme of goods versus the good. The princes of Morocco and Arragon, equating the gold of love with earthly treasure, choose unwisely and are thus "[n]ever to speak to lady afterward/ In way of marriage" (2.1.41–42). They do not deserve a wife, because they do not properly value one. Bassanio, overcoming his selfish tendencies, chooses wisely, realizing "[t]he world is still deceiv'd with ornament" (3.2.74). But, here too, in a truly golden exchange of rhetoric, Shakespeare has Portia speak to Bassanio humbly of herself in mercantile terms:

> I would not be ambitious in my wish
> To wish myself much better, yet for you,
> I would be trebled twenty times myself,
> A thousand times more fair, ten thousand times more rich,
> That only to stand high in your account,
> I might in virtues, beauties, livings, friends,
> Exceed account. But the full sum of me
> Is sum of something.
>
> (3.2.151–58)

This is Shakespeare's point in making friendship, a form of love, the centerpiece of his play. For it is not the goods with which we are possessed (an almost demonic idea) that tender us valuable; rather, it is the good that we possess, and that we give freely, that gives value to our lives and to our friends' lives. Shakespeare includes friends in Portia's list of goods. Aristotle is less poetic, writing, "[W]hen a good person becomes a

friend he becomes a good for his friend."[39] Shakespeare may
have had "small Latine and lesse Greeke", but he knew his
Aristotle: friends *are* goods.

An expensive item holds a *dear* price, and those we love
are *dear* to us. Feelings are described as *tender*, and so is currency. It is a question of what we value. This is why in life, as
in *The Merchant of Venice*, the nomenclature of commerce lends
itself so easily to the language of love. But while love may be
a venture, it is not capital. And while it is a good, it is not a
commodity. Bringing these concepts together, we can rightly
say that we are goods to the Good, as Saint Paul tells us: "[Y]ou
were bought with a price" (1 Corinthians 6:20). This is the
prime metaphor and fact of Christianity: that we were *redeemed*
by a Redeemer, a banking metaphor if ever there was one. In
The Merchant of Venice, love is examined in terms of finances,
finances in terms of love. But the greatest of these, Shakespeare reminds us, is still love.

[39] Aristotle, *Nichomachean Ethics* 1158b.

CONTRIBUTORS

James Bemis is an editorial board member, weekly columnist, and film critic for *California Political Review*. His work appears regularly on the Web sites Catholic Exchange and Catholicity and in the *Saint Austin Review* (*StAR*). Bemis is a frequent contributor to the *Wanderer* and to the *Latin Mass* magazine. He serves as cochair of the annual Catholic Writers Conference at Thomas Aquinas College. His five-part series "Through the Eyes of the Church", on the Vatican's list of the forty-five "Most Important Films in the Century of Cinema", was published in the *Wanderer*. Bemis is a member of the Society of Catholic Social Scientists and is currently writing a book on Christianity, culture, and the cinema.

Raimund Borgmeier is professor emeritus of English literature at the University of Giessen, Germany. Several times he was visiting professor at the University of Wisconsin, both in Madison and Milwaukee. His research fields are Shakespeare, eighteenth-century and Romantic literature, special genres (science fiction, crime fiction), and contemporary literature.

Michael G. Brennan has taught Renaissance literature and Shakespeare at the School of English, University of Leeds, since 1984 and is currently professor of Renaissance studies there. His most recent books include *The Sidneys of Penshurst and the Monarchy, 1500–1700* (Ashgate, 2006) and a study of early modern English travelers on the Continent, *The Origins of the Grand Tour* (The Hakluyt Society, 2004).

Crystal Downing taught Shakespeare for several years at UCLA before taking a position at Messiah College in Pennsylvania, where she is professor of English and film studies. In addition to presentations at academic conferences, her work on Shakespeare has appeared in *College Literature* and *Literature/Film Quarterly*. Her two books explore the relationship between postmodernism and Christianity: *Writing Performances: The Stages of Dorothy L. Sayers* (Palgrave, 2004) and *How Postmodernism Serves (My) Faith* (IVP Academic, 2006).

Anthony Esolen is a professor of Renaissance English literature at Providence College. Among his books are a three-volume translation of Dante's *Divine Comedy* (Random House 2002–2004), *Ironies of Faith: The Deep Laughter at the Heart of Christian Literature* (ISI Press, 2007) and *The Politically Incorrect Guide to Western Civilization* (Regnery Publishing, 2008). He is also a senior editor of *Touchstone* magazine.

James E. Hartley is a professor of economics at Mount Holyoke College, where he teaches courses on macroeconomics and money and banking, as well as a year-long interdisciplinary course on Western civilization. Currently, he is also serving as the director of the first-year seminar program at Mount Holyoke.

Daniel H. Lowenstein is professor of law emeritus at the University of California, Los Angeles. Previously he was the first chairman of the California Fair Political Practices Commission. His specialty is election law, but he also has published commentary on Shakespeare, Dickens, and other authors. He is the director of the UCLA Center for the Liberal Arts and Free Institutions.

Michael Martin teaches English at Marygrove College in Detroit, Michigan. His criticism, essays, and poetry have appeared in many journals and magazines. Michael lives on a small farm outside of Ann Arbor, Michigan, with his wife and eight children.

Joseph Pearce is associate professor of literature and writer in residence at Ave Maria University in Florida. He is author of *The Quest for Shakespeare* (Ignatius, 2008) and editor of the *Saint Austin Review* (www.staustinreview.com).